# Briton, Boer, and Yankee

# BRITON, BOER, AND YANKEE

THE UNITED STATES AND
SOUTH AFRICA
1870-1914

THOMAS J. NOER

THE KENT STATE UNIVERSITY PRESS

Copyright© 1978 by The Kent State University Press
All rights reserved
Library of Congress Catalog Card Number: 78-16749
ISBN: 0-87338-216-1
Manufactured in the United States of America

**Library of Congress Cataloging in Publication Data**

Noer, Thomas J.
　　Briton, Boer, and Yankee.

　　Bibliography: p.
　　Includes index.
　　1.　United States—Foreign relations—South Africa. 2.　South Africa—Foreign relations—United States. 3.　United States Foreign relations—Great Britain. 4. Great Britain—Foreign relations—United States. 5. South Africa—Politics and government 1836-1909. I. Title.
E183.8.S6N63　　　327.73′068　　78-16749
ISBN 0-87338-216-1

# CONTENTS

# Acknowledgements

Thanks are due to the Carthage College Research Committee for a small but needed grant to help final research, to the editors of *The American Neptune* and *Phylon* for permission to use in Chapters I and VI material I have published there, to Carthage students Brian Mildebrandt and Jeff Jones for assistance in proofreading and preparation of the map, and to the helpful staffs of the University of Minnesota Library, the Sterling Library at Yale University, the Manuscripts Division of the Library of Congress, and particularly to Milton O. Gustafson and his staff at the Diplomatic Section of the National Archives.

I owe unpayable intellectual debts to Doniver Lund of Gustavus Adolphus College for first interesting me in history, to Edward Bennett of Washington State University for luring me into the study of American diplomatic history, to David Kieft of the University of Minnesota, who helped guide me through the complexity of European diplomacy, and especially to Kinley Brauer of the University of Minnesota, who was a suitably demanding, but always cheerful and helpful, dissertation adviser. I also must thank my colleagues in the history department at Carthage for their suggestions, comments, and unfailing good cheer: John Bailey, John Neuenschwander, Jonathan Zophy, and the late Nelson Peter Ross.

My largest debt is to my wife, Linda, who not only lived with this topic for several years, but lived with me while I lived with it. Only she and I know how large her contribution was. It is to her that this book is affectionately dedicated.

# Introduction

An essential goal of American foreign policy has been to encourage and even to help establish in foreign nations governments favorable to the interests of the United States. Like all nations, the United States has assisted governments that reflected its ideas about economics, politics, and basic liberties. It has been rare, however, that a nation totally conforms to the American ideals of capitalism, representative government, and liberalism. More often the United States has been forced to decide which foreign policy objectives are most crucial in determining its criteria for support of or opposition to a foreign regime. If, for example, a nation is agreeable to American economic objectives, should the United States overlook an undemocratic political system? Conversely, should a country dedicated to American notions of political democracy and individual rights, but hostile to American trade and investment, receive support? During World War II, for example, Washington assisted all countries willing to contribute to an Allied victory regardless of their domestic policies. Similarly, during the Cold War, the United States was often willing to ignore foreign political repression in nations that had an acceptable anticommunist stance. Recent statements by President Jimmy Carter on the importance of human rights in determining American attitudes towards foreign governments have implied potential diplomatic conflict with nations that are militarily and economically supportive of the United States, but lack the American concept of political freedom.

The present situation in Southern Africa has forced the United States to reexamine its justifications for support of or opposition to foreign governments. While the blatant racism of apartheid is repugnant to such American ideals as majority rule, freedom of expression, and individual dignity, the present white minority regimes are generally favorable to American economic and strategic interests. Foreign policy "realists" have long argued that a nation's domestic policies are of relatively little concern as long as it supports American diplomatic and economic objectives. Others contend that there is a moral element in foreign policy. The mere fact that a nation tolerates American trade and investment and supports the containment of communism does not qualify it for American benevolence.

There is little consensus among Americans on which interests should determine this country's policy towards Southern Africa. A variety of internal and external pressure groups have attempted to influence the United States to make a clearcut decision either to support or oppose the present governments of South Africa and Rhodesia. Domestic liberals and blacks, as well as much of the international community, advocate diplomatic isolation, withdrawal of American investments, and even encouragement of black revolutionaries, as acceptable methods to erase the stain of apartheid from Africa. While also condemning the racist policies of the white rulers, certain business groups, conservatives, and military strategists argue that the present governments have been supportive of American investment, provide stability and order in an unstable continent, and accept the major objectives of American foreign policy. Although at variance with American ideals, they are more beneficial to the United States than the alternative of immediate black rule.

Dedicated to peaceful and gradual change, America has tried, rather unsuccessfully, to walk the middle ground between unqualified support and open condemnation of white minority regimes. It has pressured Rhodesia to accept a gradual transformation to black rule, but it has also worked to guarantee the continued rights and prosperity of whites. The United States has encouraged South Africa to eliminate "petty" apartheid, such as segregation of restaurants, parks, beaches, and the like, and to prepare for a gradual extension of the vote to the black majority. America has not, however, joined with the majority of the world in the outright censure of South Africa and the severance of economic and diplomatic ties. Until recently, the United States persisted in the purchase of Rhodesian chrome despite international opposition. America placed its military and economic interests ahead of humanitarianism. The recent American decision to support an arms embargo against the Union of South Africa reversed American priorities by putting opposition to South African repression above monetary gain.

As a result, America's choice between competing factions in Southern Africa is often perplexing and controversial, but it is far from new. Like nearly all contemporary problems it has deep historical roots. Over seventy-five years ago the United States faced nearly the identical questions: Which group in Southern Africa is most favorable to American goals and what methods should be used to support that faction? While today the alternatives are white or black, in the past America was forced to decide between competing white groups. The Union of South Africa is today a unified nation under white dominance, but the minority white population is split between Afrikaner (Boer) and English elements. It was between these two groups, Boers and British, that America was first forced to choose. Then, as now, the choice was determined by which group was more supportive of the multiplicity of American diplomatic objectives.

In the late nineteenth and early twentieth centuries, the Afrikaners and the English had radically differing visions of the future of Southern Africa. The Boers, descendants of Dutch immigrants to the Cape of Good Hope in 1652, had their own culture, religion, language, and concept of what South Africa should be. The independent Boer states of the South African Republic (the Transvaal) and the Orange Free State were in a bitter struggle with British expansionism. Britain was dedicated to the destruction of Boer independence, the elimination of Afrikaner culture, and a unified South Africa ruled by London. The Boers not only wanted to maintain their political and cultural independence, but envisioned a South Africa dominated by their blend of pastoralness and pietism. They felt that the British notions of industrialism and modernization would destroy their unique society.

Just as American diplomats must now weigh the advantages of white or black rule, in the past they were forced to evaluate the benefits of continued Boer independence or British rule. In the past, as in the present, the determining factors in America's decision were economic self-interest, humanitarianism, and its self-proclaimed mission to mold the world in its own image.

Recent studies of American diplomacy have strongly emphasized the importance of economics. Agricultural and industrial overproduction drove the United States to search for overseas markets to avoid domestic crisis. This interpretation implies that other factors traditionally emphasized by historians of American foreign policy were subservient to increasing exports. This stress on economics has somewhat obscured the implicit humanitarianism of America's open-door policy and the importance of racial ideas in foreign policy. America's involvement in global politics was motivated by ideas of race, religion, and mission, as well as trade and investment.

American policy towards Southern Africa in the period 1870-1914 reflected prevailing concepts of economic expansion, evangelism, and racism. There was little conflict between the desire to create a market for American goods in South Africa and the sincere belief in America's mission to shape the area into a Christian, capitalistic, "civilized" nation on the American model. Gradually economics, a sense of Anglo-Saxon mission, and racism reinforced each other, became interdependent, and blended in a policy of supporting "progress" in South Africa.

American objectives in South Africa were thus similar to those in other underdeveloped areas, such as Latin America and Asia, during the same period. What was unique about America's involvement in South Africa was the problem of dealing with an entrenched European population. The long conflict between the English and the Boers for supremacy in Southern Africa forced the United States to adopt a strategy different from its aggressive unilateralism in Latin America or policy of multilateral balance of power in Asia. To obtain its goals in South Africa, the United States had to accept inclusion in the bitter struggle between Britain and the Boers.

Forced to decide between support of continued Boer independence or a unified South Africa under direct British control, American leaders gradually became convinced of the advantages of British imperialism. Americans modified their traditional anti-imperialism and Anglophobia when they decided that British control was necessary for the economic development, social changes, and racial policies the United States desired in the area.

Although Americans initially viewed South Africa almost exclusively in terms of raw materials, the discovery of gold and the resulting influx of population and capital stimulated interest in the area as a potential market for American goods. The United States assumed that industrialization and economic development would not only attract a large white population but also expose the African to a capitalistic moneyed system and eventually create a huge bloc of black consumers. Economic development would open new areas for American capital in South African mines, industry, and transportation. "Progress," defined as industrialization and expanded trade opportunities, was basic to American hopes for South Africa.

The United States quickly linked economic progress with British control. Americans felt that only Great Britain could develop South Africa's mineral potential and mobilize the black labor force necessary for industrialization. The militantly agrarian Boers, noted for their opposition to industry and development, became identified as barriers to change and their subjugation was considered an economic necessity. The United States assumed Britain would open the area to trade and investment denied by the Afrikaners. England would impose an efficient and honest government necessary for economic development. English would become the language of government and business, to the direct advantage of the United States in its trade rivalry with Germany and other European powers.

A few Americans warned that direct British control, while a possible aid to development, would lead to economic restrictions on foreign nations. Traditional American Anglophobia and distrust of European imperialism delayed America's commitment to British expansion. Most interested Americans, however, were convinced that Britain's policy of free trade and the growth of American economic influence in areas controlled by England illustrated the obvious benefits of British rule. Buoyed by dramatic increases in exports to South Africa, American businessmen were certain that even if Britain should attempt to close the area, it could not drive out America. While British rule might not create a completely open door, it would result in a nearly equitable competition between

Great Britain, Germany, and the United States—a contest American business felt it could dominate.

Aside from direct economic advantages, Americans assumed British rule would facilitate the Anglo-Saxon mission of bringing Christianity, education, and good government to South Africa. English control would assure the development of South Africa along liberal democratic lines. Since America had no interest in acquiring colonies in Africa, it could best export its political and economic system vicariously through Britain. Americans felt Britain's governmental system, although tainted by aristocracy and class lines, most nearly approached American republicanism. British institutions were clearly superior to the patriarchal and anachronistic system of the Boers, or the assumed reactionary and exploitative rule of Britain's colonial rivals in Africa.

American support of Great Britain was also aided by the growing notion of Anglo-Saxon solidarity. United by language, institutions, and a common heritage, Britain and the United States drew closer near the end of the nineteenth century. England actively cultivated this rapprochement. British aid to American missionaries in South Africa and English support of the United States in the Spanish-American War strengthened the American belief in the necessity of British rule in Africa.

Finally, Americans were convinced that British supremacy was essential to the general betterment of the black African. Although few American leaders accepted the equality of the races, most believed in a "white man's burden." While white Americans assumed the African was incapable of self-rule or advanced industrial development, they considered the blatant exploitation of the black population by the Boers to be a rejection of the Anglo-Saxon mission to Africa. American blacks, missionaries, and governmental officials all argued that British control would lead to dramatic improvements in the quality of black life. Britain's avowed policy of "uplift" of the African was extremely attractive to the paternalistic racial views of American leaders.

America's decision to actively support British domination in Southern Africa was based on the assumption that English control would be advantageous to the American economy, the black African, and global progress towards liberal democratic government. The United States was successful in facilitating British hegemony, but failed to gain the larger goals. Although there was a brief boom after England's success, the assumed South African market for American products did not appear. Rather than "uplift" the African, British rule continued and, in many areas, even intensified racial segregation and exploitation. Belatedly, America recognized that British political control did not carry with it American notions of progress.

Although American policy towards Southern Africa was essentially a failure, it reveals much about American diplomacy and American society in the four decades prior to World War I. American policy was an extension of assumptions that made support of British imperialism nearly inevitable. Analysis of these assumptions and the policies they provoked is significant because, although modified by time and circumstance, many of them remain dominant in American diplomacy today.

# Briton, Boer, and Yankee

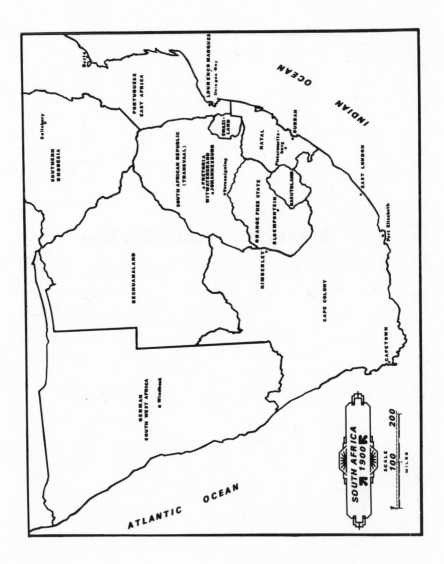

## CHAPTER ONE

# Strains on Isolation

## America's Search for a South African Strategy, 1870-1886

During the first century of its independence, the United States had minimal interest in black Africa. American foreign policy was primarily concerned with avoiding political entanglements with Europe, establishing hegemony in Latin America, and penetrating the untapped China market. Africa had neither the economic nor strategic importance of nearby Latin America, nor the assumed potential consumer population of Asia. Americans were attracted by the mystery of the "dark continent" and were curious about the African native, but the United States had no real African policy. A policy is preceded by interests, and prior to the American Civil War, concrete economic and political interests in Africa south of the Sahara were negligible.

American interest in the future of black Africa developed in the last three decades of the nineteenth century, and resulted from three major circumstances. Foremost were changes in the internal situation of Africa. European colonialization and the resulting development of Africa's raw materials and creation of a potential market for manufactured products stimulated the economic interest of the United States. Second, the growth of American industry created industrial and agricultural surpluses that led to a more assertive American commercial policy dedicated to a global search for new markets and raw materials. Finally, domestic pressure groups gradually grew powerful enough to influence a more active interest in Africa. Businessmen stressed the economic potential of Africa; American missionaries argued the need to Christianize Africa; and, to a lesser degree, American blacks became more aware of their African heritage and concerned with the development of the black African.

The two decades following the Civil War witnessed a gradual awakening of American interest in black Africa. While few

Americans had more than a rudimentary knowledge of Africa, a small group grasped the economic and humanitarian opportunities available, and outlined a strategy based on the assumed potential of Africa. As one student of American foreign policy in this period has summarized:

> . . . a few missionaries, strategists, businessmen, and publicists thought that they discerned the outlines of future American interests. Disapproving of colonialism, anxious to preserve an open door into Africa, yet fearful of violating isolationist traditions, they urged the State Department to explore the possibilities of commercial treaties and other manifestations of disinterested friendship through which the United States might expand its influence in obscure corners of the world.[1]

American attitudes towards South Africa reflected this gradual awareness of Africa's potential, and slowly and sporadically, contact with South Africa increased. American traders, missionaries, and publicists were active in Southern Africa throughout the nineteenth century, although general American interest remained slight. As early as 1784, merchant vessels out of Salem, Massachusetts, began regular stops at Capetown. Trading tobacco, lumber, and grain for African hides and Dutch imports from Asia, New England shippers prospered under the rule of the Dutch East India Company (which controlled the Cape until the British occupation in 1795) and during the early years of English control. But American trade declined sharply following the British decision to place the Cape under the Navigation Acts in 1815. Trade revived after negotiation of a most-favored-nation clause in 1830. By the time of the Civil War, America purchased nearly 20% of South Africa's wool and over 35% of its hides and skins. Trade, again declined, however, when American wool growers succeeded in placing a duty of nearly 60% on wool imports in 1867.[2]

American missionary societies also had continual contact with South Africa in the first half of the nineteenth century. In 1834, the American Board of Commissioners of Foreign Missions established the first American missions in Natal. With the aid of British authorities, America had 18 active missionary stations in South Africa by 1860. The influence of American missionaries on United States policy was not significant, however, until the last decade of the century.

This scant involvement produced few problems for American representatives in South Africa. An American consul, John Elmslie of Philadelphia, was posted to Capetown in 1799. His duties proved to be so slight that he was recalled in 1807, and America had no official representative in South Africa until 1834. Although American missionaries did protest Boer treatment of blacks in the Transvaal, they were ignored. Commander Andrew Foote of the U.S. brig *Perry* visited South Africa in 1850 and wrote a book to arouse American interest in South Africa as a source of raw materials, but it provoked little response. The only American diplomatic problems resulted from the activities of the Confederate raiders *Alabama* and *Tuscaloosa* during the American Civil War. Both ships were welcomed and supplied in Capetown in the summer of 1863. Protests by the American consular agent finally resulted in an embargo on supplying "American privateers and ships of war."[3]

By 1870 the United States had a meager trade with South Africa, a few missionary settlements, and little interest in the domestic politics of the area. America maintained a consul in Capetown to represent it in the British regions of Cape Colony and Natal, but had no diplomatic contact with the Afrikaner settlements to the north. In the next sixteen years the United States recognized the independent Boer states, became increasingly active in the economic penetration of Southern Africa, and was drawn steadily into the conflict between Britain and the Boers for control of South Africa. But even by the time of the discovery of gold in South Africa in 1886, America was still searching for a clear policy towards South Africa.

The circumstances surrounding American recognition of the Boer republics in 1870 are illustrative of the prevailing apathy towards Southern Africa. The Boers were the first permanent white settlers in South Africa. The Dutch East India Company had used the region near Capetown as a stopping point on voyages to India since the late sixteenth century. In 1651 it decided to establish a permanent settlement on the Cape of Good Hope. The Company commissioned Jan van Riebeeck to organize an agricultural settlement in the Table Valley to raise fruit and vegetables for Dutch sailors passing to and from India. In 1652, van Riebeeck and 200 Dutch settlers arrived.

The Dutch settlement grew steadily under the guidance of the East India Company. In 1794, however, the Company went bankrupt, and a year later the British arrived at the Cape to prevent the French from seizing it. The British never left. The Dutch in South Africa considered the British invaders: the English had a different language and governmental system, and lacked the fervent Calvinism of the Dutch.

The Dutch also resented the strict legal and economic controls of the British. After nearly 150 years of the rather casual authority of the trading company, British military control seemed an attack on individual liberties. More important in the development of tensions between Dutch and English were the issues of culture and race. The Dutch were committed to an agrarian economy and their own stern Calvinism. They feared a loss of cultural identity under British control, a fear that seemed justified when Britain declared English the official language of the Cape. Schools, the courts, and businesses refused to recognize the distinct Afrikaans language of the Dutch farmers.

Racial disagreements widened the gap between Englishman and Boer. The decision of Great Britain to abolish the slave trade in 1807 and slavery itself in 1833 outraged white South African farmers. Although most farmers depended on paid black labor rather than slavery, they feared England was moving towards racial equality.

By 1834, the descendants of the early Dutch settlements decided that only physical separation from the English invaders would allow them to maintain their political and cultural freedom, so they organized a vast migration to the north. The "Great Trek" of 1834-1838 was the first of numerous attempts to flee English control. Taking the Dutch word for farmer (Boer) as symbolic of their desire to maintain an agrarian lifestyle, the Trekkers made a brutal and costly march to the east and north of Capetown. Fighting nearly constant battles with the Zulu, the Boers finally carved out the independent nations of the South African Republic (the Transvaal) and the Orange Free State.

The Great Trek symbolized the determination of the Boers to preserve their distinct society. The British finally concluded that the infant Boer republics were neither strategically nor economically important enough to conquer. In 1852, England formally denied its claims to the nations and two years later recognized Boer sovereignty.

Although most European nations followed England's lead and recognized the Boer republics, the United States made no move to acknowledge their existence until Friedrich Kaufman Höhne, Governor Secretary of the Orange Free State, formally asked President Ulysses S. Grant to extend recognition on 6 November 1869. Secretary of State Hamilton Fish formally granted recognition to the Orange Free State in October 1870. Six weeks later Fish also recognized the South African Republic as a sovereign state.[4]

Recognition meant little more than an exchange of diplomatic notes. The Orange Free State established a consulate at Philadelphia in 1872, but, despite the strong urgings of the American Consul at Capetown, Willard Edgecomb, Washington made no move to extend its consular service north from Cape Colony to the Boer States. Through the efforts of Edgecomb, the United States did eventually sign a treaty of friendship, commerce, and extradition with the Orange Free State in 1872.[5]

American recognition was significant only as a convenient reference point, since it dates the beginning of a more active economic involvement in South Africa. It was not followed by political entanglement. The United States refused to interject itself in the dispute between Great Britain and the Boer republics. Prior to recognition, Fish was careful to make certain Britain did not still claim control over the two states. Similarly, America totally rejected attempts of the Orange Free State to draft the United States as a mediator in its border dispute with the English.[6] The domestic situation in South Africa was not yet important enough to provoke action by American diplomats.

American economic interest did quicken after recognition, and the press and the consular service were intrigued with reports of rich diamond fields in South Africa. Similar interest in rumors of gold discoveries were tempered by pessimistic reports from American representatives. The prospect of sudden wealth did, however, manage to lure over 1,000 American miners to the South African diamond fields by 1876.[7]

Despite the development of the diamond mines and the gradual emergence of a consumer market that followed, American trade with South Africa remained slight. The United States continued to view South Africa largely in terms of raw materials, such as wool, hides, and luxury items like diamonds and ostrich feathers. American exports were confined almost exclusively to the area near Capetown because of the lack of internal transportation and the limited American contact with the Boers to the north. While there was a slight increase in American exports following recognition, the United States continued to have a trade deficit in its South African exchange. As late as 1877 American exports amounted to only $629,000, while imports from South Africa totalled over $900,000.[8]

Despite these pessimistic figures, there was a gradual awareness of the potential of South Africa as a market for American products. John Hay, then Assistant Secretary of State, previewed his later strong interest in the South African market in a stinging despatch in 1879, berating the American consul at Capetown for his lack of aggressiveness and for his failure to send reports on trade opportunities to American manufacturers.[9] The Boers were quick to sense the growing American interest in South Africa. They began a campaign to attract American trade and gain the backing of a sympathetic "sister republic" in the impending conflict with Britain. In an address to the American Geographical Society in late 1876, a Boer representative offered the possibilities of American commercial gain among the Boers in exchange for tacit support of the Transvaal against English encroachment:

America's coming into the country would respect and uphold its government, and this new future would add strength and force to the administration. At the present time America is seeking about for new markets to support her increased manufactures . . . . It is in the natural course of events that the construction of a railway from the Eastern coast into these South African republics will develop the mineral and agricultural wealth of the country, and open up a market which would drain America of its surplus manufacture, and add tenfold to its prosperity. . . . The wealth of the republics which has not been inconsiderable . . . all has gone towards enriching the commerce of England, and it would now appear that she is no longer satisfied with this, but wants the republics entirely. Now it seems to me that, by making the country better known . . . I, at least, give people a chance of judging how fair such a monopolization would be. Nations, like persons, are more cautious when they know they are being watched.[10]

Increased American contacts with the Boer states, combined with bad harvests in South Africa and a stronger effort by American consuls to stimulate commerce, resulted in a near doubling of American exports to South Africa in 1879 and a trade surplus for the United States. The American representative in Capetown, noting the increase in American trade and the general economic advantages in South Africa, predicted confidentially that "in a few years the area will doubtless be under the domination of the white man from the Cape to the Zambezi; thus offering a vast territory for trade and more especially in manufactured articles as there is not a manufacturing of any description in the Colony."[11]

Such reports, combined with the growth of American trade, served to gradually alter American economic thinking about the area. American business expanded its vision to include not only the British colonies of Cape Colony and Natal, but also the untapped Boer republics to the north. The United States also began to view Southern Africa as a potential market rather than as simply a source of raw materials. This new awareness of South Africa's potential forced a gradual realization of the conflict between Britain and the Boers for political control. America slowly recognized the links between political control and economic development, and the limiting effects of instability on trade.[12]

Accompanying this awareness of the political problems of South Africa was a growing American consciousness of the importance of the racial situation to the area's development. The first inklings of .black American awareness of Africa, along with a desire to "redeem" the African, coincided with a rising white American concern for the status of the black under European colonialism. American shippers were warned not to bring black sailors into South African ports, and the American press began to print reports of beatings, floggings, and murders of South African blacks.[13]

While racism was not new to the United States, American missionaries were shocked by the Boers' brutality and their exploitation of the black African. The more moderate racial policies of the British in the Cape Colony seemed in marked contrast. Gradually, the United States began its early identification of British rule with an "enlightened" racial policy that proved crucial in later American attitudes towards South Africa. The American Board of Commissioners for Foreign

Missions hailed British colonialism as an example of "the practical subjugation of the natives" in contrast to the exploitative policies of the Boers in the Transvaal and the Belgians in the Congo.[14] Similarly, the *New York Times* applauded the "civilizing power" of English rule and the "Christian zeal" of the British on behalf of "those dusky millions that still kow tow to wood and stone." America's early contacts with South Africa convinced it that Britain was performing a world service by bringing Christianity to South Africa and breaking down the tribal organization of the "pagan native," while the Boers chose to ignore their religious obligation to the African.[15]

While American knowledge of and trade with South Africa increased in the decade following recognition of the Boer states, the American government maintained a strict political isolation. American officials refused several opportunities to aid the Boer republics in their conflict with Great Britain because of fear of involvement in the internal policies of South Africa. The State Department, afraid of possible British misinterpretation, rejected requests from the American consul at Capetown to follow the European example and send warships on periodic voyages to South African ports to boost American influence and prestige. More important, the United States rejected invitations from the South African Republic to sign a treaty of friendship similar to the 1872 agreement with the Orange Free State. The State Department also rejected requests to send a consular representative to the Transvaal.[16]

The most significant example of American isolation was its inaction when Britain arbitrarily annexed the Transvaal in 1877. As Britain moved to consolidate its control of the Cape Colony and Natal in the 1870s, it also began plans to incorporate the Afrikaner states into its empire. British Colonial Secretary Lord Carnarvon, an avowed imperialist, launched a scheme to bring all of South Africa into a federation under the Crown. After an abortive conference to discuss federation, Carnarvon sent Theophilus Shepstone to the Transvaal to persuade the Boers to join a political union with Natal and the Cape Colony under English rule. While some Boers felt a union with England necessary for defense against the Zulu, as well as for financial reasons, many within the Republic were violently opposed to foreign rule. Citing financial mismanagement and the threat of Zulu attacks, Carnarvon announced on 12 April 1877 that Britain was annexing the Transvaal as a colony.

Many Afrikaners adamantly denounced what they saw as naked aggression and, convinced of America's traditional opposition to imperialism and Anglophobia, appealed to the United States for help. The South African Republic sent an emotional note to Washington asking "that the influence of the United States' Government be exerted in our behalf" and denouncing the British move as a violation of the will of the people. Boer leader Paul Kruger sent a personal appeal for an American protest.[17] The United States made no reply.

America continued its diplomatic silence despite repeated Boer requests for a sympathetic statement or a direct protest to London. When the Boers rose in rebellion against British rule in 1880, the United States took little notice. After the British defeat at Majuba Hill in 1881, the Transvaal regained internal independence, but was forced to acknowledge British suzerainty. After its surprising military victory, the South African Republic requested "a sympathetic greeting to our new born republic" from the United States. The State Department merely acknowledged receipt of the note.[18]

America's diplomatic inaction was the result of a dilemma that would continue for several years. Increasingly, Americans viewed the Boers as reactionary barriers to the economic development of South Africa. They were dubbed "uncultivated," "unprogressive," condemned for their apparent backwardness, lack of education, and "indifference to dirt." Americans repeatedly compared them with the Southern slaveholders of antebellum America. Support of continued Boer independence would not only antagonize Great Britain, but buttress the forces of reaction and opposition to economic development.[19]

At the same time, the United States feared the growing British empire in Africa and was wary of the forceful subjugation of the Boers. It was one thing to applaud British conquest of black tribes to bring the benefits of civilization, but the forceful annexation of a white republic populated by descendants of the first white settlers in Southern Africa was quite a different matter. Although America felt that British expansion in Africa was necessary for economic development and improvement of the black African, total British control of South Africa would be a triumph of monarchy over republi-

11

canism. A total commitment of the United States to British designs would be a tacit approval of imperialism and aggression.[20] Rather than alienate either side in the conflict for control, America, at this time, officially ignored the struggle. Later, when American interests were greater and the choice between Britain and the Boers clearer, the United States abandoned its neutrality for a policy strongly supportive of England.

All the trends apparent in America's first tentative contacts with South Africa in the 1870s crystalized in a series of perceptive reports by Commodore Robert W. Shufeldt of the United States Navy. Shufeldt's writings were crucial because they were the most detailed summary of conditions in Southern Africa and the importance of American interests in the area. Shufeldt succinctly presented the alternatives facing the United States, and outlined a strategy that Washington eventually adopted and maintained until the conclusion of the Boer War in 1902. His reports represented the most advanced American thinking on South Africa, and effectively summarized many of the arguments just beginning to be advanced by interested Americans.

Shufeldt's reports were written during a world cruise aboard the *Ticonderoga* sponsored by the State Department and the Department of the Navy.[21] He arrived in Capetown in early August 1879, and immediately prepared a highly detailed summary of shipping rates, tariffs, native customs, climate, terrain, transportation systems, agriculture, and the effectiveness of the American consular service.[22] A month later, as he sailed north from Capetown, he prepared a long manuscript on "The Political and Industrial Questions of South Africa." Although never published, copies of the article circulated among State Department officials, consular agents in South Africa, American businessmen, and military officers, and portions were presented to the press.[23]

Shufeldt began his report by castigating American businessmen and diplomats for their inaction in South Africa. He predicted:

> The British possessions in South Africa, so little known in the United States, are in the process of becoming an important factor in the civilization of Africa and a central point for the exchange of production of that Continent for the manufactures of Europe and

America. They are in fact in the process of crystallization into a new nation possessing all the characteristics and qualities of Anglo-Saxon nationalities and energized by transplantation into the soil of a new country.

Given this rapid growth, Shufeldt argued, the economic potential of South Africa as a trading center and as a source of raw materials "is nearly unlimited."

Economic development must be preceded by a stable, unified government, however, and Shufeldt was convinced that this government would be British. The Boers will remain "surly in their immense farms—never learning and never forgetting anything—the political control of the country will pass out of their hands." The future of the area was confederation under British administration. British supremacy would be beneficial not only to economic development but also to the black African:

> Tribe after tribe will come under its [the British Government] jurisdiction by virtue of the same laws which have extended our territory from the Mississippi to the Pacific. In this way the whole of South Africa . . . will be brought into direct contact with the civilizing influences of commerce and intercourse with superior races.

British control was the inevitable result of the triumph of civilization in all of black Africa. Through French control of northwest Africa, the British in South Africa, and American influence in Liberia, "the whole of the 'dark continent' will be brought so to speak, 'into the market.'" This would aid black Africans by bringing them into contact with commerce and Christianity and elevating them "to a higher plane of civilization." Simultaneously, development would result in an economic boom to the "civilizers." In Shufeldt's view: "The conquest of Africa will be a benevolent act . . . for in the act it will rebound to the good of its people and to the benefit of the whole world."

The barriers to this blend of economic and Christian mission were the Boers and the racial situation. Shufeldt urged firm American support of Britain in the inevitable showdown with the Boers. He felt the outcome predetermined by British racial and military supremacy. He was less sure of the solution

13

to the racial problem. "The social barrier is absolutely impossible," he wrote, "whether Hottentot or Kaffir he is stigmatized as 'nigger': it is declared that he will not work: that he will lie, steal, etc.—These statements sound like echoes from our own country." The race problem would block full economic development and be a source of instability even after British control. Shufeldt saw no solution. Like the American Indian, the black African would have to give way to the white settler: "to both civilization means extermination." While harshly critical of white atrocities against the black, Shufeldt saw no alternative to the march of the superior Anglo-Saxon race.

Shufeldt concluded his report with a series of suggestions for American policymakers "in view of the . . . steady growth in the potential and commercial importance of South Africa." He urged a policy of "firm cooperation" with Great Britain in South Africa, as this would help insure the rapid establishment of a stable and efficient government necessary for trade and development. This was to be accompanied, however, by efforts to penetrate the South African market. He proposed new consulates at Port Elizabeth in the Cape Colony and at Delagoa Bay in Portuguese East Africa (the nearest port to the Transvaal); doubling the staff and salary of the consular agency at Capetown; and replacement of present consuls with younger and more forceful men. He dismissed the present American consular service in South Africa as "beneath the dignity of the country it represents" because of low salaries and the incompetent men they attracted.[24] Finally, Shufeldt was among the first Americans to recognize the crucial importance of Delagoa Bay to the development of South Africa. A natural harbor only two hundred miles from the capital of the Transvaal, Delagoa Bay would eventually become the natural outlet for the wealth of the Boer republics and imports from the United States and Europe. A railway from Pretoria to Lourenço Marques (the major city on Delagoa Bay) would, Shufeldt predicted, eliminate the costly overland route from Capetown to the Transvaal and avoid dealing with English middlemen in the trade with the north.

Essentially, Shufeldt argued that a unified South Africa under British control was both necessary and inevitable. Thus the United States should help in its creation for both economic and humanitarian reasons. Support of Britain should be accompanied by a vigorous effort to develop American trade through more aggressive commercial policies and considerations of the importance of the emerging Transvaal and Delagoa Bay. An Anglo-American partnership in business and civilization in South Africa should be courted. The race question was essentially insolvable, but bringing the benefits of commerce and Christianity, even at the point of a gun, was necessary and good.

Shufeldt's strategy delineated many of the assumptions that would eventually shape American policy towards South Africa. He combined a belief in the Anglo-American mission with profit incentive, and helped develop the stereotypes of Great Britain as the agent of progress and the Boers as the symbol of reaction and as barrier to economic development. Finally, Shufeldt based his strategy on the potential of South Africa rather than the modest American involvement of the 1870s.

Following Shufeldt's reports, the United States gradually increased its economic efforts in South Africa. The American Consul at Capetown, John Siler, urged expansion of direct steamship service between New York and Capetown and the establishment of new consular agencies in the Orange Free State and the South African Republic.[25] As trade grew at a steady rate in the early 1880s, America saw the future of South Africa increasingly in terms of a market for American industrial and agricultural surplus. The United States continued to be interested in reports of South Africa's mineral potential, but now saw it as a means to industrialization and development of a consumer market.[26] The *New Orleans Republican,* for example, feared losing the African market to European colonialization unless the United States intensified its efforts:

> While European nations . . . are carving out markets for their future commerce, the United States, the most active and enterprising among all civilized powers, cannot afford to be indifferent. . . . Is it not the part of statesmanship while Europe is stretching out her hands to Africa, this land of vast commercial possibilities, that we also should hasten thither to compete with her in the future?[27]

Despite past American indifference to their struggle, Boer representatives still hoped for American support. Colonel

15

Alfred Aylward, a Boer official, journeyed to the United States "to induce men of influence in this great republic to invest some of their capital in trading enterprises in such a way to bring these deserving, rising, prosperous men into the family of nations, from which the jealousies and intrigues of England seek to exclude them."[28]

While America generally adhered to Shufeldt's plan for a more vigorous commercial policy, it remained reluctant to commit itself to a firm pro-British stance. In a report to Congress on American trade with Africa, Secretary of State Frederick T. Frelinghuysen argued that America's disinterest in direct colonialization and lack of identification with any European power was a benefit to trade: "The fact that the American flag carries with it in Africa no reminiscence of conquest or war is recognized by the crude tribes as well as by the more civilized people, and favorably affects the commercial relations of the United States with them."[29]

Other circumstances also worked to delay support of Britain. Many Americans viewed Britain's temporary annexation of the Transvaal in 1877 and the following war with the Boers as crude aggression. A number of American politicians were dependent on Irish-American votes and denounced any support of England. To a number of large-city congressmen, it was a political necessity to continue to "twist the lion's tail." Distrust of England and English imperialism died hard. The Boers still had support among American journalists and politicians. The *New York Tribune*, for example, approved of the British annexation of Egypt, but denounced British actions in the Transvaal as "an inexcusable and reprehensive act of national piracy."[30]

Continued British resistance to American economic expansion in South Africa enhanced Anglophobia. American merchants complained that they were forced to go through English representatives to gain credit, transportation, or a wholesaler for their goods. American businessmen protested to Frelinghuysen that such "middle-men" gave favorable treatment to British firms at the expense of their American competitors. An American importer in Capetown bluntly informed the Secretary of State that England and the United States were locked in "a trade war at the Cape" and demanded that the State Department pressure England for more equal competition.[31] British spokesmen admitted they feared the rapid development of American and German trade with South Africa. They argued that the colonies must pay for British military protection through commerce with the mother country. They suggested that foreign imports to South Africa be limited to products unavailable from British firms.[32]

American business discovered that it faced competition from Germany and Portugal as well as England. The State Department feared a joint Portuguese-British agreement to control trade to and from the Transvaal through Delagoa Bay. Consul Siler repeatedly warned of a possible alignment of the South African Republic with the new colonial power in Africa— Germany.[33]

Despite such demands for stronger diplomatic support of American commercial activity, State Department officials remained hesitant to become involved in the politics of South Africa. Fearful of the diplomatic effects of a trade war with European colonial rivals, they rejected the calls for a more active policy.

By 1884, it was evident that Shufeldt's recommendations for a pro-British policy had not been adopted. Although the logic of his strategy seemed clear, America remained hesitant. The United States had no desire to become involved in either a war between Britain and the Boer republics, or in a diplomatic conflict with Germany or Portugal. Britain had shown little desire for a South African entente and remained hostile to American economic efforts. England's military campaign against the Transvaal cast it in the familiar role of bully to many Americans. Combined with the general distrust of active involvement in the internal affairs of Africa, America's negative view of British imperialism blocked any consensus for support of Great Britain.

Although it rejected alignment with England, America was even more reluctant to support the Boers. American representatives in South Africa continued to stress the opposition of the Boers to investment and development, and their commitment to maintaining a pastoral state.[34] Equally important was continued American fear that any encouragement of the Boers would lead to an incident with Great Britain. This was clearly illustrated in America's rejection of a proposed commercial treaty with the South African Republic in 1884.

Americans in South Africa had long urged a formal commercial agreement with the Transvaal to insure equality of trade opportunities in that area.[35] In July of 1884, the official representative of the Transvaal in Europe, G. J. T. Beelaerts Van Blokland, approached the American Minister in the Netherlands, William G. Dayton, with the offer of a commercial treaty similar to those he had recently negotiated with Switzerland and Portugal. Paul Kruger also urged Dayton to press his government for the agreement. Both assured Dayton that the proposed treaty would not violate the treaty of February 1884 between Britain and the South African Republic, conceding British control of the Transvaal's foreign policy. American diplomats were not as sure. Dayton told Van Blokland that "the United States was ready to consider any proposal looking to an extension of its commerce in Africa," but privately informed the State Department of his fear of English opposition.[36] Frelinghuysen shared Dayton's doubts. After a careful study of the 1884 treaty, and consultation with the American consul in Capetown, he concluded that England retained the "right of veto" on all treaties by the Transvaal. Assistant Secretary of State A. A. Adee prepared a long memo on the question, setting forth the legal limits of such an agreement. Adee's major objection, however, was fear of arousing England by apparent support of the Boers. In February 1885, despite Blokland's recently concluded similar agreement with Germany, the United States flatly rejected the treaty.[37]

Despite such attempts to avoid entanglement in the domestic problems of South Africa, the continued rapid economic development of the area drew America into the struggle. The forced opening of the vast northern territory of Bechuanaland in 1884-85 by Cecil Rhodes and a mixed force of British and American adventurers revived both the conflict between England and the Boers and American interest. The American consul warned that Rhodes's incursion into territory bordering on the Boer states marked "the final struggle for supremacy of the two nationalities in South Africa."[38] The first rumors of gold in the Transvaal provoked renewed demands from American business for freer access to the area, and a greater emphasis on reports of Boer resistance to foreign emigration and trade. American caution seemed to many to be in marked contrast to the active diplomatic support of commercial efforts by Britian, Germany, and Portugal.[39] In a long despatch on 3 August 1886, Clifford Knight, the acting American Consul at Capetown, chided the State Department for its refusal to send commercial agents to the Boer republics and its rejection of the proposed commercial treaty with the South African Republic. Knight warned that the lack of a trade agreement with the Boers meant that proposed tariff legislation in the South African Republic would be "almost exclusively directed towards the United States." The gold fields of the Transvaal, when linked with the port of Delagoa Bay, "will open to the trade of the world a market of great and rapidly increasing capacity" with mineral wealth "rivaling that of California and Australia in riches." Unless the United States adopted a more favorable policy towards the Boers, Knight predicted it would gradually be squeezed out of the new market by other nations. Knight enclosed an editorial from the Capetown *Cape Argus* predicting that "Uncle Sam will have to remonstrate with oom Paul [Paul Kruger] or he will lose a considerable amount of his South African trade."[40]

The gold rush in the Witwatersrand area of the Transvaal forced the United States to review its entire South African policy. The passive neutrality of the previous 16 years had done little more than antagonize both the Boers and some segments of the American business community. The United States faced three rather unattractive alternatives. If it continued its refusal to support the Boers, it risked the loss of influence in the rapidly developing area and its share of the mineral wealth and potential new market on the Rand. A second alternative, adoption of Shufeldt's pro-British stance, would totally alienate the Boers and temporarily abandon the riches of South Africa in hopes of eventual British control. Considering the less than impressive British military showing in the war with the Transvaal in 1880-81, this was risky. Despite rumors of imminent conflict, British control might well be decades in the future. A third policy, firm support of the Boers, would risk rupture with England and possible economic exclusion should the predicted British annexation materialize. In the decade that followed the opening of the Rand gold fields in 1886, America became convinced that the long-term advantages of British control outweighed any short-range benefits of a pro-Boer policy. It gradually abandoned its neutral policy and moved towards the active pro-British stance so forcefully advocated by Robert Shufeldt.

## CHAPTER TWO

# God, Gold, and Good Government

## The Economic and Social Basis of America's Pro-British Policy, 1886-1895

The decade between the discovery of gold in the Witwatersrand region of the Transvaal in 1886 and the abortive attempt by Cecil Rhodes to overthrow the Kruger government in 1895 was a period of rapid change in South Africa. Increasingly, the United States was directly involved in the struggle for political and economic control of the area. The rush to the gold fields of the Witwatersrand (the Rand) served as a catalyst in the long conflict between Afrikaner and Englishman. Lured by the wealth of the mines, thousands of foreigners (Uitlanders) flocked to the South African Republic until they eventually outnumbered the white Boer burghers. The conservative, pastoral Afrikaners were inundated with adventurers and overwhelmed by various schemes, syndicates, and speculators. The natural tensions provoked by this migration were intensified by a renewed drive on the part of Britain for control of Southern Africa. The discovery of gold heightened British determination to create a unified South Africa under English rule. The grandiose plans of Rhodes and his British South African Company (chartered in 1889) for an industrialized South Africa under British control made no provisions for continued Boer independence.

The uniqueness of Boer civilization made it particularly unsuited to the disruptions of the gold strikes.[1] The Boers felt they were on a divine mission in Africa to create the perfect society in the "dark continent." They were convinced that the black African, the British, and the money-crazed foreigners living in their nation were all agents of the devil sent to test their commitment to a godly society. The Boers felt that they were the new Israelites led by God to the promised land. They had fled the "English pharaoh" through the Great Trek, subdued the Zulu, and established their divine society of patriarchal family units. Their language, religion, and agrarianism

21

were symbols of their uniqueness and God's favor towards their mission. But suddenly there were grave threats to their society. England threatened their political independence and, even more immediately, their cultural independence was being attacked by the effects of the gold strikes. The Boers viewed their conflict with the British and the Uitlanders as far more than a political struggle: it was a battle for their survival as a distinct culture, and a holy war for the Lord.

The Afrikaners were appalled by the aggressiveness and materialism of modern capitalism, and the corruption of their language, religion, and governmental system by hordes of temporary residents interested only in a quick profit and an equally rapid exit. To meet this perceived threat to their way of life, the Boers tried to slow the invasion by placing restrictions on the Uitlanders. The Transvaal government refused to accept Uitlander children in its schools, rejected the use of English in either business or government, and raised resident requirements for the franchise from one year in 1882 to 14 years by 1890.

Kruger and his government also attempted to control the mines through government grants, monopolies, and concessions. They tried to limit the expansion of the mines by regulating imports of dynamite and other materials necessary for their operation. The Transvaal created a dynamite monopoly controlled first by a German firm, later by a French syndicate, and finally by a joint Anglo-German trust.[2]

The Boer campaign to slow the growth of the mining industry and limit the impact of the Uitlanders only alienated those drawn to the wealth of their country. Furthermore, the widespread corruption and graft within the Boer government angered foreign businessmen. Low-salaried, untrained officials were swamped by the rapid increase in population and the demands for services and favors. Bribes became commonplace, and even these did not always bring results.

To many foreign observers, all the Boer traits of stubborness, suspicion, corruption, and seemingly irrational opposition to change and economic development were epitomized in their legendary leader Paul Kruger. Conservative and obstinate even by Afrikaner standards, Kruger was unalterably opposed to the surrender of Boer culture and independence to either the Uitlanders on the Rand or the English at the Cape. Driven by a fundamentalist religious conviction that God was with him and his people, Kruger eschewed any compromise with industrialization and represented a solid barrier to European and American notions of democratic government and economic progress.

Kruger's rival to the South, Cecil Rhodes, also possessed a sense of personal mission—to unite South Africa under the British flag. Rhodes was as fully committed to his role as the agent of British imperialism as Kruger was dedicated to preserving Boer uniqueness and independence. To many, Rhodes, a self-made millionaire, symbolized a future South Africa united under British rule and committed to economic development, foreign investment, and white immigration.

Kruger and Rhodes represented the two major alternatives for South Africa and thus the two choices for the United States—support of the reactionary but still sovereign Boers to gain temporary economic benefits at the risk of alienating Rhodes and England, or alignment with Britain in the hopes of future, long-range gains. The third alternative, continued political isolation and neutrality, was increasingly difficult to maintain due to the dramatic growth of America's stake in the future of the area.

The Uitlanders included over 1,000 Americans. More important, a large number were mining engineers deeply involved in the Uitlander cause. Americans were among the confidants of Rhodes and other capitalists and shared the frustrations of doing business with the Boers. Further, American trade with South Africa mushroomed after the discovery of gold, particularly after the influx of American mining engineers to the Rand. Annual American exports to South Africa remained less than $2,000,000 prior to 1890, but jumped to over $3,000,000 in 1893, doubled to $6,000,000 in 1895, and skyrocketed to over $14,000,000 in 1896. By 1894, America was second only to Great Britain in exports to South Africa—a position it retained until 1907.[3]

American awareness of the economic potential of South Africa quickened after the announcement of the discovery of gold in 1886. As a result of the gold strikes and the resulting improvement of internal transportation, the American consul at Capetown predicted that "South Africa will awaken from her long sleep of lethargy and open her eyes to the light of the new destiny which is in store for her."[4] Despite this and other similar optimistic reports of the potential of South African

mines and the South African market, the United States made
no change in its policy of official neutrality. It continued to attempt economic penetration with little encouragement of either
side in the South African conflict.

In 1888, America's passive neutrality was questioned by the
new Consul at Capetown, George F. Hollis of Arlington, Massachusetts. Hollis was fervently pro-Boer and attempted to
shift America to his position. The consul felt America's refusal
to support the Boers in their struggle with Britain amounted to
a defense of imperialism. Furthermore, it was poor business.
The Boers were in control of the gold on the Rand and American aid to Kruger would give the United States an economic
advantage in the developing area. British political control
would mean British economic control and the decline of American economic influence.[5]

After a tour of American consular agencies in the fall of
1888, Hollis submitted a detailed report entitled "Notes on
South Africa." Hollis argued the wisdom of increased support
of the Boers and recommended new consular agencies in Pretoria and the Orange Free State. Receiving only lukewarm
response from the State Department, Hollis arranged an unauthorized meeting with Paul Kruger. Encouraged by Kruger's warm reception, he met with American businessmen in
the new city of Johannesburg in an attempt to convince them
of the advantages of cooperation with the Boers. Hollis continued to flood the State Department with demands for consulates among the Boers and gloomy predictions of the future
of South Africa under Great Britain. American support of the
Boers in "the imminent revolution" was, argued Hollis, absolutely necessary to insure continued economic gains in the
Transvaal.[6]

Hollis's arguments for a pro-Boer strategy fell on deaf ears
in Washington. His credence was undermined by strong opposition among American businessmen on the Rand and by
the consul's own behavior. The State Department strongly
reprimanded him for his unauthorized meeting with Kruger
and for his open hostility towards British officials at the Cape.
Gardiner Williams, the American Consular Agent at Kimberley and a mining engineer with the DeBeers Consolidated
Mines, totally rejected Hollis's position and assured the State
Department that American merchants and engineers were
united in their support of Britain. Williams also filed a series

of reports on Hollis's private life. He accused Hollis of having financial ties with the Boers and of running up bad debts in Capetown. Williams also reported a number of drunken parties at the American consulate in Capetown that ended with Hollis passed out on the front steps.[7]

While the State Department did follow Hollis's recommendations for consular agents in Johannesburg in the South African Republic and Bloemfontein in the Orange Free State, it rejected any active support of the Boers. When Hollis persisted with his argument, he was abruptly and unceremoniously fired.[8]

Despite its failure, Hollis's campaign was significant, for it represented the last major attempt to ally the United States with Kruger and the Boers. After 1891, American attitudes towards South Africa were influenced primarily by mining engineers, businessmen, and missionaries. All three groups were frustrated by the policies of the Boers and opposed any support of what they considered the forces of reaction. By the early 1890s, the possibility of America's adopting a pro-Boer policy was remote. The United States faced a choice between continued neutrality and support of Great Britain.

Just as the gold strikes in the Transvaal heightened American interest, the growing mineral potential of South Africa also attracted increased British attention after 1886. Fearful of Germany's new colonial empire, humiliated by the Boer success in 1881, and suddenly aware of the wealth of the Rand, Britain adopted a more assertive commercial and political policy. Britain shared America's fears of industrial surpluses, and saw South Africa as a natural spot to absorb its goods and idle population, thus avoiding depression, unemployment, and potential domestic unrest. As its trade with South Africa increased, Britain recognized that, next to Egypt, South Africa was the most important colonial area in Africa. It became apparent that Britain felt it was destined to rule all the territory south of the Zambezi, and this meant incorporation of the Boer states.[9]

Cecil Rhodes and his British South Africa Company personified Britain's new aggressive policy. In the decade of the 1880s, Rhodes gradually consolidated the holdings of financial magnates such as Barnett Barnato and Alfred Beit. In 1891, Rhodes served both as premier of the Cape Colony and head of the DeBeers Consolidated Diamond Corporation, which controlled 90% of the diamond production of South Africa. Rhodes's growing wealth was accompanied by an increased dedication to the expansion of British territory. After securing British control of the vast territory of Bechaunaland in 1887, Rhodes began his drive north into Matebeleland and Mashonaland (present day Rhodesia). Then in 1888, Rhodes's agents met with King Lobengula, nominal ruler of the northern tribes, and parlayed 1,000 rifles, 100,000 rounds of ammunition, and a steamboat for the king to cruise the Zambezi into an exclusive monopoly on all the minerals in Lobengula's kingdom.[10] With this claim in hand, Rhodes was able to induce London to charter the British South Africa Company and grant it exclusive commerical rights in the territory north of Bechuanaland. In 1891, Rhodes began the bloody "opening" of the north that eventually resulted in the death of Lobengula in 1893 and the triumph of the Chartered Company's control of all the territory between Cape Colony and the Zambezi—except for the South African Republic and the Orange Free State.[11]

Many Americans were convinced that the British South Africa Company was the instrument that would establish British control over all of South Africa and bring the expected commercial and social benefits to America. The *Commercial and Financial Chronicle* hailed the Company and its drive north as a boon to civilization, economic development, and to American business. The *New York Times* contrasted the company's aggressiveness and commitment to economic development with Boers' hostility to trade and investment. Optimistic reports on the mineral wealth of "golden Mashonaland" prompted one American observer to portray the region as "a veritable El Dorado for enterprising spirits from Europe and America."[12] It was assumed that American economic penetration would naturally follow the opening of the new areas by Rhodes. America assumed it could duplicate its successful Asian policy of "hitchhiking imperialism," thereby securing the advantages won by European military operations.[13]

Much of this euphoria resulted from American impressions of Rhodes. Although deeply committed to British control of all Africa and fearful of American influence, Rhodes carefully cultivated American support of his ventures. He aided American missionary settlements first in Natal and later in the north through land grants and military protection. He also made known to American businessmen and consuls in South

Africa his great admiration for American capitalism and government. He even claimed that he always carried a copy of the Constitution to remind him of the wisdom of American federalism. More important were Rhodes's contacts with American engineers and businessmen active in the South African trade. Rhodes repeatedly reminded Americans of the commercial potential of South Africa and hinted that the United States, Britain's cultural and linguistic sister, would gain more than its share of the expected economic windfall.[14]

While Rhodes was evidently sincere in his admiration of American federalism and in his belief in Anglo-American solidarity, his plans for South Africa clearly did not include influence by any power except England. Rhodes never considered equality of trade in South Africa. At the same time that he courted American support, he feared that America would become Britain's major economic rival in South Africa. The Chartered Company, although viewed by the United States as an instrument that would serve its interests, was designed to insure British exclusiveness.[15] It was a mark of either Rhodes's successful propaganda, or American naivete, that the United States linked its economic interests with the success of Rhodes. America's vision was clouded by assumptions of the advantages of British control. It saw the British South Africa Company and Cecil Rhodes as the fulfillment of Shufeldt's prediction of the inevitability and necessity of British rule. This positive view of England and Rhodes was reinforced by America's negative impressions of Britain's major colonial rivals in Southern Africa— Germany and Portugal.

America regarded German and Portuguese colonialism as an exploitative extension of reactionary governments. The United States saw both nations as interested exclusively in immediate commercial gains rather than in the establishment of white colonies, the Christianization of the African, and the civilization of the dark continent. Americans identified German and Portuguese colonialism with the type of exploitation practiced by Leopold II in the Belgian Congo.[16] Increasingly, the United States distinguished between "good" and "bad" imperialism—between "civilizing" and "exploiting." Colonialism designed only for immediate profit ignored the white man's mission to Africa and the necessity of opening the continent to trade and missionary activity from all nations. Only colonialism that recognized the long-term obligation of the European

27

nations to development, education, and evangelism deserved American support. Great Britain shared with the United States a common language, a dedication to liberal capitalism, open trade, and representative government. England also had committed itself to the spread of Christianity and civilization. Britain's rivals, while equally convinced of their own cultural superiority, seemed to represent only totalitarianism and greed, being dedicated to profit rather than "progress."[17]

America's suspicion of Britain's rivals in Southern Africa was heightened by entanglements with Portugal over the proposed Delagoa Bay railroad that would connect the Rand with the Indian Ocean. Nearly all Americans from Shufeldt on had stressed the economic importance of Delagoa Bay and the railway connection inland. With the discovery of gold in the Transvaal, control of the railroad connection with the port of Lourenço Marques took on new urgency. By 1884, British lines from Capetown had reached the border of the South African Republic. Kruger, however, steadfastly refused to grant access through the Transvaal. In the same year, he granted a Dutch-German syndicate the rights to build the Transvaal portion of the Delagoa Bay line. Kruger's grant raised British fears of a Dutch-German-Boer alliance to block British influence. Similarly, the Boers feared British control of the railway would give England a stranglehold on the gold fields.[18] Strangely, it appeared that America held the key to the railway and to the development of the entire region.

In 1883, an American financier, Colonel Edward M. McMurdo, secured a concession from Portugal to build the section of the line from Delagoa Bay to the Transvaal border.[19] While McMurdo's line made little progress, the possibility of American control of a section of Delagoa Bay's only link with the Transvaal remained. In July 1888, McMurdo wrote the American consul in London of the possible benefits of the Delagoa Bay line. McMurdo argued that he had "full control of the road and its tariff." While it was presently necessary to ship goods through the British port of Durban and pay an ad valorem tariff of 15%, the rate at Lourenço Marques was only 3½%. With American support, McMurdo argued, he could open the line to Delagoa Bay and the wealth of the Rand to American trade:

The Delagoa Bay Railway is practically a monopoly for the trade of this whole country. There is a black population of about 30 millions with a white population bordering upon 100,000 . . . . From these figures you will readily perceive the magnitude of the markets that are to be opened up. . . . The old population composed of Hollanders . . . have endeavored to keep the country in their own hands but the influx of Anglo-Saxons has been so great that there will be a change almost immediately.[20]

While McMurdo had a clear claim, he had no railroad. In the spring of 1889, McMurdo died, and Portugal, pointing to the absence of any significant progress, seized the line and took over construction. The American consul in Mozambique strongly protested the seizure and argued that "this is only the commencement of the alliance between Portugal and the Transvaal to rid and keep out of either country all English and United States enterprise." McMurdo's widow turned to Henry White, the American Secretary of Legation in London, for support of her claim to the line, and he assured her of America's help.[21]

The volatile new Secretary of State, James G. Blaine, pressed Mrs. McMurdo's claim. In June 1889, there were reports that Blaine would actively intervene in the railway squabble between Portugal, Britain, and the Transvaal. It was even rumored that the United States would send a warship to Delagoa Bay to support McMurdo's claim.[22]

President Benjamin Harrison called attention to the incident in his annual address to Congress and warned Portugal that America would not tolerate the seizure of an American citizen's property. Blaine sent a belligerent note to Lisbon protesting the "defiant attitude of Portugal" and proclaiming his "hopeless impression" of Portuguese intentions. Receiving no satisfaction, Blaine turned to London for support. Robert Lincoln, the American Minister to Great Britain, met with Prime Minister Lord Salisbury and presented Blaine's summary of the situation and copies of Blaine's protests to Portugal.[23] Salisbury was sympathetic but typically cautious. He was far more concerned with British interests and with avoiding a conflict with Portugal than in assisting America, and he refused to commit Britain to support of the McMurdo claim.[24]

With Portuguese construction of the railway already begun, and having received no support from London, the United States dropped its demand for control of the line and went to court to gain a settlement for McMurdo's widow. In March 1900, she finally received an award of nearly $300,000 from a Swiss tribunal.[25]

Intrigues among the British, the Boers, the Portuguese and the original Dutch-German syndicate over railway construction continued until the Boer War. The controversy over the McMurdo claim, however, confirmed America's negative impressions of the Boers and Portugal. American officials assumed the Boers had worked with Portugal to sabotage McMurdo's claim.[26] Railroad rivalries seemed to Americans another example of the continued bickerings that blocked full development of South Africa. British control offered the stability necessary for trade and investment, and America thus refused to be drawn into any further agreements with the Boers. Despite renewed offers from the South African Republic for a commercial treaty, the State Department refused, citing possible British opposition.[27]

American support of British imperialism received an important boost from the immigration of Americans to the Rand gold fields in the early 1890s. Although American engineers had been active in South African diamond mines since the 1870s, the discovery of gold resulted in a desperate need for additional mining experts. American engineers, because of their training in the American West, Latin America, and Asia, were eagerly sought out by the new mining magnates of South Africa.[28] In 1887, for example, Cecil Rhodes appointed Gardiner Fred Williams, a California engineer, manager of his DeBeers Consolidated diamond works. Williams remained in this position until 1905, when he was replaced by his son. Another American, Hamilton Smith, was plucked from management of a silver mine in Nevada in 1891 to become consulting engineer for the Rothschild interests, and visited South Africa several times to assess the value of the gold fields. In 1892, he shocked the engineering world with his prediction that the Rand would surpass the United States in gold production within a decade. Smith also encouraged several of his associates to come to South Africa. A group of mining engineers, including Hennen Jennings, H. C. Perkins, Thomas and William Mein, and Charles Butters, all of whom had worked together in the American West and Latin America, eventually became mine managers on the Rand. By 1896, over half of the mines in South Africa were controlled by American engineers.[29]

By far the most influential American engineer in South Africa was John Hays Hammond. Hammond became the most important American in Africa and the prime spokesman for American attitudes towards South Africa. An 1876 graduate of the Sheffield School of Mines at Yale, Hammond continued his education at the German Royal School of Mines in Saxony. From 1879 to 1892, he worked in the gold fields of the American West and Latin America. In 1893, he left a mine in Idaho to accept an offer of $50,000 per year from Barney Barnato to manage his mining properties on the Rand. Six months later, Cecil Rhodes hired him away for a salary of $75,000, a share of all profits, and unlimited expenses to become Rhodes's personal consulting engineer. Eventually he occupied the same position with the British South Africa Company. With a staff of over a dozen young and talented American engineers, Hammond was the virtual czar of South African mining by 1894.[30]

A staunch Republican and a strong spokesman for American business expansion, Hammond constantly lobbied for a more active American policy towards South Africa. A firm admirer of Rhodes and Great Britain, and possessed of a strong hatred for the Boers, Hammond hoped to ally America with Britain as he was aligned with Rhodes.[31] Hammond was confident of the commercial potential of South Africa and actively recruited American engineers and businessmen to come to South Africa to work with England in the development of the region.[32] Because of his knowledge of South Africa and the mining industry and his contacts with Rhodes, as well as with American bussinessmen, and politicians, Hammond exerted great influence on American policy.

With the aid of Hammond, Williams, and the sixty other American mining engineers and managers, the United States rapidly became the largest supplier of South African mines. Hammond and others were most familiar with American equipment and were also eager to increase American ties with South Africa. As a result, they often directed contracts to American firms, informed American companies of the highest bids acceptable on equipment, and generally promoted American involvement in the Transvaal. In 1894, for example,

Hammond informed the Ingersoll Drill Company that he could arrange exclusive rights for supplying mining drills on the Rand. Similarly, he wrote his friend W. J. Chalmers of the Fraser and Chalmers Company that he would grant American firms a contract even if their prices were higher than those of another nation. He also solicited American companies to supply wood, railroad ties, and agricultural implements to the growing South African market.[33] American firms, taking advantage of special legislation that allowed mining, railroad, and agricultural supplies to enter the Transvaal duty free, doubled their exports to South Africa from 1894 to 1895 and dominated heavy industry imports to the Rand.[34]

Hammond and other Americans were not satisfied with this increase. They were contemptuous of the efforts of American consuls and critical of Washington for its neglect of the South African market generally and the potential of the Transvaal in particular.[35]

American engineers were also important in shaping American opinion of the Boers. Exposed to the restrictions of Kruger's government and able to observe first hand Afrikaner society, American engineers were incensed by the monopolies, graft, and inefficiency of the Transvaal's government. Hammond repeatedly complained of the dynamite monopoly, the necessity of bribery, and the general inability of the Boers to understand capitalism, industrialization, and progress. Gardiner Williams, who doubled as America's consular agent at Kimberley, was equally outspoken in his opposition to the Boers, and he was particularly critical of America's "pro-Boer" representatives at the Cape.[36]

American businessmen shared the complaints of the engineers. American firms were particularly upset with the favoritism shown Dutch and German firms and the refusal of the Boers to conduct business in English. They also protested the casual attitude of Boer officials towards time of delivery and changes in prices.[37]

Boer obstinacy seemed in marked contrast to apparent British cooperation. Nearly all the mining engineers owed their jobs to British capital (although the Boers did eventually appoint an American, E. H. Woodford, as the Mining Engineer of the South African Republic) and worked closely with Rhodes and the British South Africa Company. Also, most of them admired Rhodes and his contribution to the development of the area. Hammond felt Rhodes was "the greatest personality I ever met" and "the greatest Englishman of his times." Hammond argued that Rhodes was actively seeking Anglo-American cooperation in the development of Africa.[38]

Rhodes welcomed this image, and continued to stress his vision of Anglo-American world domination. Privately, however, he retained a fear of American involvement in Africa and warned of an "American-dominated anti-British Republic in the Transvaal." He forecast a future commercial war with America and in 1899 told one of his associates that: "We shall have trouble in time to come with America. Americans are our greatest danger."[39]

The actions of Hammond and his colleagues gave some justification to Rhodes's fears. Despite their high salaries and influence, American engineers were not content to limit themselves to working for Rhodes and his associates. Therefore under the leadership of Hammond, they formulated several rather grandiose plans for direct American investments in South Africa that would be independent of either Boer or British control. In 1894, for example, Henry Butters managed to secure a contract to build an electric tramway system around Capetown. He received the enthusiastic backing of Hammond, who advised him to make it "an American project" rather than secure international financing. While the project eventually fell through, Hammond did manage to receive 27,000 shares of stock in the tramway company, which was financed by British funds.[40]

Hammond had even more ambitious plans. He suggested that a group of American investors purchase land on the proposed Cape-to-Cairo Railway (Rhodes's pet project), and then resell it to Rhodes at a substantial profit.[41] Undeterred when the project fizzled, Hammond organized a large American syndicate to speculate in mining interests in Matabeleland and in railway connections in Portuguese East Africa and the Transvaal. Rebuffed by Portuguese officials reluctant to make concessions to an "English company," Hammond replied that:

It is our intention to make it an American concern, the Syndicate having its Head Quarters in New York. While I can see no objection to the co-operation of English capitalists still I think our ends would be best subserved by making the Syndicate distinctly American.[42]

Hammond also initiated mining projects designed to be controlled by American capital. In 1895, he sent members of his staff to Rhodesia to prepare detailed reports on the potential for gold, diamond, and coal mining, as well as railroad construction and agriculture. Hammond hoped to use the report to entice American investors into a South African syndicate with Hammond at the head. If successful in South Africa, the syndicate would become global.[43] In December 1895, Hammond wrote Charles W. Truslow, a wealthy New York lawyer, of his plans to expand his interests from Africa to America and Latin America as well:

> I hope to be able to run over to New York in the early part of next year. I have a scheme for our Company (this is strictly *sub rosa)* to operate extensively in American mines, and I think that I can count on your assistance in this scheme. We have a large amount of unemployed capital, and can control, if necessary, millions of dollars for such a scheme.[44]

Hammond's deportation after his participation in the Jameson Raid cut short such projects (see Chapter III). But the influence of Hammond and other mining engineers as well as the rapid growth of American exports to South Africa revived British fears of American economic influence. A British importer in Capetown felt Americans were "pushing their way" into South Africa and were more aggressive and successful than either the British or the Dutch. The correspondent for the London *Times* was even more alarmed. He noted that prior to 1889, Britain supplied nearly all of the machinery used in the mines of South Africa. By late 1893, however, one American firm, Fraser and Chalmers, supplied over 40% of the mining machinery on the Rand. He observed similar trends in boilers, agricultural implements, and other heavy equipment. He feared that British firms were "losing ground every day" to more aggressive American companies. Rhodes also voiced his fears of American influence, telling one engineer that he did not want too many Americans on the Rand, as they were more committed to America than to Africa.[45]

The growing influence of American engineers and the increased importance of the South African market to American business raised America's stake in the political future of South Africa. American economic success had paralleled British expansion, while increased contacts with the Boers had confirmed earlier unfavorable impressions. The United States increasingly identified Britain with economic opportunity and the Boers with economic restrictions. Meanwhile America had shifted its view of South Africa from an area of raw materials only to a potentially lucrative market for American goods and capital.[46] The economic rationale for a pro-British policy was thus nearly completed by 1895.

During the same period there was a corresponding, although less complete, growth of the humanitarian and racial justification of British control. It is impossible to separate America's sense of mission from its belief in economic expansion. It was assumed that trade carried with it "civilization." The education and Christianization of the African would, in turn, create a consumer market that would further stimulate trade. Economic penetration not only aided the United States by avoiding unemployment and unrest, but helped to elevate "lesser" races and develop backward areas. This interdependence of trade and civilization was applied by American business to South Africa. The *Commercial and Financial Chronicle* argued that America had a mission to bring education and religion to the African through trade and missionary activity. Acceptance of America's Christian duty was not only a moral responsibility, but would also be profitable. By helping to elevate the black South African, "[we would] add millions to the list of world consumers. . . . Their improvement will be our gain."[47] Hammond also recognized the civilizing impact of commerce, and he argued that business and trade must be judged not only by their profits but also by their impact on society.[48] Thus, the American sense of mission, as well as economic gain, contributed to a pro-British stance.

The conflicting racial policies of Britain and the Boers also shaped American attitudes towards the political struggle in South Africa. Although far outnumbered by the black population, few white South Africans were willing to consider the African a political or social equal. In contrast to the Boers, however, both British and Americans assumed it was necessary to Christianize blacks and guide them in the use of the tools of civilization. While most white Americans at home and in South Africa shared the racist assumptions common during the period, they accepted the argument that the "superior" races had an obligation to the "inferior." Although assumed to be incapable of self-government, the black African was entitled to the paternalistic guidance of the white race. Americans tolerated and even encouraged the destruction of traditional tribal society in the name of progress, but condemned ruthless racial exploitation.

American missionaries were the most vocal critics of white racial policies in Southern Africa. They repeatedly protested the floggings, rape, and sale of liquor to Africans in the Portuguese settlements near Delagoa Bay. They also complained of harassment of Protestant missionaries by Catholic officials in Portuguese territory.[49] American missionaries were most concerned, however, with Boer policies in the Transvaal.

The Boers had a long history of racial conflict. The abolition of slavery in the Cape Colony in 1833 was one of the major reasons for the Great Trek to the north. The Afrikaners excluded the black African from their government, churches, and social organizations, since the Boers felt no Anglo-Saxon "mission" to the African. They viewed the black as an obstacle to be removed rather than an individual to be saved. The bloody wars with the Zulu, combined with a religious interpretation of the African as cursed by God, resulted in a near fanatical hatred of the African and anyone that attempted to interfere with Boer racial policies. While the Cape Colony had no restriction on suffrage by "class or colour" (although property requirements effectively excluded blacks), the Boers specifically expressed their belief in the biological inferiority of the African. The Transvaal's constitution of 1858 declared: "The people desire to permit no equality between the coloured and white inhabitants, either in Church or State." In 1876, the Transvaal Volksraad (assembly) affirmed that: "No person not regarded as belonging to the white population of the South African Republic shall be enrolled as a burgher possessing the franchise." After regaining its independence from England, the Transvaal again passed a law excluding "all coloured people" from citizenship.[50]

The Boers not only denied racial equality and suffrage, but showed little inclination to bring Christianity or the other facets of "civilization" to the black. The Boer churches were limited to whites, and rejected any obligation to spread the faith to blacks. More galling to Americans, they opposed the efforts of other nations to bring the Gospel to the black African.

American missionaries were increasingly active in South Africa in the decade following the gold strikes. By 1889, America had over 30 major missionary stations in Natal, the Cape Colony, and the Transvaal. Missionaries from the United States were shocked by the Boer's apparent rejection of their obligation to black Africa. While they admired the Boers' piousness, American missionaries noted that they had undertaken no effort to spread their faith to nonwhites. An American working among the Zulu noted that the Afrikaners' Christianity "does not extend so far as to caring for the salvation of the heathen perishing around them."[51] Even more repulsive to Americans dedicated to the Christianization of Africa was Boer reluctance to allow foreign missionaries into their territory. Convinced of the superiority of their own faith, fearful of the effects of education on the African, and generally hostile to any additional foreigners in their land, the Boers placed strict limits on the number of missionaries allowed into the Transvaal and the Orange Free State. When missionaries were admitted, they were closely watched by local burghers who carefully scrutinized their teachings, lest they mention racial equality or preach "incorrect" theology.[52]

Americans could not understand the exclusiveness of the Boers or their lack of concern for the souls of the Africans. The American Bible Society complained of the arrogant superiority of the Afrikaners and their refusal to join in "the worldwide movement" to spread the Christian faith.[53]

Britain seemed more in accord with the American dedication to Christian evangelism. The *Missionary Review of the World* argued that British colonialism was superior to that of other European powers, as it was dedicated to the spread of Christianity and the "uplift" of the black rather than merely to profit.[54] This interpretation was promoted by the actions and rhetoric of Rhodes and other British officials in South Africa. Rhodes invited American missionaries to accompany him in the pioneer drive to open Matabeleland in 1891-92. Rhodes stressed the necessity of a joint Anglo-American campaign to Christianize the area and keep the Boers away from the African. More tangible was his offer of money, land, and free transportation to any American missionaries willing to settle in the new area. In 1893, the American Board of Commissioners of Foreign Missions accepted Rhodes's offer and received a promise from the British South Africa Company of

3,000 acres of land for each missionary family. Eventually American missionaries were granted over 24,000 acres in the new territory of Rhodesia.[55]

Rhodes's actions, combined with Boer hostility, convinced many Americans that the Chartered Company was the key to progress and Christianity in South Africa. One American missionary wrote from South Africa:

> I thank God that the British South African Company dominates so large a territory populated by tribes which for centuries have been sunk in superstition and addicted to barbarous customs. . . . God in His providence has sent the Anglo-Saxon race to the southern part of the continent to prepare the way for the dissemination of His truth.[56]

Other Englishmen joined with Rhodes to stress the benefits of British rule for the native. Arthur White, Secretary of the Royal Scottish Geographical Society, in a book and in articles directed towards America, emphasized the humanitarian and social aspects of British colonialism. White even argued that with the development of a British Africa, American Negroes would emigrate and become "leaders of native society."[57]

The growing notions of Anglo-Saxonism and the Anglo-Saxon world mission also influenced missionary thought. Britain was not only a progressive, capitalistic, and democratic nation, but was also Protestant and English-speaking. All of these traits were admirable, but American missionaries were particularly impressed with the last two. Britain and the United States would combine to make South Africa a bastion of Protestantism against the forces of Catholicism in French and Portuguese Africa, and Islam in West Africa. "Great Britain and the United States, the two Protestant and Teutonic powers that wield the moral headship of humanity," wrote the chairman of the American Missionary Congress on Africa, "are the powers of most influence in the spiritual regeneration of Africa and those most endowed for the betterment of her peoples."[58] The *Methodist Review,* in an article entitled "The Mission of the Anglo-Saxon," argued that England and America were the only forces for progress in Africa.[59] Thomas Fortune, editor of the Negro newspaper the *New York Age,* summarized the American missionary view of the development of South Africa:

I believe that the nationalization of Africa will be along British lines, as that of the United States, in its language . . . , in its system of government and in its religion. The English language is the strongest of all languages, the most elastic in its structure, the most comprehensive in its use as a vehicle of human thought and expression. The English system of civil government is the best that has been devised because it allows the greatest possible freedom to the citizen . . . . The Christian religion is destined to supplant all other religious systems of belief, because it is the best code of moral philosophy ever given to man . . . . The English-speaking people are to-day the strongest force in Africa.[60]

Missionaries shared with American businessmen the assumption of the civilizing influence of trade and commerce. They felt that British encouragement of economic development would also be a valuable tool in the spread of the faith. Commerce and industrialism would expose the black African to a "superior race" and the advantages of work, morality, and Christianity. The head of an American missionary station in Natal argued: "Commerce is another successful missionary agent which is preparing the way for Christianity in Africa. . . . The Christian merchant has proved to be a valuable adjunct of the missionary."[61]

Industrialization and increased contacts with whites would be aids in the evangelism of Southern Africa. The imposition of industry and commerce would assist the breakdown of the old tribal organization. Industry would concentrate the African in cities such as Johannesburg, Pretoria, and Kimberley, where a single missionary could preach to a larger audience in one day than he might see in a year in the bush. Blacks returning from the cities to the villages would carry the torch of Christianity to every section of South Africa.[62]

British attempts to tax the African also impressed American missionaries and businessmen. They assumed that such a tax, payable in cash, would force blacks to work for wages in the mines. This would provide the mines with a desperately needed labor force and also weaken the power of the pagan chiefs. American businessmen argued that such laws were necessary for continued economic development, while missionaries saw such legislation as a method of destroying tribalism and the older animist religions.[63]

39

Although they generally had a low opinion of the potential of black South Africans, American mining engineers also saw the necessity of Christianity and education. Most felt that Britain was the best agent for this mission. Hammond, although a defender of flogging to encourage work, argued that British administration was "a blessing, not only for the whites, but for the natives as well." Other engineers agreed that education and the spread of the work ethic were crucial to the economic development of the area and could be best achieved by British rule.[64]

American diplomatic representatives in South Africa joined missionaries, businessmen, and engineers in criticism of Boer racism and exploitation. American consular agents were plagued by problems of black Americans visiting the Boer states. In 1894, a black minister from Atlanta, John Ross, was publicly whipped for using the sidewalks of Johannesburg. Ross protested this humiliation of an American citizen to Charles Benedict, the American Consul in Capetown. Benedict sent a report to Washington deploring the incident, but explained that he could not contest the law of a foreign nation. Benedict did send Gardiner Williams, the Consular Agent at Kimberley, to Johannesburg to investigate. Williams reported that "no nigger is allowed to promenade on the sidewalks of town under penalty of being whipped. There is also another law that all niggers found in the streets after 9 p.m. without a pass from their employer, are to be imprisoned for the night."[65] The American consular agent at Lydenburg, a small town northeast of Johannesburg, did protest the incident. He reminded the South African Republic that "in the United States there is no distinction in citizenship between white and coloured."[66] The State Department instructed Benedict to protest the event, but the matter died when Benedict claimed that new information revealed that Ross was whipped for insolence to the police rather than merely for using the sidewalk.[67]

Perhaps it was ironic that representatives of the United States should protest racial injustice. Given America's racial segregation, any complaint about South African discrimination must have appeared hypocritical. In fact, some Americans agreed with the legal inequality of the Transvaal. W. H. C. Brown, a representative of the United States National Museum on a scientific expedition to South Africa, argued that "Oom Paul and his folk know what is due the nigger, and we are risking much in allowing the black man to think that he is equal to the white."[68] Brown was in the minority. Most Americans accepted the obligation of the white to guide and develop the black. Most also were convinced that Britain was best able to oversee this project.

American black leaders shared this confidence in the humanitarianism of British colonialism. Black interest in Africa led to the gradual growth of the movement to "regenerate" Africa through missionary activity by black Americans.[69] In 1895 white missionaries organized a "Congress on Africa and the American Negro" in Atlanta. White and black leaders emphasized the duty of "advanced" black Americans to liberate Africa from tribalism and paganism. H. K. Carroll, editor of the *Independent,* set the tone for the conference:

> What the Christian faith, Christian education, and Christian example have done for the Negro in the United States, these influences can do for the Negro in Africa. It is natural that seven million Negroes, escaped from slavery, rising by culture, industry and economy to a high plane of civilization, should turn their thoughts to the Dark Continent, where untold millions of their race are living in a state of savagery, and that they should feel a strong desire to assist in the redemption of Africa.[70]

The interest of American blacks in Africa led to a debate over the strategy necessary to "redeem and regenerate" Africa. In the same year as the Conference on Africa and the American Negro, Booker T. Washington outlined his policy of accommodation with white rule in the United States. Washington argued that the black American should avoid political action and concentrate on self-help programs, industrial and agricultural training, and improvement of the race. Blacks should abandon social integration and political rights for economic gains.

Many black and white missionaries felt Washington's program of self-help and industrial education could be successfully applied to Africa. They proclaimed "the gospel of soap and candles, hammer and saw, and loom" and argued that accommodation with white rule would be the best strategy for the black African as well as the black American.[71]

Just as Washington's Atlanta Compromise came under attack at home, however, some American blacks also rejected its application to Africa. Black intellectuals such as Edward Blyden of Liberia contended that only a return of American blacks to Africa would free them from slavery and Africa from savagery.[72] An even stronger challenge to Washington's ideas came from Bishop H. M. Turner of the African Methodist Episcopal Church. Turner had visited South Africa and was skeptical of the assumption that Britain would dramatically improve the status of the black African. He thus rejected Washington's arguments for acceptance of white political rule. Turner returned to South Africa in 1898 to proclaim "Africa for the Africans."[73] Although he was later influential among both Africans and black Americans, Turner was in 1895 part of a small minority that rejected the assumed benefits of British rule. The bulk of black Americans concerned with Africa were convinced of the advantages of English imperialism. They worked with white missionaries to establish the type of self-help programs preached by Booker T. Washington. Less than a decade later, American blacks were accused of preaching black separatism and encouraging revolts. Prior to the Boer War, however, whatever influence American blacks exerted was directed in support of British control of all of South Africa.[74]

By the end of 1895 Americans had constructed both an economic and humanitarian rationale for support of British rule in Southern Africa. The restrictive policies of the Boers and the contrasting cultivation of America by the British seemed to illustrate the alternatives facing South Africa. The Boers represented continued hostility to industrial development and the flow of goods and capital necessary for the expansion of American trade. The corrupt and anachronistic government of Kruger blocked economic progress and fostered political turmoil and instability. The Afrikaners were reluctant or unable to provide the proper climate for capitalism. They were unwilling to develop the black labor force needed for the mines and the consumption of imports. They had rejected the duty of the white man to uplift and Christianize the black African, and not content with shirking their duty, they had also prevented others from undertaking this divine work.

Although both business and missionary spokesmen were convinced that British rule would aid both America and South Africa, the United States government was still reluctant to be dragged into the struggle between Great Britain and the Boers.

America sympathized with England, but hoped British expansion would be gradual and peaceful. Nongovernmental groups, however, were far more assertive in their support of England. They were disgusted with their government's apparent lack of aggressiveness and its refusal to give stronger support to British imperialism, and in late 1895, a group of Americans in South Africa sought to hasten the gradual British advance through support of, and participation in, Leander Starr Jameson's invasion of the Transvaal.

## CHAPTER THREE

# Reform and Revolution

**The Jameson Raid, The Great Rapprochement, and the Coming War in South Africa**

In 1835 the Boers trekked north from Cape Colony to escape British rule and establish a unique and pure society. Sixty years later that society was threatened. The lure of gold attracted a migration of foreigners to the Witwatersrand that jeopardized the government of Paul Kruger and the entire fabric of Afrikaner life. Inundated by foreign miners, directors, and adventurers, the Boers reacted with social, economic, and political restrictions. Kruger and his countrymen viewed controls on suffrage, taxation, and education as absolutely necessary to avoid being engulfed by profit-minded transients. When criticized for restrictions on Uitlander suffrage, Kruger pointed to the Transvaal's flag and exclaimed: "You see that flag? If I grant them the franchise, I may as well pull it down." Similarly, he argued that it was the Boers who had an interest in the future of the area, not the temporary residents lured by the mines. "I would pay more attention to a petition from fifty of my burghers than to one from the whole of Johannesburg," he explained.[1]

Although Americans on the Rand totaled only about 1,500, they had influence out of proportion to their numbers. American engineers ran many of the mines on the Rand, and their countrymen supplied much of the expertise and material that allowed the continued tapping of the wealth of the Transvaal. Americans formed a managerial elite united by wealth, knowledge, and close ties with Rhodes and the British South Africa Company. Thus they not only shared with other foreigners the frustrations of Boer restrictions on the vote, education, and language, but were particularly affected by economic restraints such as taxes, monopolies, and the general Boer suspicion of industrialization. When the conflict between the Afrikaners in Pretoria and the Uitlanders in Johannesburg escalated from rhetoric to violence in late 1895, Americans were in the forefront of the attempt to depose Kruger's government. To Americans living in the Transvaal, the destruction of Boer power was both a moral right and sound business.

American conflict with Kruger increased in early 1894. Plagued by raids on frontier settlements in the north, the South African Republic declared war on selected African tribes. The Volksraad levied a large war tax to finance the expedition. Kruger issued a call for volunteers, and also threatened to draft foreigners to protect the state. The threat of conscription was most serious to Americans. Unlike most European nations, the United States had no agreement with the Transvaal exempting its citizens from the draft.[2] Americans were incensed by the prospect of paying for and fighting in a war for a government that refused them the vote and other basic rights. Kruger countered with the argument that military service would be a dramatic illustration of the Uitlanders' loyalty to the nation.

Charles Benedict, the American Consul at Capetown, bemoaned the lack of a treaty with the South African Republic, but was even more angry with Kruger. He urged the State Department to deliver a formal protest and to enlist the aid of England in the effort to exclude Americans from the draft. Assistant Secretary of State Adee and Secretary of State Walter Q. Gresham both wrote to Thomas A. Bayard, American Minister in London, to seek the intervention of British Prime Minister Lord Salisbury. Bayard met with Foreign Secretary Lord Kimberley and received sympathy, but no concrete pledge of support. Adee privately admitted that the Transvaal had a case, as the conflict was not a foreign war but a matter of public defense. Washington finally decided to postpone action until the Boers actually drafted an American citizen.[3] Kruger wisely refrained from calling any Americans. This was possible because of the success of the Boer volunteers. Perhaps also, Kruger hesitated because he knew that Americans in Johannesburg, led by Hammond, had taken an oath that if they were drafted, their first shot would be aimed at a Boer commander.[4]

The debate over conscription was soon eclipsed by the general complaints of the foreign-born population on the Rand. In early 1895, the Uitlanders formed the Johannesburg Reform Committee, with Hammond as chairman, to protest political and economic restrictions by the Boers. The Reform Committee emphasized issues that concerned the majority of Uitlanders: the refusal of the Boers to build schools for foreign children; the complete lack of any voice in the municipal government of Johannesburg; the impure water and lack of a sewage system; and, most important, the lack of the vote. The Committee claimed that Uitlanders paid 75% of the taxes on the Rand, but had no say in the government. It also complained of the corruption in the Transvaal judicial system, the claimed right of Kruger to draft foreigners, and the refusal of the Boers to end the sale of liquor to blacks. Hammond also included protests over the Transvaal's grants of monopolies on materials necessary for the mines and the high freight rates on railroad lines.[5]

Hammond and his fellow engineers dominated the leadership of the Reform Committee. Americans raised the familiar cry of "no taxation without representation" and Hammond proclaimed that he would rather live under George III than Paul Kruger. Hammond denied that the Reform Committee was merely a stalking horse for British imperialism. It was, he argued, a natural reaction to the "provincialism" of Kruger. Publicly, Hammond emphasized the purely political goals of the Committee. The objectives were "to establish our actions as a genuine internal revolt having no object ulterior to that of destroying the narrow Boer oligarchy . . . and of setting up in its place a truly representative democracy on the American model."[6]

Accompanying the political and legal issues, however, were economic considerations. Hammond and other Americans on the Rand were convinced that conditions could not continue as they were without the eventual destruction of the mining industry. Hammond felt that excessive taxation, the high cost of material due to monopolies, and the general Boer attitude towards business and industry restricted investment and shackled expansion. Smaller mines and exploratory diggings were unprofitable because of the high costs. Hammond was particularly galled by Boer actions, owing to his belief that the Transvaal had actively solicited foreign capital and expertise immediately after the discovery of gold, but was now unwilling to accept the changes accompanying industrialization. He saw the conflict as between the "patriarchal, pastoral society" of the Boers and "an urban industrial civilization." The typical Boer did not understand mining, capitalism, or modern society, but "was a peasant with the conservative, reactionary, and suspicious nature of that class." Capitalism required the risk of large amounts of money in hopes of the return of a profit—a principle that was the basis of capitalism and modern society. Kruger, through taxation, monopolies, and graft, had removed the profit incentive from South Africa and jeopardized the huge investments in the mines. The Afrikaners were antibusiness and anticapitalism and must not be allowed to stand in the way of progress.[7]

Boer restrictiveness seemed in sharp contrast to the freedom of trade and investment offered by Britain. In his annual report to *Commercial Relations,* the American consul at Capetown noted the great increase in American exports in 1895 and observed:

> There is no hindrance to British colonial markets outside their being in possession of British traders and colonial sentiment in favor of the mother country. They are as free to foreigners as to British subjects, and this is all that can be expected. The increase in our exports to British Africa . . . shows that the field is ready for our exporters and manufacturers.[8]

American distrust of Kruger and his government was compounded by fears of a possible alignment of the Transvaal with Germany. Fearing encirclement by Rhodes and the British, and a revolt by a disgruntled foreign population, the South African Republic drew closer to Germany. Dr. William J. Leyds, Kruger's State Secretary, was strongly pro-German and advocated an accommodation with Berlin as a defense against England. In early 1895, Leyds sailed to Europe for talks with the German Foreign Office. Kruger followed with an address to the Germans living in Pretoria. Speaking in honor of the Kaiser's birthday, Kruger concluded:

> I shall always promote the interests of Germany, though it be with the resources of a child, such as my land is considered. The child is now being trodden upon by one great Power, and the natural consequence is that it seeks protection from another. . . . The time has come to recognize ties of the closest friendship between Germany and the South African Republic, ties such as are natural between father and child.[9]

Sensing an opportunity to exploit the conflict between the Afrikaners and Britain, Germany became the Transvaal's ma-

jor ally in its attempt to maintain restrictions on the Uitlanders.[10]

Americans feared Boer ties with Germany for both political
and economic reasons. With the support of Berlin, Kruger
would be strong enough to ignore Uitlander protests. Germany's recent annexation of South West Africa raised the
possibility of a German-Boer bloc in Southern Africa closed to
American trade and investment. Germany was already a major
trade rival in South Africa, and the United States feared being
squeezed out of the anticipated Transvaal market by a Boer-
German alliance. Hammond warned that the South African
Republic's friendship with Germany was the beginning of an
anti-American, anti-British plot to make Germany and Holland dominant in Southern Africa.[11]

By the summer of 1895, Rhodes and his top lieutenant, Dr.
Leander Starr Jameson, had decided on an armed invasion to
overthrow Kruger. Early preparations for the raid were actively supported by Hammond, the Johannesburg Reform Committee, and the American representative at Kimberley, Gardiner Williams. In October 1895, Hammond met with Williams
and arranged for secret shipments of arms to Johannesburg.
With money furnished by Rhodes and forwarded by Hammond, Williams began to smuggle guns and ammunition from
Kimberley to the Reform Committee in Johannesburg. Williams hid the weapons in empty Standard Oil drums and in
boxes of mining equipment with false bottoms. Working closely with Rhodes, Jameson, and Rutherford Harris, Secretary of
the British South Africa Company, Hammond planned an
armed uprising of Uitlanders in Johannesburg and the seizure
of the Boer arsenal to coincide with the invasion of the Transvaal by Jameson.[12]

British Colonial Secretary Joseph Chamberlain knew of the
preparations for the raid and also the role of the Americans in
the invasion. Faced with a growing conflict with the United
States over the boundary in Venezuela, Chamberlain urged
immediate action in South Africa to avoid coincidental crises
in the Transvaal and in South America.[13]

Because of either the interference of London or the confusion
among its organizers, the invasion was postponed, resched-
uled, and later postponed again. Jameson finally disregarded
late instructions to cancel the attack. Confident he knew
Rhodes's wishes, "Dr. Jim" and his 600 men invaded the

South African Republic on 29 December 1895. The raid caught Hammond and the Reform Committee unprepared. When he received news of Jameson's march, Hammond cabled Harris: "Wire just received. Expert's report decidedly adverse. I absolutely condemn further developments at present."[14]

When it became obvious that Jameson would continue, Hammond scheduled an emergency meeting of Americans on the Reform Committee. Fearful of an attack by the Boers, the group adopted a resolution supporting the Transvaal government if all the demands of the Uitlanders were met immediately. Hammond ordered two American engineers, H. C. Perkins and Hennen Jennings, to meet with Kruger in Pretoria. Jennings told Kruger:

> Although the Americans recognize the rights of the Boers, along with those of the Uitlanders, unless your Honour in some way meets the demands of the unfranchised peoples of the Transvaal, you cannot expect their support when a revolution comes. We Americans want to see the Republic preserved, but on a truer basis.

Kruger, who had full knowledge of the raid owing to the failure of Jameson to cut a crucial telegraph wire, asked: "Will the Americans be for or against the Government?" "They will be against the Government," Jennings replied. "This is no time for discussion, but a time for people to obey the law," answered Kruger ending the meeting.[15]

On New Year's Eve, Hammond called a meeting of all Americans in Johannesburg. After Hammond urged a show of support for Jameson, the Americans voted 495-5 to take up arms against Kruger. One hundred and fifty volunteered and formed the George Washington Corps to seize and hold Johannesburg until Jameson arrived. American bravado proved to be in vain. On 2 January 1896, Jameson was captured at Doornknop, 20 miles from Johannesburg. One week later, while enjoying an elegant dinner at the exclusive Rand Club in Johannesburg, Hammond and six other Americans active in the Reform Committee were arrested and charged with treason.[16]

The Jameson Raid provoked a worldwide response. Rhodes suffered a slight heart attack when he heard of Jameson's capture. The German Kaiser wanted to land marines to protect Germans in Pretoria. When Kruger wisely declined the invitation, Germany had to be content with dispatching a warship

49

to Delagoa Bay, a stern protest to London, and the famous "Kruger telegram" of 3 January, congratulating Kruger on his defeat of the invaders.

The American government, faced with the arrest of seven of its citizens for treason, was caught almost totally unprepared for the crisis. America had no full-time consul in Johannesburg and was forced to rely on J.C. Manion, a consular agent and employee of the Ingersoll-Sergeant Drill Company who was also a personal friend of Hammond. The situation at Capetown, seat of America's only full-time representative in South Africa, was also confused. The post was temporarily vacant because of a death, and responsibility went to Clifford Knight, the Vice-Consul, a British citizen with a long record of hatred of the Boers.

Despite the problems of working through a confidant of the defendant and an Englishman, Secretary of State Richard Olney took instant action to try to secure a fair trial for Hammond and his associates. He cabled Manion to "take all measures to secure John Hays Hammond protection and fair play." Acting on advice from British Ambassador Sir Julian Paunceforte, Olney also telegraphed Bayard in London and instructed him to go to Salisbury to seek British aid. Finally, Olney cabled the South African Republic requesting information and urging a fair trial. To insure American presence, Olney instructed Knight to secure an American lawyer and go to Pretoria to work with Manion for Hammond's release.[17] Adding to the muddle, Manion had already hired an attorney, and thus resented Knight's presence. He protested the intrusion of a British citizen in the trial of Americans. Although sympathetic to Uitlander grievances, Manion blamed Hammond for causing his own arrest by working with Rhodes for an armed invasion rather than continuing peaceful protest. Knight, however, defended the raid and sent despatches to Washington blaming the Boers for the entire situation.[18]

Olney managed to secure a pledge from both the British Foreign Office and the Colonial Office to try to aid Hammond and the other prisoners, but he received little cooperation from the South African Republic. The Secretary of State was particularly upset when Jameson and his band of invaders were released to be tried in Britain, while Hammond and the other Americans remained in prison in Pretoria.[19]

In late January, Manion met with Kruger, but received only the promise of a fair trial. At the same time, Knight, acting independently, continued to argue the responsibility of the Boers for the invasion. He reiterated the legitimacy of the Uitlander demands and claimed that the Reform Committee had armed only for self-defense. They were being tried for attempting "to claim the rights, by the only means left to them, that every civilized power in the world grants readily within its nations."[20]

While the Americans awaited trial, Hammond's wife and C. W. Truslow, a New York lawyer and close friend of Hammond, launched a campaign to use the influence of American engineers and businessmen to pressure the State Department and Congress to push harder for Hammond's release. Herman Butler of Ryerson Steel Company, a large supplier of South African mining equipment, circulated a petition among American businessmen active in trade with South Africa demanding Hammond's immediate release. Hammond's former associates in the American West and in South Africa flooded the State Department with demands for protection of the Americans from the corrupt judicial system of the Transvaal. Mrs. Hammond even met with Kruger in an unsuccessful attempt to gain her husband's freedom.[21]

Hammond also joined in the efforts to gain his release. He tried to enlighten Americans on the tyranny of Kruger and the need of American pressure to assure justice. He cabled Senator John Jones (Republican-Nevada):

> The Transvaal is a small unenlightened retrogressive community under the government of a narrow oligarchy, giving a bad, inefficient administration; monstrous monopolies; corruption rampant.

Hammond advised Jones that: "If the Transvaal persists in the present course, our government can only invoke the aid of Great Britain, as being the paramount South African power, to coerce the Transvaal."[22] Jones and Dr. R. W. Raymond, Secretary of the American Institute of Mining Engineers, organized another effort to force Olney to make a personal appeal for Hammond's release. The State Department finally informed the press that it sympathized with Hammond's plight, and was doing all it could.[23]

Despite these efforts, Hammond and the other Americans went on trial on 27 April 1896. On 28 April Olney received a petition from 78 senators, 172 Congressmen, and Vice-President Adlai E. Stevenson asking for direct action to "save" Hammond. On the same day, Representative Rowland Mahaney (Democrat-New York) introducted a resolution in the House urging the Secretary of State to "take immediate action to safeguard the interests" of the accused Americans. Mahaney argued that he was not defending the Jameson Raid, but did not want Hammond to be the victim of an "English conspiracy."[24]

Although American engineers introduced affidavits attesting to Hammond's "loyalty to the Transvaal Government," Hammond pleaded guilty to the charge of treason and was sentenced to death—with prior assurance that his sentence would be commuted. Olney cabled State Secretary Leyds to confirm the arrangement, but received only a vague response.[25] Robert Chapin, a classmate of Hammond's at Yale and acting consular agent at Kimberley (Gardiner Williams was being tried for smuggling arms into the South African Republic), pleaded with Kruger for clemency and urged President Grover Cleveland to make a direct appeal to Kruger. American mining magnate John W. Mackey went further. He reportedly offered $200,000 to anyone who would free Hammond through any means.[26]

Finally, on 20 May, Thomas Mein, Charles Butters, and J. S. Curtis, three American members of the Reform Committee, were released upon payment of $10,000 fines. The other Americans received lesser fines. On 11 June, Hammond's sentence was reduced to a fine of $100,000 (paid by Rhodes) and a written promise never again to interfere in the internal affairs of the South African Republic. Gardiner Williams was fined $150 for violations of the Transvaal's firearms regulations, and resumed his position as consular agent at Kimberley.[27]

Jameson's excursion and its aftermath were crucial to the future of South Africa. Although many in Great Britain were shocked by the clandestine attack, the meddling of the Kaiser provoked a wave of anti-German sentiment that combined with the jingoistic mood to transform "Dr. Jim" and his raiders into imperial heroes. Chamberlain escaped any censure from the Parliamentary Board of Inquiry set up to investigate the incident. The Board condemned Rhodes and Jameson in rather lukewarm terms. Salisbury refused to pursue the inquiry or to restrain Chamberlain's freedom of action in South Africa.

Fear of German bellicosity over the Jameson Raid did cause Salisbury to modify his hard-line policy towards the United States on the Venezuela issue. Six days after the Kruger telegram, Britain informed Bayard that it was prepared to meet American demands concerning the Venezuela boundary.[28] Salisbury's conciliatory policy, designed to secure an ally against an aggressive Germany, helped lay the groundwork for the Anglo-American "understanding" that grew steadily during the final five years of the nineteenth century.

The effects of the raid on South Africa were more immediate. The foremost casualty was Rhodes. Forced to resign from his post as Prime Minister of the Cape Colony and plagued by financial problems within the Chartered Company, Rhodes abandoned temporarily his schemes for British expansion. Equally important was the new power gained by Kruger. Kruger's hardline opposition to the Uitlanders and to industrialization was not shared by all Boers. Moderate elements within the Transvaal favored some relaxation of restrictions on foreigners and perhaps even some compromise with Britain. Kruger had narrowly survived an election challenge from more liberal forces in 1893. The Jameson Raid effectively undermined Boer progressives and drove many moderate burghers to Kruger and his uncompromising policy.

Americans, embarrassed by the active cooperation of their countrymen in a conspiracy to invade a sovereign country, generally condemned the raid. While many Americans supported the Uitlanders as "agents of progress," they viewed the raid as open imperialism led by "merchant adventurers."[29] It was a natural step to equate British aggression in South Africa with similar British moves in Venezuela. The *New York Times* warned:

There are gold fields in Venezuela as well as in the Transvaal. Though there is no great organization in Venezuela like the Chartered Company, there are individual adventurers squatting on disputed territory and claiming everything in sight, after the immemorial British manner. The South American adventurers, like the South African adventurers, are backed by the British Government.[30]

Britain recognized the effects of the raid on American opinion. One British journalist argued that the attack had permanently scarred America's favorable view of British colonialism. Britons mounted an effort to explain the raid and regain American support. They stressed the corruption of Kruger and the legitimacy of the Uitlander grievances. W. T. Stead, a close friend of Rhodes, defended the "Empire Builder" in the American press. Rhodes's actions, according to Stead, were dedicated only to the "extension of the great principles of peace, justice, and liberty" and cooperation between the English-speaking nations.[31]

Many Americans also emphasized the repeated failures of attempts at peaceful reform. Mark Twain was in South Africa during the trial of the leaders of the Reform Committee, and visited with Hammond and other Americans in jail. While sharply critical of the raid, Twain strongly sympathized with the aims of the reformers:

> What the Uitlanders wanted was reform—*under the existing Republic.* What they proposed to do was secure these reforms by *prayer, petition, and persuasion.* . . . Could anything be clearer than the Uitlander statement of the grievances and oppressions under which they were suffering? Could anything be more legal and citizenlike and law-respecting than their attitude as expressed by their manifesto?[32]

It was Rhodes and the greedy Chartered Company that seized upon the legitimate grievances of the foreigners and tried to use them as a pretext to overthrow the Boer government.

Americans made an important distinction in their assessment of the raid. They criticized Rhodes and the South Africa Company, but did not abandon their belief in the necessity of British control. They separated the military attack of Jameson from the general colonial policy of England. The *Review of Reviews,* for example, condemned the attack but argued that the Boers provoked force by their refusal to accept change. The Boers must accommodate the forces of industrialization or face similar violent attacks:

> British energy, capital, actual colonization, and demonstrated ability to perform the needed task, are redeeming South Africa for civilization and the world's progress. There is no better chance for the Boers to maintain a separate Dutch government . . . than there was for the Dutch colonists who formed New Amsterdam.[33]

The Kaiser's actions also influenced America. The Kruger telegram and the German offer of troops seemed to confirm German designs on South Africa, and raised again the possibility of an alliance between Berlin and Pretoria.[34]

The Jameson Raid resulted in temporary American antagonism towards Britain, and particularly towards Cecil Rhodes. It did not, however, cause the United States to reject its growing support of British control of South Africa. The State Department made no changes in its representatives in South Africa. Despite his British citizenship and defense of Jameson, Clifford Knight remained vice-consul at Capetown. Williams paid his fine for smuggling firearms and returned to his post at Kimberley. Hammond returned to America with his fame and fortune secure. He was still regarded as the leading American expert on South Africa, and continued as one of the key spokesmen for the British cause. He renewed his activity in Republican politics and eventually became Republican National Chairman. When George V was crowned King of England in 1911, Transvaal delegates were forced to exchange pleasantries with the official American representative— John Hays Hammond.

Americans might have been shocked by Rhodes's methods, but there is little evidence that they shifted in their support of his goals. Ultimate British success was still assumed inevitable and in the best interests of both America and Africa. Theodore Roosevelt, in a letter to Henry White, commented on the raid and summarized America's attitude:

> It looks to me, I regret to say, as though the English had [sic] serious troubles ahead of them at the Cape and in South Africa generally. I am very sorry for this, for though I greatly admire the Boers, I feel it is in the interest of civilization that the English-speaking race should be dominant in South Africa, exactly as it is for the interests of civilization that the United States ... should be dominant in the Western Hemisphere.[35]

By 1896 it was apparent to even casual observers that there was little chance for peaceful federation in South Africa. The Boers saw the Jameson Raid as the opening skirmish in a war for survival. The period from January 1896 to October 1899 was marked by acceptance of the necessity of violence to determine who would rule South Africa. Although dotted throughout by negotiations, the "interim period" between the raid and the Boer War was devoted to preparation for the ultimate battle for control of South Africa.[36]

America also accepted the inevitability of armed conflict. The United States could no longer afford vacillation and passivity. It was finally forced to choose between the British and the Boers, and the decision was not difficult. The gradual growth of assumptions concerning the benefits of British control had progressed to the point where America was firmly convinced that a British victory would also be an American triumph. The rationale for a pro-British stance, conceived by Robert Shufeldt and confirmed by American businessmen and missionaries, was widely accepted by policymakers within the American elite.

America's temporary embarrassment concerning the involvement of Hammond and others in the Jameson Raid was soon eclipsed by recognition of its economic stake in the future of South Africa. United States exports to South Africa remained near $14 million a year during 1896, 1897, and 1898. In 1899, they jumped to over $16.5 million. Noting the increase in American trade throughout the 1890s, the *Scientific American* concluded that the growth "has been little less than phenomenal" and predicted: "What the future has in store for the business relations of this country and South Africa would seem to be almost without limit." American trade also led to increased immigration. By the spring of 1899, over 3,000 Americans were employed in and near the mines of the Transvaal.[37]

The State Department also recognized the growing economic importance of South Africa. America finally established a consulate in Pretoria in the fall of 1898 to handle the increased American business interest in the Transvaal. Washington also raised the quality of American representatives in South Africa. Capetown was no longer considered a dumping ground for inexperienced consuls. Frank W. Roberts, appointed consul in 1896, had served five years as a consul in Canada and two years in Mexico. His successor, J. S. Stowe, was a wealthy Kansas City exporter of agricultural implements whose income freed him from the restrictions of the low salary of American consuls. Washington also negotiated a treaty of extradition with the Orange Free State to protect American businessmen and missionaries active in this rather neglected area.[38]

Britain also increased its activities in South Africa following the setback of Jameson's defeat. Chamberlain and Sir Alfred Milner, the new British High Commissioner for South Africa, renewed efforts to extend British control. Britain frankly admitted its objectives. Writing in *The Century* immediately after the trial of Jameson's raiders, James Bryce, former British Ambassador to the United States, claimed that the Boers "are unsuited by their ideas and habits for the task of developing the material resources of their country." The solution was simple: "The Transvaal, therefore, and all of South Africa with the Transvaal, seems destined in the future to belong to 'ue English type of civilization, and to speak the English to .gue.[39]

American journalist Poultney Bigelow echoed Bryce's belief that the Boers were simply unable to guide the economic development of South Africa. Armed with a letter of introduction from John Hays Hammond, and checking his conclusions with Hammond in New York, Bigelow toured all the states of South Africa in the summer of 1896. Bigelow met with Kruger, M. T. Stern (President of the Orange Free State), and British officials. Bigelow wrote a 10-part series in *Harper's New Monthly* entitled "White Man's Africa."[40] Although somewhat sympathetic to the plight of the Boers, Bigelow was convinced that American interests could be best served by immediate British rule. Only the English could bring the stability and freedom of trade necessary for American exports and investment: "The flag of Great Britain represents freedom of trade, freedom of thought, beyond that of any flag on the high seas, and in Africa, at least, it is the only flag strong and generous enough for our purposes."[41]

American consuls and businessmen accepted Bigelow's arguments. Americans continued to be impressed with their economic gains in territory controlled by Britain. Businessmen were particularly interested in the new area of Rhodesia and believed America could get in "at the ground floor," owing to the lack of development in the region.[42]

Despite the efforts of Bigelow and others, the dominant spokesman for a pro-British policy remained Hammond. Although he pledged to refrain from intervention in the politics of the Transvaal, Hammond maintained his contacts with American engineers and businessmen on the Rand. He also continued his investment schemes. E. A. Wiltsee, a millionaire mining magnate living in San Francisco, even approached Hammond with a plan for a multinational global investment syndicate involving "all the leading money men" to secure a virtual monopoly on world mineral rights. "The scheme must be to divide up the world through these different representatives, and you as the head ... manipulating the vast machinery of the organization," Wiltsee argued.[43]

Although Hammond declined such grandiose plans, he continued to lobby for American support of British dominance in South Africa. His argument remained the same as when he led the Johannesburg Reform Committee: the Boers were an archaic oligarchy hostile to capitalism and restricting economic development. American interests required the probusiness climate only England could create. In a long article in the *North American Review,* Hammond reiterated his view that South Africa had enormous economic potential and urged Americans to abandon "sentimental considerations" and recognize that the Boers must be removed.[44]

Hammond also carried his message to governmental officials. A frequent visitor to London, he became a close associate of American Ambassador John Hay. Hammond arranged several meetings between Hay and Cecil Rhodes at which, in Hammond's words:

> Rhodes told Hay the whole story of South Africa as only he could tell it, and Hay was won over to Rhodes and his aspirations. When Hay returned to the United States in 1898 and became Secretary of State under McKinley, he was able to impress upon the President the true situation in South Africa.[45]

When a brief depression hit South Africa in 1897, Hammond quickly blamed the Boers. He wrote Wiltsee that business and politics are so closely tied that an unstable political situation is invariably reflected in the economy. The restrictions and unrest in the Transvaal had resulted in the decline of the mining industry and thus spread to the entire economy. In another letter he blamed all the economic woes of the Transvaal on "the unscrupulous clique which at present controls the destiny of the country."[46]

Other Americans supported Hammond's interpretation. James Stowe, the American representative in Capetown, attributed the business slump to Kruger's government and its restrictions on free trade. Charles Macrum, the new American

Consul in Pretoria, complained that the Boers did not allow Americans an opportunity to bid on contracts awarded to German and Dutch firms. American investors protested the hostility of the Afrikaners to their plans for railroad financing in the Transvaal.[47]

Along with businessmen, American missionaries also increased their activities in South Africa. They also were frustrated by Boer restrictions, and continued to urge British expansion. Britain encouraged missionary support by assisting American missionary stations in Cape Colony and Natal.[48]

The period following the Jameson Raid also marked the gradual emergence of an American-supported black nationalist movement in South Africa. At a conference in Pretoria in 1892, James M. Dwane and Jonas Godulka, black South African ministers, decided to align with the African Methodist Episcopal (AME) Church, a black American sect. In 1896, Dwane went to the United States to recruit black missionaries and to meet with AME leaders. Two years later, AME Bishop H. M. Turner, a strong critic of Booker T. Washington and an advocate of black separatism, went to South Africa to establish a branch of the church independent of white control. Turner ordained 65 black ministers and claimed a membership of 10,000 Africans by the summer of 1898.[49]

White South Africans and American missionaries viewed the rise of an independent black church with trepidation. They feared the implications of Turner's slogan "Africa for the Africans." Strangely, Kruger did not seem to share this fear. He reportedly met with Turner in the summer of 1898 and told the American: "You are the first black man whose hand I have ever shaken."[50] The embryonic movement for a separate black church (Ethiopianism) was later strongly denounced by whites and provoked repressive legislation. In 1898, however, despite Turner's success, the movement was weak and rejected by both white missionaries and most American blacks.

It was Booker T. Washington's strategy of self-help programs that attracted the interest of American Negroes and of both black and white American missionaries in South Africa. They doubted both the ability of the South African black to enter the political system and the wisdom of traditional academic education for the black African. What was needed, they argued, were "industrial missions," patterned after Tuskegee Institute, to acquaint the African with the Gospel and the tools of civilization. Miniature Tuskegees would "exhibit the tangible effects and benefits of Christian civilization" as well as allow black Africans "to lift themselves out of their heathen ideas and exercises, and develop their dormant powers."[51]

Joseph Booth, a white British missionary in South Africa and later an advocate of Ethiopianism, argued in 1897 that the great progress of the American Negro under Washington's strategy could be duplicated in South Africa through the leadership of black American missionaries:

> Let the African, sympathetically led by his more experienced Afro-American brother, develop his own country, establish his own manufactures, work his own planations, run his own ships, work his own mines, educate his own people, possess his own mission stations, conserve the wealth accruing from all sources, if possible, for the commonwealth of the people and the glory of God.[52]

Few Americans in South Africa were willing to go as far as Booth suggested. They were convinced, however, of the possibilities of manual self-help programs and the necessity of British rule to foster their development. To most American missionaries, Britain remained the "civilizing factor" in Africa and the best hope for Africans. Only Britain could develop the transportation system and literacy necessary for effective mass evangelism. The spread of English through missionary schools would allow Americans to bring the faith directly to the black African rather than rely on interpreters.[53]

America assumed that British dominance was not only good, but inevitable. The only obstacle to English control would be Boer alignment with a foreign power. The United States was most suspicious of German involvement, but also feared a possible Boer alliance with Portugal or Holland. Even Stanley Hollis, the strongly pro-Boer Consul at Lourenço Marques, viewed Portuguese administration in Africa as corrupt, vicious, and hostile to American interests. He warned Washington that Portuguese colonialism would never progress beyond crude exploitation.[54] When Portugal signed a commercial agreement with the Netherlands in 1896, Americans suspected the beginnings of an anti-American plot. Because of the close ties between the Dutch and the Boers, the Transvaal might be included in an agreement with Portugal to gain political support in exchange for economic concessions.[55]

When no commercial or military alliance was signed between the South African Republic and a European power, the United States assumed the Boers would be forced to fight England alone. While many Americans were relieved at this prospect, as the war would be brief, some groups were appalled by such a potentially unequal conflict. Dutch-Americans strongly protested the impending battle between the small Boer republics and the might of the British Empire. Howard Hillegas, an American journalist, toured South Africa in 1898 and met with Kruger and other Boer leaders. Hillegas argued that the United States had a distorted picture of South Africa owing to its reliance on pro-British spokesmen such as Hammond and reports from the British press. He assured Americans of Kruger's friendship for a "sister republic" and his willingness to cooperate with American business.[56]

Other Americans sympathetic to the Boers admitted Kruger was not favorable to industrialization or foreign investment, but argued "if the Transvaal State is against the development of commerce and industry on principle, it is within its rights to be so."[57] Such arguments were hardly likely to impress American businessmen or an American government dedicated to economic expansion.

While America debated the merits of British policy in Africa, it departed on its own imperialistic adventure. In April 1898, the United States finally declared war on Spain to "liberate" Cuba. After Spain's defeat in August, American negotiators returned from Paris in December with a colonial empire. The ratification of the treaty annexing the Philippines forced America to face the problems of colonial administration that European nations confronted earlier.

The years between British capitulation to American demands concerning Venezuela and the outbreak of the Spanish-American War saw a gradual accommodation between the two English-speaking powers. This rapprochement was solidified by British support of the American war effort and the subsequent annexation of the Philippines.[58] This understanding extended to South Africa. With its own colonial war and empire, America had a new sympathy with British problems in the Transvaal. The United States looked to England as an example of enlightened colonial administration. Conversely, Great Britain encouraged American imperialism and emphasized the similarity between the benefits of British rule in South Africa and American administration of the Philippines.

Immediately after America's declaration of war on Spain, the jingoistic Senator Albert Beveridge called for "an English-speaking people's league of God" and "an English-American understanding upon a basis of a division of the world's markets."[59] Swept up in a tide of chauvinism and racism heightened by its military success, America was convinced of the superiority of the "English-speaking race" and its destiny to rule more backward races.

Britain encouraged such racial and linguistic narcissism. Edward Dicey, in an article on "The New American Imperialism," welcomed America's victory over Spain and its decision to annex the Philippines. As a colonial power, America would have new sympathy for England's problems in Africa. Lord Salisbury informed Henry White of his support of America's decision to join the colonial powers.[60] Joseph Chamberlain was also delighted. He saw American expansion as the basis for a tacit or explicit Anglo-American alliance based on non-conflicting colonial empires. The Colonial Secretary defended British imperialism as advantageous to American economic interests:

> Wherever other states have hitherto gained a footing they have made it their business, as soon as possible, to secure special and preferential advantages for their own citizens, and have endeavored to exclude all other trade. If England, therefore, had refused to pursue a policy of expansion, both she and the United States would have ultimately been shut out from participation in the vast and constantly increasing trade of the tropics.[61]

Chamberlain's virtual promise of an open door, at least for America, in British possessions seemed to verify America's belief that British control of South Africa would carry with it few economic restrictions. The increased rhetoric about Anglo-Saxon superiority and destiny helped confirm American assumptions about South Africa. The identification of British control with progress and civilization existed prior to "the great rapprochement" of the late nineteenth century. Active diplomatic support for Britain, however, was always weakened by traditional American Anglophobia and distrust of European imperialism. With the United States now also a colonial power, and with the acceptance of the mission of

"Anglo-Saxons," the obstacles to support of Britain in the imminent struggle in South Africa were nearly eliminated on the eve of the Boer War.

As America drew nearer to Britain, it continued to be frustrated by the government of the Transvaal. In early 1897, R. E. Brown, an American citizen, claimed the South African Republic illegally seized his gold claims. Brown appealed his case to the Supreme Court in Pretoria. When Chief Justice John Kotze upheld Brown's claim in March, Kruger rushed a bill through the Volksraad denying the court's right to declare any governmental action unconstitutional and authorizing the president to remove judges who claimed this right. Kotze was removed from office and Brown took his case to the American Congress. The claim languished in the courts until it was finally dismissed in 1923, but the Brown incident confirmed America's belief in the capriciousness of the Transvaal's legal system and the arbitrary power of Kruger.[62]

Businessmen also continued to protest Boer policies. American investors managed to gain tentative approval of a plan for construction of a tramway around Johannesburg. Before construction began, Kruger withdrew the contract and awarded it to a multinational group. The American consul in Pretoria protested, but received no satisfaction. Like the Brown case, this incident helped solidify American belief in the corruption and antibusiness attitudes of the Boers.[63]

While most Americans seemed confident that British control would lead to American economic gains, others cautioned that British administration would bring British exclusiveness. Hillegas defended his pro-Boer stance by arguing that American commercial interests in South Africa "are of such recent growth and such great proportions" that Britain would block further inroads on the South African market:

> That the British merchants are keenly alive to the situation which threatens to transfer the trade supremacy into American hands has been amply demonstrated by the efforts which they have made to check the inroads the Americans are making in their field, and by the appointment of committees to investigate the causes of the decline of British commerce.[64]

There were a number of reports in 1899 noting concern by British merchants over the growth of American imports. London was particularly worried about the low steamship rates

between New York and Capetown and the tendency of whole-
salers to stock American goods rather than give preference to
those of the mother country.[65]

Despite these rumblings, there is little evidence that America doubted the wisdom of its decision to favor Britain. As
Britain and the South African Republic rushed towards war in
the summer of 1899, America remained convinced of the necessity and the inevitable outcome of the struggle.

With the appointment of Sir Alfred Milner as British High
Commissioner in April 1897, Britain entrusted power to a man
determined upon war. Milner saw no compromise with Kruger.
He was convinced that South Africa must be united under the
British flag. He urged repeatedly that the Colonial Office pressure Kruger into war. Even when Kruger proposed a compromise on suffrage requirements for Uitlanders, Milner recommended that Chamberlain send more troops and prepare for
war.[66]

By May 1899, it was clear that war was imminent. The *New
York Times* saw an "irrepressible conflict" between the Boers
and the Uitlanders, backed by Britain. The paper argued that
the Boers were blocking both economic development and political freedom:

> It is not the machinations of Cecil Rhodes or any other individual
> with which the Boers are contending. . . . It is the 'Zeitgeist,' the
> 'spirit of the age' . . . . There is no room in the world for 'peculiar
> people' who insist on nonconformity, and upon taking up more
> room than belongs them or than they can use to the utmost advan-
> tage. . . . They must conform, like the Mormon, or be extinguished
> like the North American Indian.[67]

Despite such fatalism, Boer moderates made attempts to
compromise. Led by Jan Hofmeyr of the Transvaal, M. T.
Steyn of the Orange Free State, and William Schreiner of Cape
Colony, a meeting was arranged between Kruger and Milner
in late May 1899. American representatives in South Africa
drafted a memorandum on the conference at Bloemfontein
reporting the impossibility of peaceful compromise or international arbitration.[68] After the failure of the meeting between
the two leaders, Jan Smuts, the Attorney General of the South
African Republic, offered another proposal to lower suffrage
requirements. Milner rejected it. By September 1899, both
sides were committed to war.

By mid-July American representatives were convinced that war would come within a year. The American consul at Pretoria reported plans to neutralize Johannesburg during the war to insure continued gold production and prevent destruction of the mines.[69]

Immediately following Macrum's prediction of war, Rear Admiral H. L. Howison, Commander of the South Atlantic Squadron, filed a similar report. On 6 July Howison informed Macrum that he would visit Johannesburg to check on the status of Americans on the Rand and the legitimacy of Uitlander grievances. Howison rejected an invitation to meet with Boer leaders in Pretoria. The Admiral's report to the Department of the Navy (later forwarded to Secretary of State Hay) bitterly condemned Kruger and the Boers in prose reminiscent of John Hays Hammond. Howison repeated the Uitlander argument that they paid the bulk of the taxes but had no voice in the government. Kruger's government, according to Howison, was characterized by "an utter disregard of justice." He concluded with a prediction of war and British success:

> The condition of affairs cannot possibly last much longer and there is only one possible ending, namely the occupation of the Transvaal by the English. During the transition period there is a strong possibility of the destruction of Johannesburg and the Rand mines, which will mean a loss of many millions in American trade and property, and possibly many lives.[70]

American fear of the destructive effects of war on trade was outweighed by disgust over the lingering tensions and disruptions within the Transvaal. American businessmen, frustrated by the constant wranglings between Uitlander, Boer, and Englishman, felt war necessary to stabilize the territory under British rule. The *Overland Monthly* concluded that Kruger's government was "an anachronism" in the age of industry and must be eliminated. The editors argued that the Jameson Raid was wrong "from a technical standpoint" but had the correct objectives. The *Commercial and Financial Chronicle* agreed. It argued that the Boers simply "do not know how to govern." The conflict would be similar to the American invasion of Cuba in 1898: It would not be for personal gain but to bring stability and good government.[71]

Consul Stowe also defended British motives. In a confidential despatch he reiterated the complaints of American businessmen and dismissed the South African Republic as "not a Republic, but an oligarchy." Stowe echoed the arguments of Howison and Hammond concerning Uitlander rights. "Those who have developed the country and invested their money have some rights," he argued. Stowe saw the Uitlanders as victims of Boer repression:

> Under the pretext of republican liberty an industrious majority of the population are given no more rights of citizenship than beasts of burden: they are worried by an oligarchic administration, a police or secret service force which are everywhere, and commerce and industry are being crushed through a paralysis of trade.[72]

In Stowe's opinion, war would be welcomed as a means of breaking the impasse and restoring trade:

> I am of the opinion, that the state of affairs in the Transvaal is without parallel in the civilized world. . . . My concern is; however, with regard to the effect of the existing state of affairs upon trade: and on this point I am not at all sure whether war, which would undoubtedly be short and sharp, would not be preferable to the present unrest which is undermining the trade foundation.[73]

Stowe summarized much of American thought concerning the impending struggle. The war was both just and inevitable, and would be brief. England would intervene to restore order and provide the stability and good government necessary for trade and development. It would illustrate the superiority of the English-speaking Anglo-Saxon. Finally, Britain had repeatedly affirmed a willingness to grant to American business opportunities absent under the Boers. In Stowe's words: "Concessions may be looked for from the imperial government to a greater extent than from the Transvaal."[74]

Historian Walter LaFeber has argued that the most important consideration in America's decision to go to war with Spain over Cuba in 1898 was "the growing belief of many sections of the business community that somehow the disturbances on the island would have to be terminated before the United States could enjoy full prosperity."[75] A similar logic was at work in South Africa in 1899. While of much less importance to the United States than Cuba, South Africa was gripped, in Stowe's phrase, by "a paralysis of trade" due to internal conflict. The United States had no inclination to intervene in South Africa, but saw British action in American interests.

In the face of this economic argument for support of Britain, pro-Boer spokesmen were forced to rely on American sympathy with republicanism and the underdog. They blamed the crisis in the Transvaal on rich and greedy special interests. The indefatigable Stanley Hollis attempted to refute the pro-British reports of Stowe with despatches blaming the forthcoming war on British capitalists using the legitimate grievances of the Uitlanders as a pretext to crush republicanism. The issue, according to Hollis, was whether the government of the Transvaal was to be "of the people, for the people, and by the people," or "of the people for the mining magnates and their servants and followers."[76]

Hollis's argument did not alter American attitudes. In the two decades since Shufeldt's reports on South Africa, the United States had gradually adopted his assumptions and moved towards his recommendation of support of British domination. Barely two weeks before the outbreak of war, Secretary of State Hay wrote to Henry White: "I hope, if it comes to blows, that England will make quick work of Uncle Paul. Sooner or later, her influence must be dominant there, and the sooner the better."[77]

On 3 October, in a desperate attempt to postpone the conflict, the President of the Orange Free State asked Stowe to request Washington to arbitrate. Hay rejected the offer.[78] On 8 October, Sir Reginald Tower, the British Ambassador in Washington, asked the United States to assume British affairs in South Africa "in event of an attack on British forces." The next day the South African Republic issued an ultimatum to Britain. Receiving no reply, Boer troops invaded Cape Colony on 11 October 1899, and the Boer War began. The United States immediately agreed to accept control of British affairs.[79]

America had long anticipated war between Britain and the Boers. It was convinced that war would result in the "Anglization of all South Africa."[80] Chamberlain justified the war in a speech to the House of Commons as an expression of Britain's duty to bring good government and an enlightened native policy to all of South Africa.[81] This fitted nicely with American assumptions that the war would result in the triumph of Anglo-

Saxon civilization. As one letter to the *New York Times* summarized:

> The Boers detest civilization . . . . The March of civilization is responsible for the Transvaal crisis. . . . The Boers must go, civilization demands it. The Anglo-Saxon race will accomplish it.[82]

The combination of Anglo-Saxon racism, belief in the superiority of British institutions, and faith in the commitment of England to the native, formed a powerful argument in favor of American support of Britain's war effort. It remained for Hammond, however, to express an equally crucial factor in America's acceptance of war and its hopes for an English victory. In a letter written the day after the outbreak of the conflict, Hammond stated:

> Great Britain will inevitably win. The result of British supremacy and a progressive regime in the Transvaal will be a great stimulus to the development of the wonderful resources of that country. In the general prosperity all nations of commercial enterprise will be benefited. America will come in for her share.[83]

Throughout the war, America was convinced that "her share" would be the bulk of the anticipated huge postwar South African market. Although technically neutral, the United States did everything possible to assure a rapid and complete British victory.

## CHAPTER FOUR

# A British War for American Interests

## The United States and the Boer War, 1899-1902

Diplomacy, like war, combines strategy with tactics. Just as a successful military campaign depends on both the wisdom of the overall strategy and the skill of tactical maneuvers, successful diplomacy requires a broad objective and a continual series of adjustments to attain that goal. Policymakers in the United States felt that British success in the Boer War was necessary to insure American objectives in South Africa. They were forced, however, to devise a series of tactics to help assure a British victory.

The American government assumed that support of Britain would be brief. Given the might of the British Empire and the assumed backwardness of the Boers, the British triumph would be complete and rapid. As the war continued beyond the few months Americans had predicted would be necessary for a British victory, it became more difficult for the government to justify its pro-British stance, and to prevent the Boer War from becoming a domestic issue. As the war dragged on, it allowed the mobilization of a large pro-Boer movement within the United States. Democrats hopeful of a presidential victory in 1900, Irish- Americans, and a broad segment of the anti-imperialist movement were convinced that America was aiding Britain in an unequal contest to crush republicanism in Africa. The McKinley administration became caught in a vicious circle: the longer Britain floundered in South Africa, the more Washington worked to insure a British victory. This more active support of Britain led to more vocal and widespread domestic criticism of the administration.

During the first few months of the war, Washington, assuming the war would be over before effective opposition could be mobilized, used a wide variety of diplomatic tactics to aid Great Britain. The United States became a major source of supply for the British army; Hay and the State Department declined to hold Britain accountable for violations of American neutrality; Washington refused to be drawn into European intervention schemes, and rejected Boer efforts to gain American assistance, or at least true neutrality.

As the war dragged on, Congress, journalists, and the general public began to attack the pro-British policies of Hay, the State Department, and President William McKinley. The pro-British element of the American elite was worried by the ineffectiveness of the British military effort and the growing discontent within the United States. Led by prominent diplomats, businessmen, missionaries, and military officials, they launched a pro-British counteroffensive that restated their assumptions that Britain was fighting a war for American interests. This renewed effort on behalf of Britain, combined with the long-awaited English military success, contained effectively the pro-Boer movement within the United States. While the war continued to sputter through late 1901 and early 1902, American spokesmen remained convinced of the inevitability of a British victory and the wisdom of their support of London. The last year of the war was notable not so much for active American diplomatic intrigues as for preparation for the penetration of the postwar South African market.

The few studies of American policy during the Boer War have been devoted almost exclusively to discussion of American neutrality. They have illustrated, but not explained, American actions. They have not shown either the reasoning behind support of Great Britain, or America's long-range objectives in South Africa.[1] American policy during the Boer War was not a series of hasty decisions. It was the logical continuation of two decades of assumptions about the future of South Africa. Businessmen, diplomats, missionaries, and journalists were all convinced of the advantages to the United. States of a unified British South Africa. The same groups accepted the war as a means to gain that end.

Although disturbed by the possible disruptive effects of a war, American businessmen were confident that the conflict would bring the stability necessary for continued economic penetration of South Africa. Immediately prior to the outbreak of war, a group of American businessmen active in the South African trade organized to lobby for American support of Britain in the pending conflict. When war was declared, they pressed the State Department to take an active stance in favor of Britain to obtain economic benefits for American business in postwar British South Africa.[2]

Aside from future benefits stemming from British control, American merchants assumed the war would have the additional advantage of further alienating the Afrikaners from British products. *Iron Age* predicted: "America will profit hugely by the anti-British feeling among Dutch, Hollander, and Afrikaner." Weakened by the war effort, Britain would not be able to prevent American inroads in South Africa.[3]

Americans were also quick to restate their assumptions of the social benefits of British control. Commenting on the outbreak of the war, the *New York Times* stressed the outrages perpetrated by the Boers and argued that "compared to Paul Kruger's Government Tammany Hall is a magnificent illustration of freedom and majority rule."[4]

Britain encouraged the American view of the war as a struggle for good government and racial progress. One British spokesman claimed that: "The British Empire is fighting a holy war for the cause of freedom and justice for the native races of South Africa." Another assured America that a British victory would not only be of economic benefit to the United States, but would also bring "a kindliness of legislation toward the inferior races."[5]

Missionaries in the United States agreed that the war would be advantageous to both the black African and the American economy. Britain would allow the missionary a free hand throughout South Africa. The missionary, in turn, would become "a salesman for the manufactures of Christendom" by educating and improving the African.[6]

Influential politicians and members of the government greeted the war with a firm conviction of the necessity for a quick British victory. Theodore Roosevelt, John Hay, Henry White, American Ambassador to Great Britain Joseph Choate, and military strategist and historian Alfred Thayer Mahan all agreed that Britain must triumph.[7] In a letter to White, Hay summarized the thinking of this pro-British faction: "The fight of England is the fight of civilization and progress and *all of our interests are bound up in her success.*"[8]

Unfortunately for Hay, British successes were few in the opening months of the war. Britain entered the war overconfident and ill-prepared. Its armies were scattered throughout the world; British troops had to be transported to South Africa from India, Egypt, and England, whereas the Boers took the field immediately. The Boers also faced no problem of supplies or orientation. Like Napoleon in Spain, the United States in the Philippines, and France in Indochina, Britain faced a guerilla force using unconventional tactics on its own terrain.

Rather than being the rout many had predicted, the Boer War went through three distinct stages. From the outbreak of the conflict in October 1899 until February 1900, the Boers were amazingly successful. The Boers outmaneuvered and outfought the British army, culminating in a series of British defeats during "black week" (9-15 December). But, beginning with the successful relief of the besieged city of Kimberley, and ending with the capture of Bloemfontein in September 1900, Britain gained the initiative, and the major battles of the war were over. The final stage of the war was characterized by a stubborn refusal of the Boers to surrender. The ensuing twenty months of guerilla warfare and misery finally ended with the Peace of Vereeniging on 31 May 1902.

America became involved in the war immediately after the first shots. While Hay never officially proclaimed neutrality, it was assumed that the United States would remain neutral in the struggle.[9] Having assured Britain that it would assume its affairs in South Africa, America quickly moved to represent Great Britain in the Transvaal. This action provoked strong opposition from the Boers. The South African Republic bluntly informed the American consul at Pretoria that it would not regard the United States as an intermediary between British citizens and the Boers. When Hay ordered Macrum to gain information concerning the treatment of captured British officers, the Boers refused to cooperate. State Secretary Reitz explained: "We got rid of the British agent on the 11th of October last, and God willing, we will never have another one here!"[10]

Despite this rebuff, Hay remained undaunted. He personally instructed Macrum that he would be responsible for transmitting letters, packages, and money to captured British troops. The Boers again refused to accept this procedure. The impasse between the Boers and the State Department was finally broken when pro-Boer Consul Stanley Hollis worked out a face-saving compromise: The Transvaal would not officially recognize the United States as Britain's representative, but would allow American officials to distribute money and letters under the nominal supervision of Boer leaders. The arrangement was accepted only because it was made reciprocal: America agreed to undertake similar duties on behalf of the Boers, should they request it.[11]

Charles Macrum's departure from Pretoria eight weeks after the war began further strained diplomatic relations between the Boers and the United States. The post was temporarily filled by the transfer of Stanley Hollis, the former advocate of a pro-Boer American policy, from Lourenço Marques to Pretoria. Hollis was delighted with the appointment and worked closely with Kruger, Reitz, and other Boer leaders. Hollis's appointment was, however, merely a temporary appeasement of the Transvaal government. He was soon replaced by Adelbert S. Hay—the son of Secretary of State John Hay.[12]

The Transvaal viewed the appointment of the younger Hay as a direct insult. The Secretary of State was one of the most outspoken advocates of a British victory, and his son was known to share his views. The fact that Adelbert Hay stopped in London and visited with Salisbury and Chamberlain before proceeding to Pretoria confirmed Boer suspicion. When Kruger finally received Hay in early February 1900, the consul reported his cool reception and admitted he was "looked upon as an enemy and with suspicion."[13]

While the Boers were angered by American diplomatic cooperation with Great Britain, they were more upset by American moves to help supply the British army. American businessmen were well aware of the lucrative profits available to a neutral in time of war. During the first full year of the war (1900) American trade with South Africa and Great Britain increased dramatically. Direct exports to South Africa climbed from $16 million in 1899 to over $20 million in 1900. Even more dramatic were increases in shipments of war materials to England. Exports of canned beef tripled from 1899 to 1900, and sales of boots, gunpowder, and firearms to Britain showed a similar increase.[14]

Boer representatives in the United States were quick to protest American trade in armaments. Hay dismissed their protests. He asserted that the United States could sell all material, including contraband, as long as it did not refuse either side.[15] In response to Congressional attacks on this interpretation, Hay argued that the government

> works for the interests of the American farmers, American merchants, and American manufactures. It seeks, in every proper way, to extend the market for their goods and products all over the world. They have a perfect right to deal with everybody, whether belligerents or not. We should be glad to see our people furnish ... every army in the world, to feed and clothe them, and to supply them with everything they need. . . . We are perfectly free to sell to both belligerents all they are able to pay for.[16]

America's claim of the right to sell to both sides was no doubt technically correct. In fact, however, it meant only the right to supply Britain. The Boers had no navy, little cash or credit, and few business agents in the United States. As would happen again during World War I, American neutrality resulted in trade and economic entanglement with only one belligerent.

Most galling to the Boers was America's refusal to block British purchase of horses and mules in the United States and the hiring of American citizens as muleteers. Many of these muleteers enlisted in the British army after accompanying their animals to South Africa. The Boers protested the open recruiting by the British consul in New Orleans, where most of the mules were shipped, but Washington ignored their appeals.[17]

The Boer case was weakened by the fact that many Irish-Americans entered the conflict on the side of the Transvaal. Unable to gain passage to South Africa as a military unit, the "Irish Brigade" formed an ambulance corps for the International Red Cross. When they reached South Africa, the ambulance corps promptly disbanded and its members joined Boer units.[18]

The most serious test of America's position was the British naval blockade of South Africa. The United States had long proclaimed the right of neutral trade and held to the slogan "free ships make free goods." Assuming the war would be brief, Hay did not give much attention to Britain's proclamation of a blockade. As the war entered its second month, however, Britain tightened the blockade and threatened the freedom of foreign shipping.

As early as December 1899, the State Department received reports of British seizures of foreign ships near Delagoa Bay. Hollis protested that Britain treated the neutral Delagoa Bay "as if it were an enemy port."[19] Matters reached a crisis in early January 1900, when the British detained four ships carrying American goods (flour, foodstuffs, and lumber). Hay ordered Ambassador Joseph Choate to lodge a mild protest until the State Department could gather full information.[20]

Hay was clearly embarrassed by British actions, but moved rapidly to forestall domestic criticism of England. He instructed Choate to work out some sort of arrangement "in accordance with liberal and enlightened principles of justice" to have American businessmen compensated for all past and future seizures. It was formally agreed that the United States would disregard future British seizures if Britain would pay the going rate for the goods had they been sold in South Africa. Hay informed American companies of the deal in early March. Britain would pay compensation with "the understanding that no claim for damages will be made for the seizure of the goods so purchased."[21] Apparently the arrangement proved satisfactory, for the State Department ignored numerous reports of British seizures. Washington finally informed Hollis that his continued protests of British violations marked him "pronounced, openly, and avowedly hostile to one of the belligerents."[22] Hollis discontinued his protests.

The unexpected length of the war brought another test of American neutrality—intervention schemes. Hay rejected a Boer request for mediation immediately prior to the war. During the first year of the conflict, European powers made several attempts to involve America in plans to mediate the war. In early January 1900, a group of Belgian officials informally approached McKinley concerning possible American mediation. The major drive for intervention was, however, led by Russia and its Foreign Minister, F. W. Muraviev.[23]

Unlike the United States, the major European powers welcomed the Boer successes. They saw the war as an opportunity to weaken Britain by forcing an embarrassing peace. Russia spearheaded two major intervention plans. In October 1899, Muraviev sounded out major European states and America concerning a joint plan for mediation, and in February 1900, he secured an ally in the Kaiser and organized a second move for intervention.

The United States refused to be drawn into either plan. Muraviev's first effort approached the United States only indirectly. Hay rejected every invitation to discussion of the matter.[24] Europe approached the United States more directly during the second intervention scheme. Baron Theodor von Holleben, the German Ambassador in Washington, brought up the matter in a conversation with Hay on 2 January 1900. Hay bluntly told him that the United States would support Great Britain in every problem connected with the war. A month later Holleben tried again. He cited examples of British seizures of American goods as justification for intervention. Hay remained adamant. He replied that America would stay neutral even if Britain completely closed Delagoa Bay. Similar efforts by the Russian Ambassador provoked the same response.[25]

Hay's basic argument against intervention or mediation was that it would have to be proposed and welcomed by both sides in the conflict rather than by just one belligerent or a third party. After British military successes in March 1900, the Boers officially asked Hay to use his good offices to arrange mediation. Secure in his knowledge that Britain would reject any mediation plans, Hay dutifully conveyed the Boer offer to Salisbury on 10 March. The Prime Minister declined and Hay proclaimed that he had done all he could.[26] Hay later assured Henry White that he had no intention of pushing arbitration, but had merely been going through the motions to appease Irish and German-Americans "who have joined their several lunacies in one common attack against England and incidentally the Administration for being too friendly with England."[27] America later rejected another intervention effort when it declined a Dutch move to bring the Boer War before the recently established Hague Convention.[28]

Having failed to halt shipment of American arms, involve the United States in protests of the British blockade, or bring it into intervention plans, the Boers decided their best approach was to bypass the McKinley Administration and bring their case directly to the American people. With their military situation badly deteriorating in the late spring of 1900, they sent envoys to America to mobilize support for their cause.

W.J. Leyds, Kruger's former State Secretary, coordinated the Boer diplomatic efforts in Europe. In late April, the three Boer envoys to the United States, Daniel Wolmarans, Cornelius

Wessels, and Abraham Fischer, met with Leyds in The Hague to plan their campaign in America. European statesmen advised the Boer representatives that their best chance for success was to appeal to the large Irish population, and to Democratic politicans preparing for the forthcoming presidential election.[29] The American Minister in The Hague, Stanford Newel, kept Hay informed of the activities of the Boer envoys throughout their stay in the Netherlands. Newel saw the Boers' trip to America as "a sinister move by Europe" to embarrass the administration. He warned Hay that the Boers knew they would receive no assistance from Washington, but felt "they can materially aid the election of the opposition candidate Mr. Bryan who they know would intervene for the Boers." Despite the efforts of Newel to discourage them, the Boer representatives sailed for New York on 9 May 1900.[30]

After three days of noisy receptions attended by large numbers of Irish-Americans and Democratic politicians, the Boer leaders finally came to Washington on 18 May to meet with Hay and possibly with President McKinley.[31] The arrival of the envoys placed the administration in a difficult position. By the summer of 1900, there was a growing pro-Boer movement within the United States. Several Democratic senators had even accused Hay of signing a secret alliance with Britain. Clearly, a refusal even to meet with the Boers would be interpreted as yet another example of the administration's support of England. On the other hand, it was apparent that the long-awaited British military success had made foreign intervention the only means of saving the Boer republics. Any statement of sympathy for the Boers' plight would risk misinterpretation by Britain, and possibly undermine nearly a year of American support.

Hay finally decided to meet with the envoys, but not to risk any misstatement of his position. The Boers expected a long informal discussion, after which they would present Hay with a written statement of their grievances; Hay, in turn, would later reply. But Hay permitted only a brief and highly formal meeting. He was accompanied by his secretary, who kept a complete transcript of the conversation. Hay accepted the envoys' statement but, rather than studying it, countered with a prepared letter reaffirming America's position that it was ready to offer its good offices only when both sides requested it.[32]

This apparent snub incensed the Boers. They complained to the press that Hay had rejected their proposals before he had even read them. Hay's strategy did have its intended effect on Britain. White reported that Salisbury and the Foreign Office were delighted with the cool reception given the Boers. British officials told White of their gratitude for America's understanding of the situation, in contrast to the hostility of the continental powers.[33]

Hay's rejection of the Boer delegation was the culmination of America's diplomatic support of Britain during the first period of the war. The refusal to limit sales of arms or food, the tacit agreement over violations of neutral rights, the rejection of intervention plans, and the assumption of British offices in the Transvaal helped to solidify the Anglo-American "understanding." These same actions, however, combined with the heroic efforts of the Boers, stimulated a strong pro-Boer reaction within the United States. As the war continued, many Americans became increasingly critical of Washington's support of Britain. A large segment of the American public was convinced that support of England was a criminal action that was crucial in blocking a Boer victory. In addition, Democratic politicans, who had determined to make the election of 1900 a mandate on annexation of the Philippines, saw American support of British imperialism in Africa as a potentially strong campaign issue.

Hay, Roosevelt, Senator Henry Cabot Lodge (Republican, Massachusetts), and other leaders of the pro-British elite were dismayed by the early British defeats. While they never seriously doubted eventual British success, they were justifiably worried about domestic reaction to a long war in South Africa. Both American and British leaders feared that the Boers would appeal to the sporting interest of America's natural sympathy for the underdog and traditional hostility to Britain.[34]

Congress led the attack on what it considered America's pro-British neutrality. After the initial Boer victories, Senator William Mason (Democrat-Illinois) introduced a resolution stating:

*Resolved by the Senate of the United States,* That we watch with deep and abiding interest the heroic battle of the South African

Republic against cruelty and oppression, and our best hopes go out
for the full success of their determined contest for liberty.[35]

Like all resolutions concerning the war, Mason's proposal was
referred to the Republican-dominated Foreign Relations Committee, where it was killed.

Senate Democrats continued their attacks on the administration when information concerning British recruitment and
purchases of supplies became public. In late January 1900, the
Senate engaged in a bitter debate on the war. When Democrats
attacked the administration's "plot" to extinguish liberty and
republicanism in South Africa, Lodge defended American policy. He stressed the need for Anglo-American solidarity, and
reminded his colleagues of British support for the United
States during the Spanish-American War.[36]

While Republican leaders effectively defeated attempts to
dislodge from committee bills calling for recognition of the
Boers and an end to sales of armaments to Britain, the arrival
of the Boer envoys in May 1900 provoked a renewed congressional effort. William Allen (Populist-Nebraska) urged that
the Senate grant the Boer delegation the privilege of the Senate floor to plead their case. When this plan was defeated and
the press reported Hay's cool reception of the Boers, George
Wellington (Democrat, Maryland) delivered a bitter attack on
Hay, McKinley, and Lodge. Wellington argued that the administration and the Foreign Relations Committee had combined to frustrate the will of the American people. He again
accused Hay of signing a secret agreement with Britain.[37]

Despite these and other similar outbursts, Congress never
passed a resolution critical of the administration's handling of
the war or expressing support of the Boers. This was due
primarily to the effective maneuverings of Lodge and the
Chairman of the Senate Foreign Relations Committee, Cush-
man Davis (Republican-Minnesota). In the House, Representative Robert Hitt (Republican-Illinois), Chairman of the
Committee on Foreign Affairs, performed the same function
with similar effectiveness.

While the McKinley administration stifled congressional
opposition, they were powerless to do anything about journal-
istic criticism. Although Democratic politicans could be
attacked for playing politics during an election year, many

nonofficeholders (or officeseekers) were sincere in their admiration for the Boers and in their hatred of British imperialism. War correspondents, prominent intellectuals, and leaders of the anti-imperialist movement all attacked American support of England.

Critics of the administration argued that the United States had an inaccurate picture of Kruger and the Boers because of the influence of the British press and the effectiveness of British propaganda.[38] War correspondents who had first-hand knowledge of the bravery and skill of the Boer troops returned with a new admiration for Kruger and the South African Republic. Richard Harding Davis, whose coverage of the Spanish-American War had made him a national figure, went to South Africa to cover the conflict in late 1899. Davis had been strongly pro-British, but changed his views after traveling with the Boer armies. He wrote a book strongly critical of British intentions and opposing American support of a British victory. Even Poultney Bigelow, a strong advocate of British control prior to the war, was impressed with the Boers' fighting ability. Although he still viewed Kruger as a reactionary, Bigelow felt that M. T. Steyn, President of the Orange Free State, understood the necessity of industrialization and could form a government of progressive Afrikaners to rule an independent Boer state. Bigelow also discounted the humanitarian argument for aiding Britain. He concluded that neither Britain nor the Boers would do much for the black.[39]

Anti-imperialists, such as Carl Schurz, Andrew Carnegie, and Henry Adams, joined the attack on American policy. They argued that there was a parallel between British imperialism in Africa and American annexation of the Philippines. Neither could be justified as extensions of civilization but were merely examples of blatant exploitation.[40]

As the presidential nominating conventions drew near in the summer of 1900, George W. Van Siclen, a New York lawyer, and James O'Beirne, a prominent Hibernian leader, formed a large pro-Boer organization. Irish-Americans were particularly active in the pro-Boer effort. Some Fenians were convinced that a dramatic move to illustrate American support for the Boers was necessary. They approached New York Governor Theodore Roosevelt to test his reaction to an Irish-American invasion of Canada to pressure Britain to withdraw from South Africa. Roosevelt thundered that he would call out the militia and "clap them all in prison."[41] Plans for the invasion of Canada were abandoned.

While not particularly concerned with mass public opinion, Hay and other administration leaders feared a new election issue and a possible estrangement from Britain should the pro-Boer movement become too vocal. Hay wrote to Choate concerning the growth of opposition to the administration's policies:

> It is wholly illogical, but nevertheless in accordance with the observed workings of human nature, that the less the Boers need sympathy the more they get. . . . the lower breed of politicans begin to join in the outcry. A smashing victory would quiet everything considerably, but I greatly fear the effects of another British defeat.[42]

After he received word from Hay of growing Congressional criticism of American policy, Henry White also was alarmed. In a worried letter to his wife, he stressed the need of an early English victory as "apparently the pro-Boer sympathizers are getting more and more troublesome in our country."[43]

The actions of two American officials, former Consul at Pretoria Charles Macrum and Undersecretary of the Interior Webster Davis, enhanced administration fears of a rupture with Britain. Macrum's actions were totally confusing. An advocate of British control prior to the war, he was shocked when the conflict finally came. Macrum was greatly impressed with the courage of the Boers and dismayed by the brutality of the British. He was further alienated from Britain because he feared that his mail was being opened and censored by British officials.

In December 1899, as the war neared the end of its dramatic first stage, Macrum suddenly cabled the State Department urgently requesting an immediate leave of absence. Hay was astounded that he would leave Pretoria when America most needed representation. He emphatically denied Macrum's request. Undaunted, Macrum repeated his pressing need to return to the United States and threatened to leave even without permission. Finally Hay coldly told Macrum to leave and appointed Adelbert Hay to replace him.[44]

Macrum knew nothing of Hay's appointment and assumed he would return to South Africa after consultation with the State Department. He arrived in Washington in early February 1900, and informed officials of British censorship. Macrum claimed it had been necessary for him to come to the United States to make sure Washington was aware of British interference with his reports. When told by State Department official David Hill that he had been replaced, Macrum took his case to the press. He not only exposed British censorship, but claimed he had been fired for protesting British violations.[45] Macrum's charges were at least partly true. After an investigation by other American consuls confirmed British meddling, Britain apologized.[46] Macrum, however, gained a degree of notoriety as a martyr to an Anglo-American conspiracy, and toured the country pleading the Boer cause.

Webster Davis also aided the pro-Boer campaign. Davis was so appalled by what he considered a tacit alliance between America and Britain that he resigned his position with the Department of the Interior to educate the public to British atrocities. He wrote a series of pamphlets and later a book describing in gory detail the brutality of British troops in the Transvaal. Davis highlighted his brief moment of fame with a ringing speech to the Democratic National Convention in Kansas City pleading for a platform plank in support of the Boers. The Democrats responded with a statement extending sympathy "to the heroic Burghers in their unequal struggle to maintain their liberty and independence."[47]

The pro-Boer lobby stressed the brutality of Britain and the moral obligation of America to support republicanism over imperialism. Stanley Hollis gave more pragmatic reasons for support of the Boers. Hollis repeated his argument that a Boer victory would be in the economic interests of the United States:

When this country secures its full independence there is going to be a magnificent market here for goods our American people can produce, and for American brains as well. Americans will be wanted to renovate the old mines . . . to build new railroad lines and with American rails. . . . American agricultural machinery will be wanted everywhere. But supposing England wins in this war; what then? . . . imperialism would result very soon in a high tariff that would discriminate in favor of British countries, and against all non-British countries. . . . Under the English flag crushing taxation and tariff discrimination against American trade. Under the Republican flag a country nearly free from debt and with light taxation . . . and with openings for the extension of American commerce that would place the United States first in the list of countries exporting merchandise to this country.[48]

To explore further the idea of American cooperation with the Boers, Hollis made an unauthorized visit to the Transvaal in June 1900. He met with Kruger and assured the Afrikaner leader of American friendship. Kruger, in return, requested passage on an American ship should he have to leave South Africa. Upon receipt of Hollis's report of his meeting with Kruger, the State Department immediately cabled: "Confine yourself to your consular duties at Lourenço Marques. Do not leave your post again without instructions."[49]

During the latter part of 1900, a new problem emerged that embarrassed American officials for the remainder of the war: Britain began interning civilians in relocation centers—quickly dubbed concentration camps by the press. Critics of Britain were swift to equate this move with the "reconcentration" policy of Spanish General Valeriano "Butcher" Weyler in Cuba, which had been a major force in mobilizing American public opinion against Spain. Supposedly fighting a war to "civilize" South Africa, Britain was following the same policy of "reactionary" Spain. Although Hay privately grumbled that the internment policy "will stop the instant Botha and DeWet [Boer commando leaders] wish it to stop," he worked to raise and distribute American money and supplies to civilians in the camps.[50]

When it became apparent that the war would continue even after the fall of Bloemfontein, American leaders became concerned about the effects of the struggle on other areas of diplomacy. Like the other major powers, the United States saw an opportunity to gain from Britain's preoccupation with South Africa. After the Senate defeated the first Hay-Pauncefote Treaty with Britain concerning construction and fortification of an isthmian canal, Lodge urged a strong American stance to force a British retreat:

That the English should undertake to go to war about the canal seems impossible, although I admit, they have done a good many impossible things lately. If however, there is any danger of that kind, now is the time to take the step, for England is too exhausted by the African War to enter on any new struggle . . . .[51]

While some agreed with Lodge that the Boer War might offer the United States a diplomatic advantage, American policy-makers were more worried that continued domestic criticism of Britain would weaken the developing "understanding" between the two Anglo-Saxon powers. Hay, White, and Whitelaw Reid, the future Ambassador to Britain, all were concerned that a dramatic incident, such as a Fenian raid on Canada or a congressional resolution recognizing the Boers as the legitimate rulers of South Africa, could strain Anglo-American relations and threaten American economic penetration of postwar British South Africa.[52]

The risk of possible exclusion from the assumed postwar boom in South Africa and the force of the developing Anglo-American friendship provoked a strong counteroffensive by pro-British spokesmen. Governmental officials such as Hay, Roosevelt, and Choate, as well as such influential private citizens as Mahan, Hammond, and Sidney Brooks, led the campaign to restate the reasons for continued American support of Great Britain.

Members of the American elite sympathetic to Britain based their counteroffensive on the assumption that the average American, while probably pro-Boer, was uninformed and relatively unimportant. Roosevelt explained to British diplomat Cecil Spring-Rice that the typical Boer supporter was "short-sighted and in a hurry," while "all cool-headed and farsighted people realize that the war probably had to come . . . and that the interests of the English-speaking races and of civilization demand the success of the English army."[53] While the pro-Boer movement appealed to emotion and politics, the pro-British forces would depend on reason and American self-interest. Dismissing the knowledge and influence of the masses, they would direct their campaign to men of importance and influence. Sydney Brooks outlined the Anglophile argument in an article in the *North American Review*. Brooks felt that the outcry against England was the reaction of an uninformed public with no knowledge of the situation aside from an inbred hatred of Britain. What would deflate the pro-Boer forces was clear logic and a simple explanation, for those too shortsighted to see it, of how American interests would be served by a British victory. Brooks argued that while many Americans felt the war was a blunder, "I have failed to come across any who would not agree to the proposition that is was better for the world at large that England should succeed."[54]

One of the intellectual leaders of the pro-British camp was naval historian and strategist Alfred Thayer Mahan. In a series of articles and books, Mahan presented both a racial and economic argument for support of Britain. Despite early British defeats, Mahan remained firm in his "conviction of the essential righteousness of the British cause in South Africa."[55] Not only was Britain correct in its decision to go to war, but any American efforts to aid the Boers would be a rejection of the Monroe Doctrine and invite European interference in the Western hemisphere. In a book devoted to the war, Mahan emphasized the importance of the Anglo-American "understanding," the economic benefits of a unified South Africa, and the strategic importance of South Africa for the British Empire.[56]

Under the leadership of Hammond, American business interests reaffirmed the economic potential of a British South Africa. Hammond devoted nearly all his time to speeches and debates in support of Britain. Hammond not only defended British control as an economic advantage for America, but raised the specter of German influence should the Boers remain independent. He charged that Germany was arming blacks and equipping the Boer forces in hopes of gaining control of the Rand gold fields.[57]

American business journals attacked the actions of Macrum and Davis and continued to assert that British rule would be to America's advantage. Day Allen Willey, writing on "American Interests in Africa" in the *Arena,* summarized the assumed importance of the war for the American economy:

> The United States has almost as much interest in the result of the war in South Africa as Great Britain herself—from a purely commercial standpoint. The saying that has been so popular since the Spanish-American War that 'commerce follows the flag' means not only the American but the British flag, for it is a notable fact that, in many of the British colonies as well as the mother country, American exporters have been very successful whenever they have tried to find a market for their goods. And not a few instances are on record in Washington where American merchants and manufacturers have secured more of the business of a certain section under the English flag than the English themselves. . . . With such

a population as South Africa contains, and with such a country as will be developed by the extension of English control, it can safely be asserted that a market will be opened to the manufactures of the United States that is almost limitless.[58]

Consul James Stowe also anticipated a postwar open door in British South Africa. Following a long conversation with Sir Alfred Milner, Stowe predicted:

> The end of the war will be found to be of greatest good to the greatest number. Concessions will be done away with—concessions that were for the benefit of a few; the natives will be better treated, the police supervision and persecution will vanish . . . personal independence and liberty will be guaranteed. . . . Schools for the education of all will be established; no religious sect will be persecuted. . . . higher civilization will prevail, new mines will be developed, new industries inaugurated, and all men will be equal under the law.[59]

The final element in the pro-British coalition was missionaries. American missionaries in South Africa continued to be strong advocates of a British victory. The *Methodist Review* felt that British control would be "a great step forward in the interest of justice, humanity, and Christian propagandization. . . . The civil and political advance furnishing at least the 'open door' for the missionary in Africa."[60] Chamberlain assured missionaries that no segment of the population would benefit more from British rule than the "exploited natives" of the Transvaal.[61]

American missionaries also seized on the economic argument. They stressed the link between missionary activity and industrial and economic development. Britain would bring industry and Christianity. The *Missionary Review of the World* reminded the faithful that "the Boers resist the spread of Christianity among the heathen, or display an indiscriminate hostility to the missionary as such." An editorial in the same journal concluded: "we believe it to be in the interest of Christian civilization that their [the Boers'] dominance is ended in South Africa."[62]

American blacks also hoped for a British victory. The *Colored American Magazine* praised British rule in South Africa and observed that in areas of British control " the environments of the native in South Africa have been changed from a state of intellectual darkness to that of intelligence and enlightenment; from a state of superstition to facts and realization." Similarly, Dr. C. S. Morris, a black missionary in South Africa, saw the war as part of God's design for the "regeneration of the native." British victory would open the entire area of Southern Africa to black American missionaries.[63]

Fearful of the growth of the American pro-Boer movement, Britain continued to stress the humanitarian reasons for the war and the potential economic advantages for the United States. English spokesmen relied heavily on the assumed Anglo-Saxon mission and solidarity between the two English-speaking nations. On the eve of the Republican National Convention, Chamberlain publicly expressed his admiration for America's policy during the war, and reaffirmed the common purpose of the two powers. The British press continued to stress the parallel between American "civilizing" in the Philippines and British policy in South Africa.[64] In the winter of 1900, a young British officer who had been captured by the Boers toured America to enlist support for the English cause. Winston Churchill reported that while much of the general population was hostile to Britain, most governmental officials and men of influence were solidly behind Britain's efforts.[65]

British equation of their actions in Africa with America's policy in the Philippines was echoed within the United States. The anti-imperialists felt that their major effort should be to expose American atrocities in Asia rather than concentrate on Britain's in Africa. Even William Jennings Bryan, one of the most outspoken critics of British imperialism in South Africa, refused to sign a petition calling on McKinley to arbitrate the war. Bryan argued:

> Our refusal to recognize the rights of the Filipinos to self-government will embarrass us if we express sympathy with those in other lands who are struggling to follow the doctrines set forth in the Declaration of Independence. . . . Suppose we sent our sympathy to the Boers? In an hour England would send back, 'What about the Filipinos?'[66]

McKinley's reelection and the reduction of the war to bloody but minor commando raids caused the pro-Boer movement within the United States to decline. Pro-Boer forces hoped for a change in American policy when Theodore Roosevelt assumed the presidency in September 1901. Although Roosevelt had somewhat modified his outspoken pro-British stance, he refused to alter American policy during the last months of the war. Roosevelt was not as concerned with the possible economic gains of British rule as were Hay, Hammond, and others. Roosevelt's belief in the superiority and duty of the Anglo-Saxon race, however, convinced him of the necessity of British rule. The prestige of the British Empire and of the English-speaking powers demanded defeat of the Boers.[67]

As the situation in South Africa grew more desperate for the Boers, rumors circulated that Paul Kruger, living in exile in the Netherlands, would come to the United States to raise money and to make a personal appeal for American intervention. Hay instructed Stanford Newel to do everything possible to discourage the trip and to convince Kruger that he would get no help in America. Kruger abandoned the plan and remained in Europe.[68]

There were other inquiries from Afrikaners, adamant in their refusal to live under British rule, concerning possible emigration to the United States. Texas, New Mexico, and Colorado offered free land to Boers willing to resettle. The American consul in Capetown warned against such offers, citing the inefficiency of the Boers and their reliance on black labor. Despite Stowe's warnings, over 250 Boers reported in the fall of 1901 that they were ready to make the voyage to the United States. They appealed to the State Department for loans to pay their passage, but Washington refused to make the advances. Nevertheless, some Boer families did make the trek, including F. W. Reitz, former State Secretary of the South African Republic, who settled in Texas.[69]

As the war neared its end, America pressed for settlement of claims against the British for property destroyed in the fighting in South Africa. Newton Crane, an American lawyer living in London, was named to head the effort. Eventually American citizens received over $30,000—an average of over $2,000 per claimant, compared to an average of $300 for citizens of other countries.[70]

When the Boer War ended on 31 May 1902, thousands of British troops were left with no war to fight. Many turned their attention to America's continuing struggle in the Philippines. American consuls received hundreds of offers from British troops eager to bring the benefits of Anglo-Saxon civilization to the Filipino. Despite predictions that a 5,000 man army could be raised within a few weeks, Washington refused all British applications.[71]

The United States was generally well satisfied with the result of the war. Although it had taken much longer than expected, British control of Southern Africa was now complete. Many Americans agreed with the *Review of Reviews* that the war had "lurched South Africa into the twentieth century," and would revitalize the economy and government of the region. Missionaries eagerly looked forward to the new opportunities for evangelism that would follow industrialization and the concentration of blacks in urban areas.[72]

American business interests were also content. There appeared to be nothing to block the expected economic penetration of South Africa. Throughout 1902, American consuls reported a deluge of inquiries from American firms interested in trade and investment in the new British South Africa.[73] In anticipation of the postwar boom, the American consulate was moved from the old Boer capital of Pretoria to the mining and trade center of Johannesburg. At the same time, a consular agency was opened in the new region of Rhodesia in expectation of new gold discoveries and resulting opportunities for American investment.[74]

Americans expected that not only would they reap the rewards of British friendship cultivated during the war, but they would also capitalize on Boer hatred of their English conquerors. Hammond urged businessmen to launch a forceful commercial policy to capture markets abandoned by Britain during the war.[75] American merchants lobbied for the immediate establishment of direct steamship service between all major American ports and South Africa to eliminate dependence on foreign ships and to seize the opportunity to provide both white and black Africans with "the appliances of civilization."[76]

Throughout the last months of the war and the period of British demobilization, American businessmen and missionaries began to try implementing their plans to harvest the fruits of the British victory. Confident in the accuracy of their assumptions concerning British rule, and spurred by the dramatic increase in American trade during the last decade, they saw no reason to question the inevitability of continued American economic expansion and the spread of Anglo-Saxon civilization.

Even during this period of optimism, however, there were disturbing reports of future problems for the United States in South Africa. James Stowe resigned his post at Capetown in 1901 and blasted the inadequate budget and staff allowed American consuls. Stowe warned of an impending trade war with Britain in South Africa, and argued that America could not compete without more assistance from Washington.[77] Upon his return to the United States, Stowe wrote in the *Scientific American* of the growth of trade with South Africa, but also noted that Britain was becoming fearful of continued American economic influence. He predicted that Britain would initiate a policy to exclude the United States from the South African market as soon as it recovered from the war.[78]

Stowe's warnings had little effect in 1902. Americans overlooked the growth of British trade with South Africa, and neglected evidence of a growing feeling in both London and Capetown that American business was a potential threat to British control of South Africa. As early as 1900, British observers expressed alarm over American inroads in South Africa. The *British and South African Gazette* warned in October 1900:

> We can not afford to let our colonies and our new territories become the dumping ground solely for American machinery or see all the good posts filled by Americans after we have fought for them ourselves.

Confident that Britain had fought a war for American interests, the United States soon discovered that the war between Afrikaner and Briton had been replaced by a war between American businessmen and the British Colonial Office—between the open door and imperial preference.

## CHAPTER FIVE

# The United States and British South Africa

## Postwar Economic and Political Disillusionment, 1903-1914

During the two decades prior to the Boer War, economic considerations had a strong impact on American policy towards South Africa. Faced with the problems of industrial and agricultural surpluses, American policymakers were convinced that only the penetration of new markets could prevent depression and domestic unrest. Americans believed it was essential that they have access to the world's consumers and raw materials. They saw high tariffs, monopolies, and other tactics that would exclude American goods from foreign markets as jeopardizing not only American prosperity but the entire economic and governmental system.

The United States supported the creation of a British South Africa with the assumption that England would not only develop the area's resources and a large, black consumer bloc, but would be more agreeable to open economic cooperation than were the Boers. America was aware of the natural inclination of a colonial power to assist manufacturers of the mother country. British restrictions on foreign trade in South Africa had been minimal, however. The growth of American trade had, in fact, paralleled British expansion. American businessmen and diplomats assumed that the British victory would be followed by even greater American economic success.

Britain recognized America's economic ambition. During its conflict with the Boers, it cultivated American support by dangling the prospects of the South African market before the United States. Britain, however, shared America's fear of overproduction, and was convinced that the South African market was crucial to its own prosperity. The defeat of the Boers was a victory for British imperialism, and British leaders felt that trade with South Africa must become lucrative enough to justify the large expenditures that were required to end Afrikaner control.

The emphasis of historians on the Anglo-American "understanding" and the diplomatic deference of Britain has resulted in a neglect of the importance of English fears of the American economy and the intensity of the Anglo-American trade war during the first decade of the twentieth century.[1] By the end of the Boer War, the United States had replaced Germany as Britain's major commercial rival. British policy in South Africa reflected a growing concern about America's economic power. The period from the British defeat of the Boers to the unification of South Africa in 1910 witnessed a bitter conflict between the two English-speaking powers for control of the South African market. British officials used a variety of tactics to block further American economic expansion. Combined with a severe postwar depression in South Africa, Britain's policy of exclusion of foreign goods was extremely effective. After a period of success immediately after the war, America's dreams of a postwar boom in South Africa quickly evaporated. Frustrated and angry, Americans gradually realized that the "great rapprochement" in diplomatic matters did not necessarily extend to economics.

As the war between the British and the Boers struggled to its conclusion in the summer of 1902, the United States was confident that its pro-British policy had been a success. Bolstered by a ten-fold increase in American exports to South Africa in the decade from 1892 to 1902, spokesmen predicted at least an equal increase in the first 10 years of British rule.[2]

Americans dismissed reports of British fear of open competition in South Africa. The *Iron Age* reminded London that "there is plenty of room in South Africa for manufacturers of all nationalities and it is only by the clashing of the best of every country that real progress can be effected."[3] Businessmen assumed that America could capitalize on the strong anti-British feeling among the Boers and the equally strong British opposition to Germany. The United States would be the natural source for the new industrialized South Africa.[4]

The United States also assumed it would gain from the opening of the Transvaal and the Orange Free State to free trade and investment. Similarly, a new racial policy would finally bring the millions of black Africans into the economy both as workers and consumers. Americans were confident that their superiority in expertise and product quality, coupled with their lower shipping rates, would give them a competitive advantage in an open South Africa.[5]

For well over a year after the Peace of Vereeniging, it seemed that American optimism was justified. American consuls wrote glowing reports of increased exports of machinery, hardware, steel, cotton, and agricultural products. American businessmen pressed the State Department to expand consular staffs and establish new consulates to handle increased trade. Exporters urged the government to eliminate the British middleman by putting Americans "into direct commercial communication with the Afrikaner trader."[6] In his annual report for 1903, Consul William Bingham at Capetown noted that he had received hundreds of inquiries from American firms. He urged the State Department to persuade American companies to send more commercial agents and salesmen to keep up with the demand for American products.[7]

By the end of the first year of British control, it seemed to American businessmen and officials that the expected boom was at hand. American exports to South Africa hit a record high of $30 million in 1903—double the best prewar year.[8] What Americans could not foresee was that this would be the peak of their exports. The United States would not again reach even half of the 1903 level until well after World War I.

The dramatic rise in America's trade with South Africa confirmed British fears. Despite the fact that British exports also increased and still constituted over half of all industrial goods sold in South Africa, the rapid American advance was disturbing to England. Commenting on the growth of American trade with South Africa and other British colonies, Leopold Amery, one of Chamberlain's advisers, warned:

> Economically the stability of the British Empire is threatened not by Germany, but by the United States. We are thus brought to the greatest question of the future—the relations between the Empire and the United States.[9]

Other British spokesmen also voiced their alarm over American inroads in South Africa. Henry Birchenough, a special British commissioner sent to report on South Africa, concluded that "America is undoubtedly our most formidable rival present and future."[10] The National Industrial Association of Great Britain attributed the growth in American products to the influence of American mining engineers on the Rand. It predicted the United States would eventually dominate supplies to the mines. *The South African Export Gazette* reported that British businessmen were losing the South African market to their more aggressive American competitors.[11] By 1903, fears of the "American peril" had replaced earlier qualms about the "German menace."[12]

Parliament also showed alarm at American success. Members demanded an investigation of shipping rates to South Africa. One M.P. charged that "certain large and important contracts have gone to the United States for no other reason than that the freight rate thence to South Africa has been as much as 50 per cent less than from this country." Edward Grey, citing figures showing the jump in American exports, argued "trade which, under fair and equal conditions, would belong to the United Kingdom is being actually driven to America" because of lower shipping costs.[13]

During the year following the Boer War, three highly influential books appeared to alert England to the threat of the American economy generally, and the possible loss of the South African market particularly. Stafford Ransome, a former British mining engineer in South Africa, wrote a long summary of conditions in the mining industry. Ransome emphasized the continuing dominance of American engineers and technical experts in South Africa and the control of the heavy machine industry by "the Yanks." He concluded that while Britain still controlled the largest share of the South African market, "the United States is close on our heels." Ransome warned that the day had passed when Britain could merely offer its products without aggressive salesmanship. Ransome did not call for direct limits on American penetration, but urged better sales methods and a higher quality of products to meet the American challenge.[14]

More alarmist in tone was F. A. McKenzie's *The American Invaders*. McKenzie viewed America as a global threat to English markets. He was particularly concerned with the recent developments in South Africa. Like American policymakers, McKenzie was convinced of the economic potential of South Africa:

In writing of trade in South Africa we have to deal with the future rather than the past. . . . South Africa stands as the great market of the immediate future. Now that peace has come South Africa wants literally everything from pulpits to cradles, and from locomotives to pin-cushions. . . . South Africa presents trading possibilities such as we of this generation have never seen before.[15]

McKenzie feared that recent American inroads jeopardized British control of this potentially lucrative area. The economic possibilities of South Africa justified the expenses of the Boer War. He warned, however, that

British taxpayers paid, and are paying, the hundreds of millions for the war . . . the coming months may show that we have paid the price to benefit the traders of other lands, and that America especially will reap the commercial profits of our triumph in South Africa.[16]

Like Ransome, McKenzie attributed the American threat to the efforts of Hammond and other American engineers. He blamed the mine owners for hiring Americans rather than British subjects. He urged a crash effort to match American management and mechanical expertise to reverse the trend of the past decade.

The most sensational attack on American commercial penetration of South Africa was W. T. Stead's *The Americanization of the World*. Stead, a confidant and biographer of Cecil Rhodes, stressed Rhodes's early fears of American influence in South Africa. Stead even tried to blame the Jameson Raid on Hammond and other Americans. He argued, far from convincingly, that Americans on the Rand wanted to use the Jameson Raid to create an independent republic closely aligned with the United States. Stead contended that the threat of some sort of agreement between the disgruntled Boers and the United States still remained. This potential anti-British arrangement had an economic base. Stead noted the increase in American trade since 1895 and concluded: "The United States has been diligently preparing to invade the South African market as soon as the war affords them the opportunity." The United States planned "to seize the South African market" through political ties with the defeated Boers. "Few things seem less improbable," he concluded, "than that the Afrikander Commonwealth, under the leadership of Johannesburg . . . might very soon find itself in friendly treaty alliance with the United States."[17]

Like Ransome and McKenzie, Stead urged Britain to emulate American sales and management policies. Stead also, however, suggested two other steps to meet the American challenge. He called for a friendly policy towards the Boers to prevent them from being wooed by the Americans. He also urged legislation to limit imports of American goods through increased tariffs and more subsidies and grants to English firms.[18] Stead's program of a more forceful commercial policy, an accommodation with the defeated Boers, and an end of the open door for American business in South Africa, accurately anticipated the methods that would be used by Britain to block American economic expansion in South Africa.

One of the most immediate results of British fears of American commercial expansion was the movement in late 1903 for the protection of British industry. As early as March 1902, economist J. A. Hobson predicted that in response to the growth of American exports to Britain and to British colonies there would be a movement to abandon free trade.[19] Led by Colonial Secretary Chamberlain, the protectionist movement was aimed directly at the United States. As one historian of protectionism has summarized:

> Far more than fear of Germany, the growing American rivalry stimulated Chamberlain's call for a reversal of Peel's verdict of 1846. . . . American expansion was constantly used to warn Englishmen of the dire straits of their home economy and the vulnerability of their imperial markets. Similarly, American economic successes were admired and viewed as examples of what protection could accomplish for Britain and the Empire.[20]

In his famous Birmingham speech of May 1903, Chamberlain launched the drive for protection of British industry and British markets. In October, he resigned from the government to devote full time to the protectionist campaign. Owing to a variety of reasons, primarily fears of American retaliation, high food costs, and a general revival of British industry, the protectionist movement began to wane in early 1904. It remained a subject of intense debate, however, until Chamberlain's incapacitation in July 1906.

While the argument over protection raged in Britain, a similar movement developed in South Africa. The American consul at Capetown warned of increased hostility towards American business and demands by British officials for higher tariffs to discriminate against American goods. He predicted that South Africa would increase subsidies to British firms to lower their cost.[21]

Bingham's prediction soon proved accurate. Beginning in early 1904, British and South African officials initiated a campaign to weaken American economic influence. South Africa was able to mobilize effectively to meet the American challenge because both the government and economy were controlled by a small clique. Mining magnates occupied or controlled most governmental offices both in the former Boer states and in the Cape Colony and Natal. Along with control of the mines and government, this group also dominated the transportation industry, the press, and the banking system.[22] Committed to the "imperial idea," this small but powerful elite feared continued American imports and investments. After 1903, it joined English leaders in opposition to expanded American economic influence.

British and South African officials used a variety of tactics to block further American economic penetration. They first moved to limit the free movement of foreign goods and individuals. During the Boer War England required foreigners to secure official permission to enter the Boer states. When the war ended, England retained the permit system and refused to allow American businessmen to enter or reside in the Transvaal or Orange Free State without governmental approval. Hay and Henry White strongly protested this restriction on American trade, and gradually permits were issued. American businessmen, however, were still forced to endure long waits while their applications were processed, and restrictions on their movements once they were granted. Later, when Rhodesia began to develop its own mining industry, Britain revived the permit system. Americans were repeatedly denied permits for trade in Basutoland, as well as the right to bid on railroad and mining construction in the north.[23]

South Africans also moved to enforce rigid standards of quality for incoming American products. American agricultural and industrial goods were subjected to strict inspection, delays, and even rejection. South African officials met the protests of American consuls with statements that South Africa was merely enforcing minimum standards.[24]

Local officials also delayed or cancelled American contracts for municipal improvements, railroad construction, and other projects. Michael Whilby, for example, had used the friendly intervention of an American mining engineer to secure a contract to supply gasoline to several large mines on the Rand. When the Boer War ended, the American engineer was replaced and Whilby's contract cancelled. Despite protests from White and others, Whilby received neither the contract nor compensation.[25]

Whilby's plight was not unique. After 1903, American mining engineers and mine managers lost much of their influence. American businessmen, in turn, lost their most important contacts in South Africa. The American consul at Capetown noted in early 1906 that since the war few Americans had managed to secure jobs in management of the mines as "most such positions are filled with young men of British nationality." No longer did Americans such as Hammond, Thomas Mein, and Charles Perkins control the hiring and purchases of the great mines. They were replaced by Englishmen. Even those who retained their positions lost their powers of purchase and control of personnel.[26]

One of the most frustrating limits on American business was lack of credit. Nearly all the banks of South Africa were controlled by British capital. It was extremely difficult for American firms to gain long-term financing and credit from banks dominated by their trading rivals. In early 1904, a group of American businessmen on the Rand, frustrated by restrictions and delays in financing, approached Joseph Proffit, the American Consul in Pretoria, with a scheme for an American-controlled bank in Johannesburg to enable American industry to bypass Britain. Proffit was enthusiastic and advised the State Department that the plan "should be earnestly commended to all persons zealous of the promotion of American trade with this country." Although State Department officials welcomed the idea, it never developed beyond the planning stage and Americans were forced to continue to go through British and South African banks.[27]

South Africa also used tariffs and transportation costs to increase the price of American goods. American representatives repeatedly complained that high freight rates, combined with rebates to English firms, enabled Britain to undercut American prices.[28] In a bitter letter to an American railroad manager, Consul Bingham complained that the railroads were owned by the government, which was dominated by anti-American British financiers:

> The general sentiment here is that railways must be a great source of income to the Government, freights are so high that they simply choke down many business enterprises. . . . This is a good place for persons to take lessons who desire the Government to control the railway system of our country.[29]

Hollis noted a similar situation at Lourenço Marques. He reported that South Africa had adopted a general policy of a 25% rebate for British goods transported from Capetown or Durban. In Lourenço Marques, Americans had not only to pay full freight rates, but also a tariff to Portugal for using Delagoa Bay. Hollis strongly urged a reciprocity agreement with Portugal to allow American goods to enter at lower duties, thus enabling them to compete with British products. Hollis feared that the movement towards rebates, subsidies, and tariffs threatened the entire American trade with South Africa:

> A glance at the statistics of the exports of American goods to all of South Africa for the past ten years will show at once that it is necessary for us to have an 'open door' to the markets in this part of the world as anywhere else.[30]

Britain also moved to eliminate America's competitive advantage in steamship rates. Bowing to pressure from Parliament and business, the government reformed the steamship monopoly in 1905 and reduced rates to make shipping costs between London and Capetown nearly equal to those between America and South Africa.[31]

In 1906, South Africa took a major step towards preference for imperial goods. After several months of hard negotiations, South Africans adopted a new customs agreement that increased subsidies to English firms while generally raising duties on foreign products. The plan included a 3% rebate on iron and steel products imported from the United Kingdom, and slightly raised duties for heavy industrial products from other nations. Similarly, it boosted duties on wheat, one of America's major exports to South Africa, and established a rebate for grain from Britain, Canada, Australia and New Zealand.[32] Chamberlain's protectionist arguments, while ultimately rejected by England, had found a favorable audience among British colonies. Whitelaw Reid, the American Ambassador in London, commented on the movement to exclude American goods from British territories in a letter to Theodore Roosevelt:

> ... the colonies all want preference in the British markets, which cannot be given without the abandonment of free trade. ... If they don't get such preference, some of them are ready to negotiate for it with other countries without reference to Great Britain.[33]

The development of South African agriculture also hurt American exporters. The *Rand Daily Mail* of Johannesburg led a campaign to eliminate dependence on American food imports. H. E. V. Pickstone, the founder of the South African Fruit Company, argued that South Africa must not only become self-sufficient in food, but fight America for markets in Europe, Canada, and Northern Africa.[34] A movement to import Indian and Egyptian cotton rather than continue to depend on the United States was so successful that one cotton importer informed the American consul at Capetown that the market for American cotton in South Africa was virtually dead by the end of 1903.[35]

The general policy of discrimination in favor of British goods combined with a severe postwar depression in South Africa to destroy American illusions about a postwar boom. America had badly overestimated both Britain's commitment to the open door and the general economic health of South Africa. American exports to South Africa dropped from a peak of over $30 million in 1903 to less than half that figure by 1904. The decline continued throughout 1905 and 1906. In 1907, the first year of the new tariff rates, American exports shrunk to $9.8 million—the lowest figures since 1895. In 1908, the figure bottomed out at $9.7 million. For the first time, Germany passed America in exports to the area.[36] The real winner in the South African trade war, however, was Great Britain. Despite the general depression in South Africa, British exports increased in the period 1904-1909. While the United States and Germany struggled to maintain one-tenth of the market, Britain accounted for nearly 60% of all South African imports.[37]

Just as the United States was reluctant to accept the "myth" of the China market, it was slow to abandon its long-held conviction that South Africa would become a large consumer of American goods. In early 1903, *Iron Age* predicted that the anticipated postwar boom might not be as large as expected. It cautioned American business that the South African trade would increase only with improved credit and transportation systems.[38] It was not until 1904, however, that most interested Americans began to accept the possibility of declining economic influence. In a long report on "Business Conditions in South Africa," Bingham blamed the depressed South African trade on the disruption of the mining industry due to the war, a severe drought, and the ineffectiveness of black labor. He predicted that South Africa faced a lengthy depression and urged American manufacturers to be extremely cautious in their plans for South Africa. Gardiner Williams, still manning the consular agency at Kimberley, was equally pessimistic in letters to American firms. Joseph Proffit in the Transvaal recommended that the United States postpone the opening of additional consulates in Rhodesia, owing to continued restrictions on American trade and the generally depressed state of the mining industry.[39]

By 1906, America recognized that it was in danger of near exclusion from the South African market. The *New York Times* concluded a report on the decline of American trade with South Africa by admitting that "the roseate predictions" of a trade boom after English defeat of the Boers were totally in error. The *Iron Age* was equally blunt. It reported that "the importation of American goods has declined considerably, now amounting to practically nil."[40]

Despite the declining figures of American trade, many refused to admit that Britain had been successful in squeezing out foreign economic influence. American consuls devised several futile schemes to revive trade. Hollis continued to urge a reciprocity arrangement with Portugal to increase shipping through Delagoa Bay. Assistant Secretary of State Adee was sympathetic, but argued that Portugal's cooperation with Britain to maintain high tariffs and shipping costs was legal. American protests would do little except "produce ill will" in both Lisbon and London.[41]

John Snodgrass, the new American Consul in Pretoria, urged America to meet British restrictions with an aggressive trade war. He recommended that the United States work closely with the Boers to capitalize on their hatred of Britain. He also suggested that Washington ignore British restrictions and protests and establish consular agencies in Rhodesia. Snodgrass even revived the idea of an American bank in South Africa. He argued that a bank "controlled solely by American capital" would enable the United States to exchange exports directly for gold. America could thus "obtain a fair share of the gold output of this country" without dealing with Britain.[42]

The depression in South Africa was, according to Snodgrass, temporary and totally due to "mismanagement and lack of confidence on the part of the Mother Country." The establishment of an American bank and a new commercial policy would revive the South African market for the United States. Snodgrass listed over forty American companies, including United States Steel, Allis-Chalmers, General Electric, Western Electric, Remington Typewriter, National Cash Register, Armour and Company, Singer Sewing Company, McCormick Harvester, and Standard Oil, that were in favor of his plan.[43]

The proposed bank never materialized. The State Department was cool to the idea, fearing the hostility of Britain and unconvinced that such a scheme could reverse the slump in American exports. Many Americans did share Snodgrass's belief that British mismanagement was at the heart of South Africa's economic problems. Whitelaw Reid complained in a private letter to Secretary of State Elihu Root in 1906 that South Africa was badly misgoverned by the Colonial Office. Reid felt the new Colonial Secretary, Winston Churchill, "although cleverer than anybody had supposed him, is too clearly without convictions, too inexperienced, and too irresponsible."[44]

The United States did attempt to follow Snodgrass's suggestion for a renewed effort to crack the South African market. In reaction to numerous protests to the Secretary of Commerce about restrictions on American trade with South Africa, Assistant Secretary of State Huntington Wilson instructed American consuls to "protest with vigor" every "needless discrimination against American merchants." In the spring of 1908, the State Department ordered the American representative in Capetown to return to the United States for a tour of the country to interest American manufacturers in South Africa and to provide suggestions on how to expand trade with the area.[45]

Despite such sporadic efforts to revive American exports, by 1908, both trade and interest in the area had dropped to new lows. The optimism of 1903 had been replaced by disillusionment and pessimism. Bingham wrote to an American businessman in the summer of 1905 that the depression, coupled with British policies, had so crippled American trade that "it will take years to get down to a good solid business foundation again." Frederick Burnham, a mining engineer in South Africa and a close friend of Hammond, concluded in 1908 that Britain "might as well give South Africa back to the Boers" for all their administration had benefited the United States.[46]

American bitterness reflected the errors of American assumptions. Despite occasional warnings, particularly from Hollis, the United States had been nearly blind to the problems of developing a sound trade with South Africa. Only belatedly did Americans realize the limits of the transportation and credit systems and the problems involved in developing a black consumer bloc. There could be no instant imposition of "progress" and "civilization." America also overestimated the degress of hostility between Englishman and Boer that would follow the war. Despite predictions that Boer hatred of England would drive them to American goods, the rather generous British peace did not provoke the intense, lingering hatred that America had assumed. Similarly, the war did not disrupt British trade patterns and contacts to the degree American officials had anticipated. When the war ended, Britain was able to renew and expand its trade owing to its control of credit, transportation, and the government. Although the United States could not have been expected to foresee the severity of the depression that hit South Africa in 1904, it should have been apparent that the wartime boom would not inevitably blossom into the large market that America anticipated.

Aside from overestimating the effects of the Boer War, the United States also failed to anticipate the rapid changes in British industry during the first years of the twentieth century. Modernization of British industry rapidly diminished the technological and managerial advantage the United States enjoyed earlier.[47]

The most serious American misconceptions concerned the intentions of Great Britain. The growth of the Anglo-American "understanding" blinded Americans, as it has many historians, to the seriousness of the trade rivalry between the two nations. The assumption that Britain would maintain anything approaching the American conception of an open door in South Africa was a naive misreading of Britain's interests. Despite the propaganda efforts of England to insure American support in the struggle with the Boers, there was ample evidence that Britain expected South Africa to help pay for the war through increased trade with the mother country.

America's decision to support a British South Africa had been the product of a series of assumptions first enunciated by Robert Shufeldt and confirmed by two decades of American contact with the area. The near unanimity of support for a pro-British policy among the American elite makes it difficult to contemplate the United States' adopting another course. Even had the United States decided to support continued Boer independence, it seems unlikely that it would have gained more economically. The United States was correct in its belief that eventual British control was inevitable. Support of the Boers would have been futile and would have jeopardized the growing Anglo-American diplomatic rapprochement. What America had *failed* to perceive was the intensity of Britain's fear of the American economy and the English conviction that the United States' commercial penetration must be limited to insure British prosperity. Anglo-American friendship did not include free access of American products to British territories.

Despite the low level of American trade after 1904, interested officials and businessmen still hoped for a revival of the South African market. Many felt the movement for unification of South Africa would be the agent to restore American trade. As American disillusionment with British administration increased, so too did its faith in the possible economic advantages of unification. Americans had argued that one of the major reasons for the general economic stagnation in South Africa was mismanagement by Great Britain. The United States hoped that a new federation would revive the economy through unified native and economic policies. American officials also believed that a more representative government not as closely tied to the British Colonial Office would be more favorable to open trade and investment. Whereas Americans had previously argued that British control was necessary for the development of the South African market, after 1905 they attempted to reverse the argument: a lessening of direct British control would be to America's economic advantage.

The steps towards the eventual unification of South Africa began in early 1906. The return of the Liberal Party to power under Sir Henry Campbell-Bannermann led to a movement for more decentralized rule in South Africa. Campbell-Bannermann also made it clear that Downing Street would not block eventual unification of South Africa with a degree of self-government. The effect of the Prime Minister's actions was to transfer the emphasis in the political development of South Africa from London to South Africa.[48]

The drive towards unification accelerated in January 1907, when the moderate Lord Selborne replaced Alfred Milner as High Commissioner. Selborne immediately began to explore the possibilities of unification. In July 1907, he presented the influential "Selborne Memorandum," pointing out the advantages and possible steps to a unified South Africa. Throughout 1908, representatives of the South African states met and debated the proposed union. After interminable discussions on the location of the capital, customs rates, language, and native policy, delegates finally agreed to a tentative plan for federation. Approved by Parliament in August 1909, and proclaimed by the King on 2 December the new government of the Union of South Africa took power on 31 May 1910—exactly eight years after the conclusion of the Boer War.

Americans observed carefully the movement towards unification. Julius Lay, the American Consul at Capetown, prepared a detailed report on the Selborne Memorandum. Lay argued that the proposed union would stabilize the economic situation, increase productivity (thanks to a uniform racial policy), and result in a new opportunity for American trade.[49] The *Nation* shared Lay's optimism concerning the economic benefits of the union, but was fearful of the plight of the black African under direct Boer control. Many Americans were still skeptical of the Boer interpretation of the "white man's burden," and joined British liberals to warn of the need to prevent a return to earlier Boer exploitation.[50]

Despite occasional concerns for the status of the native population, most Americans supported unification as a means to revive the dormant South African market. In his annual report to *Commercial Relations* in 1908, Lay predicted that American trade had reached its low point and would rebound dramatically after unification was completed. He felt that the union of the South African colonies would break Britain's growing monopoly on trade and give local officials, who tended to be less committed to England, more control of the economy. Trade policy would no longer be subject to the whims of London, but to the demands of the South Africans.[51]

American support of unification continued to be somewhat hindered by fears of the future of the black population. When details of the new Union were made public in 1909, it was clear that "a unified native policy" meant exclusion of nonwhites from the political system. Suffrage laws were to remain as they had been prior to unification. Thus non-Europeans could legally vote in the Cape Colony (although property qualifications barred most), but were excluded in other states. In addition, the Boers demanded and received a clause limiting office holders to "British subjects of European descent."[52]

The suffrage restrictions provoked a storm of opposition from radical and liberal members of Parliament. Those critical of the new nation's racial policies contended that blacks had been "sold out" to assure agreement on other matters. Noted South African author Olive Schreiner warned of eventual race war should Britain accept official racial inequality. J. A. Hobson called the whites-only clauses "an outrage" and predicted:

At best the South African Union will be a close replica . . . of the Southern States of the American Commonwealth, where the races subsist side by side in the same land in no spiritual contact with one another, each race suffering the moral, intellectual, and industrial penalty of this disunion . . . .[53]

Some liberals in the United States also found it difficult to support the official acknowledgement of racism and the denial of the "white man's burden." The *Independent* rejected the popular argument that the new union would emulate American federalism: "The contrast between the American Constitution and the South African is very marked: ours says the Negroes shall vote; the South African definitely says they shall not." The *Nation* also criticized the suffrage laws, but hoped "that in time the Cape franchise will be extended to the whole of South Africa."[54]

Despite such protests, many Americans felt that the African was not ready for political rights, and supported the Union's race laws. The American Board of Commissioners for Foreign Missions argued that Americans did not fully understand the backwardness of black Africans and did not appreciate the educational progress the new Union would bring. Similarly, the *Colored American Magazine* contended that although unification meant blacks would have to abandon immediate political rights, it would mean more jobs, education, and missionary activity. The same journal also expressed a common American assumption: Britain would never allow a return to the extreme and open exploitation of the prewar years. Should the Boers attempt to reimpose their abuse of the African "the British Government, which has been always quick to recognize the cries of the oppressed, should not, and we think will not, tolerate this state of things long . . . ."[55]

Generally, Americans concentrated on the potential political and economic benefits of the Union rather than concern for the plight of the black African. Throughout the meetings and deliberations leading to unification, American consuls impressed on Washington the commercial advantages to the United States. Lay predicted that the new federation, while retaining ties with England, would be more open to free economic competition among all nations. Elected South African officials would be more interested in low prices and high quality than appointed British administrators with sentimental and political ties to English firms. Thus the old three-cornered rivalry between Britain, Germany, and the United States would be restored under more equal conditions. Americans also assumed that unification would lead to a reduction of tariffs and transportation costs as well as internal improvements financed by American capital.[56]

Many American businessmen shared Lay's optimism. *The Commercial and Financial Chronicle* suggested that the new Union might finally bring the expected South African boom. *Iron Age* subtitled an editorial on unification "Emerging from Seven Years of Depression." It argued that the trade decline had been due primarily to "political fickleness," but:

The unification of the several states into a consolidated form under the union government will, it is hoped, spell the death knell of racial, political, and tariff barriers, which have so long rendered general progress impossible.[57]

As American firms gradually regained their interest in South Africa, the State Department and the American consulate in London reported a flood of letters inquiring about the economic possibilities resulting from unification. American consuls prepared reports on new opportunities for railroad investment, expected tariff reductions, and anticipated demands for American goods.[58]

Americans were not unanimous in their predictions of increased trade. The irrepressible Stanley Hollis again lodged a long and well-reasoned dissent. Hollis argued that unification would not free South Africa from British dominance. English protection, loans, and guidance remained essential for South Africa. Hollis was worried that "in return for this protection, the merchants and manufacturers of Great Britain will be given . . . concessions in the South African markets that our merchants and manufacturers will find it difficult to compete with."[59] As in the period prior to and immediately after the Boer War, Hollis had little influence. Although not nearly as widespread or as intense, belief in the benefits of unification strongly resembled earlier assumptions concerning the results of British control.[60]

Hope that unification would revive America's declining trade with South Africa proved as illusory as earlier convictions of the advantages of British rule. South Africans, as well as Englishmen, still feared American economic control, and were reluctant to abandon tariffs and preference for British goods. Despite changes in the governmental structure, there was no significant alteration of economic policy. Americans continued to be excluded from government contracts, investment schemes, and management positions. Tariffs and freight rates remained high.[61] While American exports rose slightly after unification, the increase was moderate. From a low of $9.7 million in 1908, exports increased to $12.9 million in 1911 and $15.7 million in 1912—a steady but hardly dramatic increase, and still barely half of the 1903 total.[62]

Despite the failure of the expected South African market and the tightening system of racial discrimination, some Americans were well satisfied with the results of British control and the unification of South Africa. Theodore Roosevelt, in an address in London on the first day of the Union of South Africa, praised British colonialism in Africa as "a great work of civilization." Roosevelt called for continued Anglo-American cooperation in black Africa. Hammond, in a speech to the American Society in London, hailed the Union as "a great step in the progress of Anglo-Saxon civilization."[63]

American missionary spokesmen also praised Britain's policies. South Africa had not only committed itself to the Christianization and education of the African, but had allowed him contact with a more advanced civilization. Britain had also aided the missionary through encouragement of industrialization and urbanization:

> In the old days the missionary had to seek the natives in the remote and scattered villages. . . . To-day the natives from these same villages are coming to the missionary by hundreds and thousands. Not infrequently a preacher in a mining compound in Kimberley or Johannesburg has more than a thousand persons in his audience.[64]

American belief in the economic possibilities of South Africa died as hard as did the assumption that Anglo-Saxon rule had greatly bettered the black. After the initial flurry of anticipation surrounding unification, however, predictions concerning the South African market became more realistic. In 1914, a report by the Commerce Department on the possibilities for American cotton products in South Africa stressed the potential of the area, but argued it would take time to develop the customers necessary for the absorption of American products. The report noted that "the custom of wearing clothes is growing very rapidly among the natives" and predicted a continued increase in the market for American manufactured goods. The growth of American exports would, however, be linked directly to the pace of industrialization and civilization, which would be gradual. There would be no instant market, but only a slowly expanding trade as the economy developed and the black tribes became more dependent on industrial goods.[65]

This more realistic appraisal was symbolic of the change in American thinking. The United States finally realized that there would be no instant South African bonanza. Transforming words like "progress," "industrialization," and "civilization" into tangible programs would take time. Just as the United States finally realized that China would not instantly absorb American surplus, so too did it recognize that the black African would not immediately demand a cotton shirt and new shoes from the factories of New England, or beef and wheat from the American Midwest. Even if Africans wanted American products, they lacked the purchasing power to pay for them. Equally important, America belatedly recognized that British manufacturers and politicians were determined to maintain economic control of the area.

The disillusionment of the period 1903-1908 did not destroy American optimism, but it did temper predictions of the benefits of unification. When the years following the Act of Union did not meet even these limited expectations, America finally accepted its diminished role in Southern Africa. By 1908, Americans had decided that "half a loaf" was better than none. By 1914, they realized that a "slice" was the most they could expect in the immediate future.

As its economic involvement in South Africa dwindled, so too did general American interest. Following World War I, Woodrow Wilson and the State Department were involved with the disposal of the former German colony of Southwest Africa as a mandate to the Union of South Africa. Economic interest in the area was high during the aggressive commercial policy of Secretary of Commerce Herbert Hoover in the 1920s. But never again did America voice its earlier confidence in the potential of the South African market. Whereas its predictions of British control had proved correct, the roseate hopes of a booming market for American products and capital proved false.

CHAPTER SIX

# Segregation and the Origins of Apartheid

### The United States and South African
### Racial Policies, 1903-1914

The United States supported British control of South Africa for reasons other than economic self-interest. American policymakers justified English imperialism as acceptance of the Anglo-Saxon duty to "inferior" races. American diplomats, missionaries, and blacks shared the belief that British rule would hasten the development of the black South African. Repeated British rhetoric concerning their plans for racial progress and support of American missionaries confirmed American assumptions about the humanitarian aspect of British colonialism.

Encouraged by England to accept the "white man's burden" in Asia, the United States reciprocated with support of Britain's "duty" in black Africa. American Ambassador to Britain, Whitelaw Reid, felt "the Anglo-Saxon race" sought a common goal of "civilizing" in the Philippines and in South Africa. Joseph Chamberlain concluded that American rule in the Philippines "will make for the happiness of the native population, while an experience in the problems of government, under such conditions, will help the American people understand our world work."[1]

The period from the end of the Boer War to the outbreak of World War I tested American assumptions about the intentions of Britain and the applicability of American racial policies to black Africa. American predictions of social change in South Africa proved to be as inaccurate as their economic forecasts.

To most interested Americans, Britain's triumph over the Boers signaled the beginning of a new era of progress for the black South African. Education, jobs, and Christianity would replace the reactionary policies of the Boers. The civilizing forces of industrialization, missionary activity, and progressive government would swiftly elevate the African from ignorance and primitiveness. The United States also assumed that the more advanced American Negro would be both an example and an instructor for the black African. Immediately after the conclusion of the Boer War, the *Review of Reviews* reminded Americans:

> The authorities of British South Africa are observing with interest the progress of Negroes in America, and are expecting advice and help from them in promoting the advancement of the Negro tribes that now come under their jurisdiction.[2]

American blacks agreed that they would be in the vanguard of the movement to "regenerate" black Africa. Blacks in the United States felt they could cooperate with the Anglo-Saxon in missionary activity and in developing African models of Booker T. Washington's self-help programs.

White America generally welcomed Washington's strategy of industrial education, race improvement, and abandonment of political expectations. Many British and South African officials also urged implementation of such programs in South Africa. They viewed Hampton and Tuskegee Institutes as "safe" institutions that improved the Negro but did not threaten white control. South Africans were impressed with the discipline at Tuskegee and Hampton and the emphasis on religion and practical training.[3]

Washington's stress on work and manual training was especially attractive to white South Africans frustrated by the problems of creating a black labor force. Alexander Davis, a South African journalist and businessman, bemoaned the African's "abhorrence of all hard work" and advocated establishment of institutions like Tuskegee throughout South Africa to teach both skills and the work ethic. Sir Edward Grey and other British officials invited Washington to visit South Africa to suggest programs "based on his gospel of excellence of labor."[4]

White South Africans also had noneconomic reasons for supporting Washington's programs. They felt that the American plan would present an alternative to the Ethiopian movement of the AME Church and its slogan of "Africa for the Africans!" Washington and his followers not only condemned political action by black Americans, but were outspoken critics of black separatism in South Africa. Moderate black leaders in the United States, committed to Washington's "accommodationist" strategy and financed by white supporters, labelled Ethiopianism an "insidious poison" that was "a racial rather than a religious movement." They argued that it would destroy racial cooperation in South Africa and provoke repression from fearful whites.[5]

There was widespread white enthusiasm in South Africa for Washington's program of industrial education in the years immediately following the Boer War. Black Americans, with the encouragement of South African officials, established a "miniature Tuskegee Institute" at the American Zulu mission in Natal. Both black and white American missionaries hailed the Natal project as a model for the rest of South Africa.[6] White missionaries were convinced that "Christian industrial training on the Tuskegee model" was the only effective strategy for black South Africa. It would not only improve the skills of the black African, but provide a practical example of racial cooperation to illustrate the "lunacy" of the Ethiopian doctrine of black separatism.[7]

With the encouragement of the British Colonial Office, Washington sent teams of Tuskegee graduates to South Africa to train African aides to spread his programs.[8] Students and missionaries endorsed by Washington were able to secure a degree of trust and cooperation from white officials that more militant blacks could never obtain. South Africans generally assumed that Washington's program was highly successful in the American South and could safely be applied in South Africa.[9]

Despite the desire of American blacks to export their racial programs to South Africa—and the interest of many South African and English officials in their efforts—the campaign was generally unsuccessful. Problems of finance and language plagued black missionaries. Training programs were at a much more elementary level than in the American South, and the few skilled workers that did emerge lacked opportunities for employment. White employers were reluctant to replace skilled white workers with blacks. Black labor was conceived almost exclusively in terms of work in the mines. Equally important in the failure of American sponsored industrial missions were white fears of agitation among the black majority by militant black Americans. By 1909, South African officials identified American blacks with political agitation and rebellion (see below).

Despite its lack of success, interest in some type of Tuskegee-Hampton program for South Africa continued until World War I. In early 1909, a private American firm approached the American consul at Capetown with a program of industrial training for South African blacks modelled on Tuskegee and using black American teachers.[10] Tuskegee sponsored conferences in 1911 and 1912 to revive its programs in Africa. Black leaders from South Africa visited Tuskegee in 1912 to try to rekindle plans for "a Tuskegee educational system in South Africa" and a program of scholarships for South Africans interested in black American colleges.[11] Even as late as 1913, the South African Minister for Native Affairs instructed D. D. T. Jabavu, a black South African, to "furnish a full report on the Tuskegee curriculum and educational methods . . . with views on their suitability and adaptability to the conditions of the native under the Union." Jabavu visited Tuskegee and prepared a detailed report that praised the program, but concluded it was not workable in South Africa. He felt the American Negro was much more advanced than the South African black and had "the habit of industry absent in South Africa." In addition, the Negro church had given a sense of community and sharing that "cannot be paralleled in South Africa."[12]

While British and South African officials actively encouraged the activities of black American missionaries in the period immediately following the Boer War, they reversed their position by 1906. Whereas South Africa conceived of industrial missions and American Negroes as alternatives to black nationalism, it rapidly began to view Americans as leaders of black militancy. Britain's reluctance to eliminate economic and social restrictions on the African produced a strong reaction among many American Negroes. Black Americans active in South Africa became disillusioned with Britain's racial policies and moved increasingly towards support of black separatism. The links of American black missionaries with Ethiopianism, in turn, convinced many South Africans of the dangerous influence of any contact between black Americans and the African. American blacks became caught in a spiral of disillusionment and hostility. The greater South African fears of possible racial unrest were, the more stringent their restrictions on American blacks became. The more rigid South African policy became, the more resentful and militant American Negroes grew. The procress culminated in the expulsion of most American blacks, and bitter Afro-American attacks on the racial policies of South Africa.

Black disenchantment with South African racial policies was at least partly attributable to a general American over-optimism of the effects of British control. Britain did have a sincere desire to improve the condition of the African, but had made it clear that racial policy was secondary to economic development and unity among white South Africans. Britain was determined that the advancement of the black African would not be achieved at the price of South African stability. As early as 1903, Chamberlain assured South Africans that racial policy would be controlled by South Africa and not dictated by London:

> Your fate is in your own hands. . . . Do not anticipate any other meddling on the part of Downing Street, or of any section of the British people . . . the good sense of the British people will never tolerate any intermeddling in the purely domestic concerns of the people to whom it has conceded the fullest liberties of government.[13]

Despite such announcements of British intentions, the United States was confident of dramatic changes in South Africa. Black Americans felt that the British victory over the Boers, while not bringing racial equality, would open the area to black American missionaries and remove much of the racial discrimination prevalent under the Boers. Immediately after the Boer War, American consuls were inundated with complaints from black Americans concerning their treatment in the new South Africa. The Reverend A. M. Middlebrooks, a black minister from Pinebluff, Arkansas, wrote Secretary of State Hay protesting Britain's refusal to allow him to preach and baptize converts in the Transvaal. The Department instructed the American consul in Capetown to investigate and lodge a protest if Middlebrooks's complaint was justified. Bingham reported that the charge was essentially correct: Britain had a general policy of refusing black missionaries access to blacks unless they were under white supervision. The consul observed that, despite the opinions of many Americans, the British victory had not greatly altered South Africa's racial situation. Both Englishman and Boer "have the old idea that existed in the Southern States that the colored man should be kept in ignorance ... they claim that if the Kaffir is given an education he could not be handled as submissively as he could if he were kept in ignorance."[14]

Black Americans also complained of social restrictions. There were numerous protests over the denial of the use of public transportation and threats of imprisonment for using public sidewalks.[15] In response to protests of such discrimination, the American consul in the Transvaal attempted to impress upon the State Department the depth of racial prejudice in South Africa. He described in detail the segregation system in the Transvaal and admitted that the recent British victory had made little difference: "The old prejudices still exist, and physical conflicts engendered by this old prejudice are not unusual."[16] The American consular agent in Johannesburg denied charges that he refused to intercede for black Americans. He pointed out the rigid system of separation, however, and warned American Negroes "there is a great prejudice against the black man in this country and the American colored man would not be able to obtain the same treatment in this country as at home." He advised all blacks to avoid South Africa. The American representative at Kimberley issued a similar warning.[17]

Despite such notices, American consuls continued to face the problem of racial discrimination against visiting Americans. In August 1904, a group of sixteen black Americans petitioned the American representative in Johannesburg demanding their rights "as natives and citizens of the United States." They complained of harassment for attempting to use the sidewalks and trains and the arrest of one of their party, Thomas Brown, for trying to purchase a bottle of liquor. Brown claimed at his trial that as a citizen of the United States he could vote and hold office in America. "A man who is entitled to vote in his own country is surely entitled to have a bottle of sherry in this country," he argued. The judge was not convinced and declared that as a Negro, Brown was bound by the laws applying to black South Africans.[18]

Proffit deplored the decision, but pointed out that South African restrictions on integrated transportation and drinking "does not differ in any essential way from the laws . . . in many of our Southern States." The problem was not citizenship but color. American blacks received no special treatment because they were American citizens. While Brown's sentence was eventually suspended, Proffit warned that "colored Americans should remember that they are guests here and abide by the rules, however harshly they might press upon him."[19] When Proffit formally protested the treatment of black Americans in late 1904, South African officials claimed the matter was a domestic concern.[20]

The discrimination against black Americans caused some to question the altruistic intentions of Britain. This disappointment increased when it became apparent to Americans that there would be little immediate change in the status of the African. Foreign Secretary Grey reinforced American disenchantment when he dismissed demands for increased educational opportunities for the South African black as unnecessary. "The mines of Rhodesia are the best schools to which the natives of South Africa can go," he argued.[21] Liberals in Parliament, journalists, and missionaries criticized Britain's "abandonment of the native." One M.P. argued that Britain left the African to "the unconverted mercies of the white people." He caustically asserted that freedom in South Africa meant "freedom to 'whollop his own nigger.'"[22] Missionaries from America and England reminded the government of the pledges for uplift of the black, and the lack of commitment to this goal. One church official predicted in 1906 that "the future of South African missions is sufficiently gloomy if they continue to follow their present lines." J. Du Plessis, one of the most influential missionaries in Africa, concluded in 1907 that "not only has the position of the native not been bettered since the war; in some respects it has even grown worse."[23]

Despite these and other equally gloomy reports from American missionaries and consuls, American faith in the commitment of England to the black African died hard. Large numbers of Americans, both white and black, remained convinced that England was dedicated to the advancement of the "native races." *The Voice of the Negro,* in an editorial on the death of Boer leader Paul Kruger, blamed the continuing racism in South Africa on the recalcitrant Boers. It argued that as Britain consolidated its rule, it would grant more rights to the African. In a later article, the same journal attributed lack of racial progress to the fact that "the Boers are working hard to keep England from giving any recognition to the black man as a man." White American missionaries agreed that the barriers to racial progress were the defeated but obstinate Boers.[24]

One reason for this reluctance to abandon faith in British intentions was the white fear of black militancy. American missionaries, diplomats, and journalists were nearly unanimous in their denunciation of the activities of the AME Church and its doctrine of "Africa for the Africans." White America, as well as a large segment of black moderates, viewed Ethiopianism as a "barbarous movement" that preached racial hatred, violence, and a return to tribalism. Many assumed that the racial restrictions imposed by Britain were necessary to prevent violent uprisings led by extremists.[25]

But as racial restrictions intensified in 1904 and 1905, disillusioned American blacks became more receptive to black nationalism. Blacks expressed impatience with the policies of England and the seeming lack of "progress" in South Africa.[26] One of the first, and most important, denunciations of British racial policies was a series of articles in the *Colored American Magazine* by A. Kirkland Soga, a black South African editor of a Bantu language newspaper, *Izwi Labantu* (Voice of the People). Soga emphatically rejected Booker T. Washington's strategy of accommodation as unsuccessful in the United States and unworkable in South Africa. He accused Washington of being a tool of white money, unconcerned with the plight of the black African. Soga quoted Jefferson and Mill on the rights of man, and American Revolutionary War propagandists on taxation without representation. He concluded that Washington's "sterling advice" to abandon political agitation was "a betrayal" of the basic freedom of the black man.[27]

In a later article Soga rejected the theory that Britain was working to better the condition of the black South African. He charged that Chamberlain and other officials were uninterested in the progress of the black man and ignored discrimination in the courts, education, and employment. South Africa was ruled by "an oligarchy of wealth that made a mockery of justice."[28] In a three-part open letter to Chamberlain, the African journalist argued that the denial of the suffrage to blacks meant permanent acceptance of inferiority. Britain's verbal commitment to the advancement of the African was a sham: "Our experience in the past leads us to know how little we can expect from such professions."[29]

Soga's condemnation of both the philosophy of Washington and the intentions of Britain opened a new phase of militancy among black Americans. His arguments were repeated and amplified by others equally disillusioned with British rule. Charles Hall Adams, in an angry article entitled "Let the Native of South Africa Have Justice and Education," attacked the discrimination prevalent in South Africa. Adams described the "white side of South Africa" as "a huge cesspool of treason, a menace to the British nation, a toppling mockery, a nauseating farce." To Adams, it was "a wonder of wonders" that blacks had been able to endure "such a hell of oppression." Adams stopped short of endorsing the separatist Ethiopian movement, but did reply to its critics:

> Now and then we hear reports from the Negro-haters and alarmists that the Negroes of South Africa are likely, some day, to set up the cry of 'Africa for the Negroes.' If this be so, it is quite natural; it is simply carrying out of the old saying that, 'What is sauce for the goose is sauce for the gander.' The narrow, prejudiced, bigoted, stupid, tyrannous white people of South Africa force all the self-respecting, brave, liberty-loving, loyal Negroes into this attitude, or frame of mind, or unrest, by constantly prating and shouting from the house-tops, about 'white domination.'[30]

While Adams did not support Ethiopianism and its program of black separatism, two influential Afro-American journals did. The *Colored American Magazine,* which published both Soga's and Adams's articles, proclaimed in April 1905 that "Afro-Americans might with every assurance of effectual work, throw themselves into the breach of the Ethiopian movement, and hold the light while the natives fight for liberty."[31] *The Voice of the Negro* was also convinced that American blacks should move away from missionary and self-help programs towards a more militant stance. It defended Ethiopianism as the natural result of racism. South Africans "regard American Negroes with distrust and misgivings," it argued, because the Americans would not bow before white exploitation. In June 1905, *The Voice of the Negro* charged that South

Africa "has gone further than even Mississippi has dared to go" in racial restrictions.[32] In an editorial on South Africa a month later, the *Colored American Magazine* demanded "Africa for the Africans, and for the African NOW!"[33]

This more militant mood was spurred by South African reprisals following black revolts in Natal in 1906. American blacks bitterly condemned new restrictions on black missionaries that followed the revolt. Even some whites, although shocked by the Natal uprising and highly critical of Ethiopianism, were convinced that black unrest was the inevitable result of the restrictive policies of South Africa. *Harper's Weekly* blamed the bloodshed on "the crass stupidity with which Britain's representatives are handling the native question."[34]

Ironically, the Natal revolts convinced many South Africans that they had been too *lenient* rather than too harsh in their policies towards both the Ethiopians and American blacks. South Africa had become steadily more uneasy over the rhetoric and influence of American blacks in the period 1903-1905. In late 1903, the South African Native Affairs Commission began an investigation of the AME Church and the Ethiopian movement. In 1905, it published a five volume report condemning the movement as a plan for the eventual ouster of whites. It blamed much of Ethiopianism's militancy and influence on American missionaries and financial aid from American blacks. It also argued that many of the Ethiopian leaders had studied at black American colleges. The *Report* did not call for suppression of the sect, but warned leaders of the AME Church to avoid "mischievous political propaganda" if they wished to continue to be active in South Africa.[35]

Other South Africans concurred. In May 1904, journalist Roderick Jones published a study of Ethiopianism entitled "The Black Peril in South Africa." Jones dwelt heavily on the influence of American blacks and the political emphasis of AME ministers. A year later he again attacked the group. Jones denied that the movement was religious:

> When Ethiopian missionaries, saturated with American democratic ideas, go up and down the land telling the Kaffirs that South Africa is a black man's country, and that the blacks must 'stand

up for their rights,' it is impossible to ignore the political aspect of the propagandism.[36]

Jones was particularly concerned with the influence of "American Negroes, whose teachings, if not deliberately seditious, implant in the native mind crude ideas about the brotherhood of man, and fosters a separatist spirit wholly incompatible with strict loyalty to . . . white rule." He reported a growing feeling in South Africa to "bundle the American Negro, bag and baggage, out of the country, under a law excluding undesirables."[37] White American missionaries sensed this growing hostility towards their black countrymen. They warned against further political involvement and urged concentration on the Gospel. The Reverend Frederick Bridgeman, an American missionary in Durban, noted that antiwhite statements of AME leaders were widely quoted by whites fearful of black unrest. Bridgeman cautioned black missionaries to curtail their rhetoric or accept responsibility for white repression and possible race war.[38] The American consul at Capetown expressed similar fears. He wrote to the American representative in Liberia:

. . . above all the American colored man should not come here, for there is a great prejudice against him by the whites. They are very fearful that he will teach the native colored man some modern ideas, which will enlighten him to such an extent that they cannot handle him. . . . The Government is claiming that these men are teaching the doctrine . . . that Africa is a black man's country and the white man has no business here. This is all laid to the American Negro some of whom come here with good educations.[39]

In the summer of 1905, the government of the Transvaal confirmed these fears by refusing to allow any more American ministers of the AME Church to enter its territory. A few weeks later a British official in Central Africa asked the American consul at Capetown about reports of "radical American negroes" calling for revolution in South Africa.[40] This growing hostility towards Ethiopianism and black American missionaries culminated in the revolts in Natal and the strong South African reaction. The Natal uprising began in February 1906, in response to increased rents and taxes. It continued sporadically until it was finally crushed in July. It has been estimated that nearly 4,000 blacks were killed in the field or later executed for their part in the rebellion.[41]

Like the American South prior to the Civil War, South Africa lived with constant fear of black revolt. The rebellion in Natal convinced South Africans of the dangers of black nationalism, American blacks, and any relaxation of white supremacy. Immediately after it crushed the uprising, South Africa moved to eliminate American influence among the Africans. The head of the American Zulu mission in Natal, a black follower of Booker T. Washington and a strong opponent of Ethiopianism, reported a climate of fear and hostility among white South Africans:

> The missionaries are blamed on all sides as responsible for this rebellion because they teach the natives that they also are men with souls like white men. . . . Ethiopian teaching has been used as an argument to interfere with the work of missionaries.[42]

In late 1906, white officials, fearful of a repetition of the Natal disturbances, closed the major American missionary station in the Transvaal. South African leaders defended "whites only" voting clauses in the new constitutions of the Transvaal and the Orange River Colony as necessary to prevent black revolts. Natal rushed through a resolution requiring a white missionary to live at each mission station to prevent the spread of Ethiopianism.[43]

Although recent scholarship has shown that the influence of Ethiopianism and black Americans on the Natal revolt was greatly overestimated, South Africans placed a major share of the blame on Afro-American missionaries and Africans who had studied in the United States. Colonel Frederick Tatham, a member of the Natal legislature, attributed the entire uprising to AME teachings. The semiofficial military history of the conflict blamed it on the growth of mining centers, where blacks "became acquainted with that insidious American negro propaganda called Ethiopianism."[44] The official report of the Natal Native Affairs Committee pointed out that over 150 black South Africans had studied in the United States and 20 had participated in the revolt. The Committee concluded:

> The natives must be made clearly to understand and to realize that the presence and predominance of the White race will be preserved

at all hazards, and that all attempts to destroy its hegemony, whether overt or covert, such as the Ethiopian propaganda, will be promptly punished instead of being disdainfully treated, as in the past.[45]

Throughout 1906, American consuls noted a severe tightening of restrictions on black Americans not only in Natal, but throughout South Africa. New laws were hastily drafted curtailing the freedom of movement of all nonwhites—African and American. Natal and the Transvaal barred black ministers even remotely connected with the AME Church from preaching in their territory. By late 1906, black Americans were synonymous with Ethiopianism and violence. South Africa viewed even conservative black missionaries from the United States as threats to white rule.[46]

The identification of American Negroes with racial unrest continued throughout the period from the Natal revolt to the unification of South Africa. South Africa continued to intensify its harassment and restrictions of black missionaries. In a long confidential despatch in early 1909, Julius Lay, the American Consul at Capetown, attempted to explain the severe limits on black American missionaries. Lay interviewed several governmental officials and concluded: "They consider the influence exerted by the American colored . . . interferes with their control of the natives." He agreed that "American representatives of the AME Church have not always conducted themselves in such a manner as to entitle them to the confidence of the authorities."[47]

Theodore Roosevelt also justified South Africa's actions. In a speech to the AME convention in Washington in January 1909, the President castigated the violence implied by Ethiopian rhetoric. He urged the delegates not to allow "occasional wrong-doings" to overshadow "the fact that on the whole the white administration and the Christian missionary have exerted a profound and wholesome influence in savage regions."[48]

The annual report of the South African Native Races Committee for 1909 continued to link the Ethiopian movement with black Americans. The committee concluded:

This close connection between the Ethiopians and the negroes of the Southern States is viewed with grave misgivings by many

South Africans, who fear that, by stimulating the spirit of racial jealousy and exclusiveness, it may have a sinister influence on the future of South Africa.[49]

In response to this widespread criticism, many Americans active in the AME Church sought to disassociate themselves from violence and insisted that they desired only "to foster and encourage loyalty and obedience to lawfully constituted authority and not to breed disaffection. . . . "[50] Black ministers in South Africa even urged Booker T. Washington to come to South Africa to explain to whites that their programs were designed "to uplift their brethren and not to incite sedition."[51]

The South African Native Races Committee was also extremely critical of Joseph Booth, a white missionary. Booth had toured black colleges in the United States in 1898 and was greatly impressed with the racial pride and economic advances of American blacks. After the Natal revolt, Booth became active in the Ethiopian movement in Nyasaland. Along with John Chilembwe, an African who had studied in the United States, Booth preached a militant and even violent program of black nationalism. Chilembwe publically dismissed Booker Washington's philosophy as "petty-Bourgeois" and claimed in 1912 to have discussed the prospects of a black revolt in Central and South Africa with W.E.B. DuBois, the emerging leader of black protest in the United States. Three years later, Booth and Childembwe launched a bloody revolt in Nyasaland. As in the case of the Natal rebellion, American missionaries, both black and white, received a large share of the blame for "inflaming the natives."[52]

The identification of American Negroes with racial violence and black separatism seriously weakened the influence of the United States on South African racial policies. By the time of the unification of South Africa, even moderate Afro-Americans were under suspicion and surveillance by white South Africans. When South Africa formalized the racial policies for its new union, it used the United States as an example of the tragic results of declaring the black man the equal of the white.

The Southern United States offered an obvious parallel to many in South Africa. While South Africa was aware of the crucial difference in numbers (blacks were a large majority in South Africa, but a minority in the American South) they expressed a keen interest in America's "native problem." South Africa sent several delegations to the United States to observe the enforcement of white supremacy. The *Rand Daily Mail* argued that "every fresh study of the negro problem in America is of particular interest to South Africa. . . . This country may learn much from the policy adopted towards a people of a lower civilization in another part of the world."[53]

South Africans who studied or visited the American South in the period prior to World War I arrived at one major conclusion: the United States had made a series of tragic blunders in its handling of the Negro. The major mistake had been official proclamation of the equality of the races. South Africans were nearly unanimous in their opinion that the Fifteenth Amendment to the United States Constitution was a fundamental error. The decision to grant blacks full political rights was a rejection of the overwhelming evidence of their inferiority and a serious danger for the nation. It led to violence, corruption, and a cynical bidding for the "nigger vote." The United States was forced to resort to "legal gimmicks," such as the grandfather clause and literacy tests, to disenfranchise the black man. South Africans dismissed this as hypocrisy and sham.[54] Better to have expressly stated the inferiority of the black and officially deny him the vote than to first grant legal equality and then be forced to use violence and trickery to maintain white control.[55] The *Rand Daily Mail,* a leading advocate of studying the American racial system, concluded after a series on the American South:

> Is it not better to learn a lesson from the experience of the United States, and from the first refuse to build up false hopes amongst the native population, or provide a possible foundation for raising up of endless charges of political trickery in the future? The race problem of Southern America has been made more difficult by the well-meant, but unstatesmanlike, fifteenth amendment of the constitution, which has produced nothing but bitterness and allegations of bad faith.[56]

South Africans saw ample evidence of the mistake of granting political equality in the American experience after the Civil War. South Africans viewed American reconstruction as a disastrous experiment in black rule. Repeatedly, South Africans pointed to the "wild orgy of American reconstruction" as an example of the folly of black suffrage and the stupidity of

Northern politicans.[57] South Africans defended their decision to deny the vote to nonwhites by pointing to the American experience. Throughout the debate on suffrage laws for the Union of South Africa, American reconstruction was used as graphic proof of the dangers of political equality. Former British Prime Minister Arthur Balfour defended Britain's decision to let South Africa set its own racial policies by comparing the situation to post-Civil War America. Rather than impose equality like northern American Republicans, Britain should leave the matter to those living with the black man and more able to judge his ability. The *Spectator* also supported the Union's rejection of racial equality by citing the American example:

> We certainly have no ambition to imitate that kind of premature and theoretical generosity, which has ended in tricking the majority of Negroes out of their vote, and hanging and burning a Negro occasionally, as tho to make quite certain that no pretension can exist to equality under the law.[58]

South Africans echoed this interpretation of the failure of America's experiment with legal equality. Journalist Violet Markham summarized the South African view of American reconstruction:

> It seems incredible that the politicans of the North should have thrust manhood suffrage and full political rights . . . on a mass of emancipated savages, for the majority of whom . . . the highest form of pleasure prior to the possession of these privileges has been to caper to the strains of a banjo. . . . We safely affirm that the racial antipathies of the present are the product less of the war, than of the orgy of misgovernment which followed the peace. A white race handed over to a majority of savages, armed with votes and exploited by the basest type of white political adventures.[59]

Similarly, Maurice Evans, a Natal official, made an extended tour of the American South and concluded that the proclamation of political equality and its subsequent denial had poisoned race relations in the United States: "Equal political opportunity means equal conflict, the weaker must and will be worsted in the fight. The position of the Southern United States is often quoted as a warning and indeed is, I think, appropriate."[60]

The heritage of political equality, South Africans argued, was not only hypocrisy and trickery, but violence. South African leaders were shocked by the terror used to maintain white supremacy in the South. The press carried detailed reports of lynchings and violence and editorials condemning American approval of white crime. Similarly, South Africans were appalled by the blatant injustice of Southern courts. The violence necessary to enforce disfranchisement and segregation not only made a mockery of law, but debased both black and white. South Africans again used the American example as an argument for direct assertion of racial inequality. They argued that South Africa must not become an "armed camp" like the American South. Laws must be firm but fair to both races. Corporate punishment was necessary as an alternative "to the horrors that from time to time are seen in the Southern States of America." Evans devoted an entire chapter of his book on the American South to the problem of white violence. He rejected the argument that white crime against blacks was necessary to insure control. Violence resulted from false theories about equality that raised black expectations and forced whites to retaliate with terror.[61]

If the United States was a model of how not to handle political rights, South Africans hoped it might offer a clue to the persistent problem of black labor. South African leaders were generally impressed with the quality of Negro labor in the American South. While they dismissed the graduates of elite institutions such as Tuskegee and Hampton as "unrepresentative," they were interested in the motivation of the average black worker. In 1907, "a prominent member of the Government" approached the American consul at Capetown requesting information on the quality and training of black workers in the United States. Lay wrote the Governor of Alabama and the State Department requesting information. The Department of Commerce sent a copy of its publication on "Negroes in the United States" and an apology that there were no studies dealing directly with black labor.[62]

In early 1908, the Transvaal released a study on black labor in South Africa and the United States. While fearful of the possible effects of black workers on white jobs, authors of the report were generally impressed with the productivity and diversity of Negro workers in America. They urged additional study of the American system of training and organizing black labor.[63]

South Africans also visited the United States to appraise the quality of black workers. In 1906, H. E. V. Pickstone, a leader of the South African fruit industry and a constant critic of the quality of African labor, toured the American South "to look into their constructive policy, if any, towards the Negroes. . . . I am looking into the economic position, which is the vital side of the question for us in Africa." Pickstone was impressed with the quality of black workers, but was disturbed by what was to become a common theme in South African reports on the American South; the reluctance of the white man to do manual labor when a black labor force was available.[64]

South Africans feared the "decadence" that resulted when whites became convinced that manual labor was fit only for a black man. The "po' white trash problem," as one South African dubbed it, was seen as a warning to South Africa. Evans saw the degeneration of the white race in the American South as a possible portrait of South Africa in the near future. He feared a large class of whites would "look upon labour, with its antiseptic medicinal virtues, as a degradation."[65] The American consul in Pretoria reported fears of South African officials that

> South Africa will duplicate the experience of our Southern States where the white man directs and the colored does the work and the relatively incapable white man is . . . unable to maintain his position as an aristocrat in the economic world and must either merge with the colored population or become a parasite on the white community.[66]

Despite their interest in the use of black labor in the United States, South Africans found little they could apply to their own labor shortage. The major conclusion South Africans drew was that they must avoid the creation of an unskilled, violent class of "mean whites" that had developed in the American South.

To many white South Africans, America's "native policy" provided not only an example of the horrors of black suffrage, but a powerful reminder of the tragedy of unclear distinctions between the races. The United States had been unable to decide between segregation and assimilation. The result was a hodge-podge of integration and forced white supremacy that produced exploitation, violence, and miscegenation. America had drifted towards "fusion" of the races and "sham assimilation." A much more honest and peaceful solution, argued South Africans, was "real" segregation. The white man should openly affirm that the black was neither his social nor political equal. Acceptance of the absolute superiority of the white race was the only basis of an effective racial policy. The white man would be relieved of the temptation to vie for the black vote. He would avoid the debasing experience of having to use violence and sham to rob the black of legal rights. Similarly, the African would know his exact position in society. He need not worry about violent reprisals or manipulation by white politicans. The black would be free to develop and improve without the obligation of political involvement. Dependent on the assumed good intentions of the white man (a key point for liberal advocates of "real segregation"), the black would gradually improve to the limits of his capacity.

This idealistic view of separate racial development, one of the justifications for the later policy of apartheid, was a common theme among South Africans familiar with the American experience. Pickstone, for example, formulated a program of five "grades" for non-Europeans based on length of employment, education, and wealth. The lower grades would be confined to black reservations and to periodic employment in the mines. Each increase in grade would bring more social and political rights. Pickstone outlined his plan to Booker T. Washington, who was lukewarm, and to Theodore Roosevelt who, according to Pickstone:

> ... seemed favourably impressed and said: 'Such a scheme as you propose is impossible in our country. It would involve an alteration of our Constitution. . . . but there is nothing in the British constitutions to prevent such a scheme . . . within the British Empire.'[67]

William Wybergh, a South African who toured the South in 1908, also argued for separate racial development. He dismissed the American solution as "sham assimilation" that frustrated both races. South Africa should profit from American blunders and seek a parallel development of separate cultures.[68]

It was Maurice Evans who most articulately expressed South Africa's response to American racial policies. Evans argued that his observations of the United States convinced him that rigid segregation, with equal justice, was the only solution for South Africa. The intermingling of the races in the American South produced fears and violence in both races. The Southern white mistakenly believed that he was protecting his home, job, and wife through terrorism. Corruption in the Southern courts and the use of terror was paving the way for eventual race war in America.[69]

The lesson to South Africa was, argued Evans, not false equality but complete separation. Thus Evans strongly advocated the creation of black reservations in South Africa. Given his own land, the black would develop his own economy and institutions and maintain his language and traditions. Evans advised the American South to consider a similar program:

> The wisest friends of the American Negro, both white and black, after all these years would welcome a separation of the races such as is still possible for us in South Africa. . . . We still have black States and large reserves, and yet short-sighted ones would break them up, and force the landless inhabitants to become vagabonds or industrial serfs, scattered throughout the length and breadth of the land. To such the experience of the South should serve as a warning. . . . I frankly recognize the differences of the races and believe we must accept this in our practice. I advocate territorial separation, the conservation of what is good in native life and custom, and the gradual teaching of what they can assimilate from our civilization . . . . Too late it may be for the South, but I feel that if some of her best men . . . could counsel us, they would say that on such lines and not in the way that it was forced upon them by the conquering North, lies our hope for the future of South Africa.[70]

While many white South Africans such as Evans were sincere in their belief that rigid racial segregation would benefit both black and white, the need for black labor made total separation as impossible in South Africa as in the United States. It was a short step from well-intentioned arguments for the acceptance of inequality as a prelude to separate development to use of a perverted form of the argument for the justification of permanent white supremacy and economic exploitation.[71]

South Africans also looked to the United States for examples in how to deal with another racial group—the Orientals. The use of Chinese labor in South African mines was a major subject of debate in the period following the Boer

War. Mineowners cut wages for black workers in the mines nearly in half following the British victory in 1902. This made recruitment of black workers difficult. Many blacks refused to sign labor contracts until wages were restored. When efforts to recruit blacks from Portuguese East Africa failed, South Africans decided to import workers from China. With the approval of the Colonial Office and British High Commissioner Lord Milner, South Africa began the massive importation of Chinese in 1904. By the end of 1905, over 50,000 Chinese were employed in the mines. Despite assurances that the Chinese would take no white jobs, and written restrictions on the treatment of Orientals, the issue provoked intense debate in London and South Africa. Liberals in Parliament were outraged by reports of the mistreatment and starvation wages paid the Chinese. White South Africans were dismayed by strikes, desertions, and crime among the imported workers.

American problems with Japanese immigrants in California served as an example to both sides in the South African debate. Opponents of Chinese labor repeatedly pointed to the problems in the United States, particularly the controversy between San Francisco school officials and President Roosevelt over discrimination against the Japanese. Those favoring the continued use of Oriental workers defended the policy by citing figures on the cheap labor costs and high productivity of Asian workers in the United States.[72]

Certain members of the State Department, particularly those in the Far Eastern Affairs Division, felt America could use South Africa's problems with the Chinese to its diplomatic advantage. They argued that the mistreatment of the Chinese in South Africa and the brutal conditions in the mines made American discrimination against the Japanese seem minor by comparison. Washington ordered American consuls in South Africa to prepare detailed descriptions of the conditions of Chinese workers on the Rand. These were relayed by the State Department to the American ambassador in Tokyo to illustrate the more moderate American policies.[73]

The decision by South Africa to expel the Chinese after their labor contracts expired also involved the United States. Desperate Chinese laborers, fearing starvation if returned to China, flooded American consuls with applications for immigration to California. Caught in the embarrassing position of admitting Chinese immediately after working out the "Gentleman's Agreement" with Japan to exclude further Japanese immigrants, the United States rejected all applications.[74]

Despite the brief flurry of activity involving the Chinese, it was South Africa's policies towards blacks that continued to concern Americans. Following political unification, South Africa began to tighten its official policy of racial segregation. The Native Labour Regulation Act of 1911 made breach of a labor contract by an African worker a crime. The Mines and Works Act of 1911 prohibited blacks from entering many skilled jobs. Most importantly, the Native Land Act of 1913 resulted in the geographic separation of South Africa into black and white lands. Hailed by many South Africans as a step towards preservation of black tribal lands, the law set aside only 13% of the land for blacks, while preserving the remaining 87% for white ownership.[75]

In the years after the English victory, South Africa also intensified social segregation. The pass laws, requiring non-Europeans to carry labor passes to justify their movement, were rigorously enforced. Discrimination in transportation, entertainment, and housing also intensified. South Africa even protested the attempt of an American firm to show films of heavyweight boxing matches featuring the black American champion Jack Johnson. Officials argued that Africans were gloating over posters "showing a black man knocking a white man about."[76]

American hopes for free access of foreign missionaries also failed to materialize. South Africa required all missionaries to gain permits from the Minister of Native Affairs before entering the country. These were severely limited and usually excluded black Americans. The State Department advised all black Americans to avoid travel in South Africa for fear of assaults on American citizens.[77]

While some black Americans accepted South African segregation as a necessary stage in the African's development, most black leaders, and some white liberals, were incensed by the official racism. American missionaries were particularly concerned about the pass laws and the compulsory labor requirements. The *Missionary Review of the World* reported:

> One can hardly believe it is possible that such legislation could be seriously proposed, but so strong is color prejudice, and so enslaved are party politicans to their political superiors, that unless

the sense of justice of the British public is aroused and pressure is brought to bear . . . this shameful wrong will be perpetuated. . . .[78]

Although American diplomats and missionaries in South Africa criticized the tightening system of segregation, its most vocal American critic was W. E. B. DuBois. DuBois, the National Association for the Advancement of Colored People, and its journal *Crisis* (edited by DuBois), repeatedly condemned South Africa's racial policies.

DuBois rejected the acceptance of segregation within the United States and the humanitarian intentions of Britain in South Africa. He argued that South Africa was the inevitable result of white colonialism. White rule, whether in America or Africa, meant racial exploitation. *Crisis* denounced South Africa for its restrictions on suffrage, lack of educational programs for the African, prohibition of mixed marriages, limits on black artisans, and harassment of black missionaries.[79] It became even more vehement with the passage of the segregation legislation of 1911-1913. Initially hopeful that the establishment of black protectorates would allow the African a degree of self-rule, the journal was shocked by the terms of the Native Land Act. Commenting on the provisions of the law, it concluded: "The civilization of South Africa, by means of theft, disfranchisement, and slavery, goes on apace."[80]

*Crisis* saw an obvious parallel between white rule in South Africa and in the American South. The South, it argued, served as an example to South Africa of the necessity of terror and violence to preserve white supremacy. In both Africa and the United States, the white man's commitment to justice was only rhetorical:

> The Union of South Africa, in imitation of the United States of America, and especially the Southern section thereof, has decreed that a white skin is always to be the *sine qua non* to the realities expressed by the high sounding phrases about 'life, liberty, and the pursuit of happiness.'[81]

Black American missionaries in South Africa also expressed their disillusionment with the racial policies of the new Union. John Dubé, the past head of the abandoned American missionary station in Natal, and a former advocate of Booker Washington's philosophy of accommodation, wrote to *Crisis* in early 1914, protesting the pass laws and the Native Land

Act. Dubé organized a delegation of Africans to go to London to seek the intervention of Britain in favor of blacks, and pleaded with DuBois to accompany them.[82]

Black protests had little effect on the racial policies of South Africa. By 1914, it was clear that the Union of South Africa had rejected legal equality, black suffrage, and integration in favor of rigid restrictions on the rights and movements of the African. Earlier American assumptions that British control would lead to the "uplift" and "civilizing" of the black African were as erroneous as their belief in the economic benefits of English rule. Britain had proved as willing to sacrifice the rights of blacks for unity between Englishman and Afrikaner as the United States had been to tolerate segregation to help heal tensions between North and South. White fears overruled the white man's burden.

Given America's own tarnished racial record, both in the United States and in the Philippines, it is not clear just how far it expected South Africa to go towards integration. Certainly, many American missionaries and blacks were extremely disappointed with British policy in the period 1903-1909, and particularly with the racial laws of the new Union. White America, however, reluctant to grant social or de facto political equality to the American Negro, should not have been too shocked by South African restrictions on the supposedly "less advanced" black African. The basic difference between the two nations seems to have been in official statements of policy. The United States continued to proclaim its commitment to equality for all races. It was disturbed by South Africa's decision to declare inequality openly and to establish laws preserving white control. South Africans argued that they were merely being more honest and practical than Americans. Observation of American segregation convinced them of the folly of first declaring equality and then using illegal means to circumvent the law. The direct statement of white supremacy seemed a far better solution than the hypocritical and violent compromise of the American South.

The differences between the American policy of legal equality and de facto segregation and the South African decision to simply deny equality seemed important to whites in both nations. But to blacks in the United States and in the Union of South Africa, the semantic distinctions were less important than the established fact of white supremacy in both nations.

# Conclusion

This study has argued that America supported British control of Southern Africa to insure economic development, a "progressive" government, and the "civilizing" of the black African. Basically this policy failed: British domination resulted in a decline of American economic influence and did little to improve the lot of the black African. Although a failure, America's South African strategy revealed changes in both the goals and methods of United States foreign policy in the period.

The decision to support British imperialism was the all but inevitable result of ingrained attitudes about economics, politics, and race. Throughout its history the United States viewed itself as a model for the rest of the world to follow. But, as historian Robert Beisner has argued, in the 1890s America's idea of mission shifted from a passive example to active attempts to export its system. In response to the surge of European imperialism in the 1890s, "the old idea of mission struck many as a dangerous luxury and a selfish abnegation of duty." The United States adopted what Beisner has called " the new American mission": a vigorous attempt to use its power to extend its political, economic, and social system abroad.[1]

In South Africa, Britain became perceived as the best vehicle to impose a replica of the American system. Having no direct colonial aims in Africa, the United States determined that British imperialism rather than continued Boer independence was most compatible with American concepts of "progress." The Boers, and to a lesser degree Britain's colonial rivals, were seen as hostile to such assumed "goods" as liberal capitalism, freedom of trade and investment, the spread of Christianity, and the education and uplift of the black African.

The "new American mission" neatly complemented the other major force in American foreign policy: economic self-interest. Economic and humanitarian considerations were so intertwined and interdependent that they were complementary rather than antagonistic. The economic prosperity of the United States was assumed to be dependent on increased foreign markets, but policymakers of the period were equally certain that the development of a progressive South Africa through the establishment of democratic institutions and a paternalistic racial policy was also an American interest. Involvement in the internal politics of South Africa was an extension of America's sense of mission and uniqueness as well as representative of a practical awareness of the link between the domestic affairs of a foreign nation and American prosperity.

American relations with South Africa reveal a shift in the tactics of diplomacy as well as its goals. Beisner contends that the 1890s witnessed the development of a real American foreign "policy." Prior to the period, American diplomacy had lacked the basic characteristics of "policy." Beisner found four major elements of "policy" that developed in the 1890s: continuity, "a new awareness of the interlacing of issues," "the increased readiness of the government to move beyond public opinion . . . or alternatively to create public support," and "a shift of the locus of initiative from the field to Washington."[2] American policy towards Southern Africa illustrated each.

Despite occasional domestic opposition, American policy displayed a continuity of support for England from the discovery of gold in 1886 until well after the Boer War. Although the intensity and method of support shifted, Washington was consistent in its belief in the necessity of British rule and the need for American assistance. This support ranged from verbal encouragement to active assistance. Few within the American policymaking elite questioned the benefits of English control and rarely did the United States vary from the encouragement of British hegemony.

The United States also recognized the importance of the South African situation to global politics. English control of South Africa, America argued, would represent a model for enlightened colonialism throughout Africa. It would be an example of the Anglo-Saxon duty for the rest of Europe. Similarly, the economic development of South Africa and the maintenance of free trade and investment would be symbolic of America's determination to have an expanded role in the world economy. While the open door was to be preserved in Asia by blocking European colonialism, it could be established in South Africa only through support of British imperialism.

The American government was both willing and able to ignore or try to shape public opinion in support of its goals in South Africa. The dismissal of the pro-Boer lobby and the public relations efforts of pro-British American leaders during the Boer War are prime examples of placing accepted American interests above the prejudices of the supposedly "uninformed" American public.

The final element in the development of "policy" was the shift of control of diplomacy from isolated, nongovernmental individuals to foreign policy professionals in Washington. A true global awareness and policy demanded centralization of foreign affairs. This is exactly what happened concerning South Africa. Businessmen, missionaries, and independent American consuls, were crucial in shaping American impressions of the struggle between Britain and the Boers. Following the Jameson Raid, when the situation in South Africa approached crisis, it was the State Department that controlled American actions and impressions. Beisner cites as an example of this shift the changes in America's relations with China. Marilyn B. Young summarized the centralization of America's Asian policy:

> Individual Americans, diplomats, missionaries, and adventurers acted independently of government direction in the belief that personal efforts could have a direct effect on the destiny of nations, even empires. . . . However, as international rivalries increased, the prerequisite for success became strong government backing, not the heroic efforts of an individual, and bold schemes on the part of restless Americans disappeared. Government initiative replaced that of the individual.[3]

Young's conclusion is as applicable to South Africa as to China. John Hays Hammond was a prime example of a "restless individual" committed to "bold schemes" to alter nations. His active role in shaping American views of Rhodes, Kruger, England, and the Boers and, most illustrative, his involvement with the Jameson Raid, were unofficial, individual, acts. When the situation in South Africa became more tense and

137

more important for the United States, it was officials in Washington rather than private citizens who established policy and took action.

American involvement in South Africa thus illustrated the major characteristics of the "new foreign policy" of the late nineteenth century: economic concern for increasing American exports and preserving free access for American investment; a "new" sense of active mission to spread American ideals; and the establishment of "policy" rather than sporadic and casual responses to international situations. American relations with South Africa reveal an additional element in American diplomacy: the inaccuracy of American assumptions and the failure of a policy.

Americans assumed that what had worked in the United States could and should be exported to South Africa. Economic development, an industrialized economy, representative government, racial paternalism, and Christianity had been judged "successful" for the United States and were considered applicable to South Africa. The first decade of British control challenged this assumption and showed the inaccuracy of American predictions for South Africa. Rather than abandon its expectations for the area, the United States sought to explain away the lack of progress. It blamed the unexpected postwar depression for the failure of American economic gain. The lack of racial progress was attributed to mismanagement by the British Colonial Office and the continued prejudice of the Boers. The enduring belief that a change in government, such as the unification of South Africa, would finally bring the expected changes, testifies to American miscalculation and a reluctance to reexamine expectations.

To question the wisdom or the possibility of imposing the American model on South Africa was tantamount to questioning American institutions themselves. Despite the differences in geography, development, racial makeup, and government between the United States and South Africa, Americans continued to assume that a slightly modified version of the "American way" would be established by Britain. Long after it should have been obvious that this theory was inaccurate, the United States still viewed Britain as the agent to apply American solutions to African problems. Only when it became obvious that the new Union of South Africa was as dedicated to the restriction of American commercial penetration as Britain and had rejected a "progressive" racial policy, did America finally begin to recognize the fundamental errors of its South African strategy.

Since 1914 South Africa has become the industrialized, urbanized nation that many Americans predicted. Similarly, as many had forecast, disputes within the white minority over cultural identity and racial policy have remained the essence of South African politics. The memory of the Boer War (or the Second War for Independence as it is known to many Afrikaners) continued to influence the nation despite attempts to unite English-speaking and Afrikaner whites. Politics have reflected the century-old struggles over the preservation of Afrikaner culture and the methods of controlling the black majority.

The response of South Africa to the outbreak of World War I in 1914 revealed the depth of dissension within the nation. Even prior to the war, whites had split on the question of loyalty to Great Britain and the British Empire. Louis Botha and Jan Smuts, leaders of the ruling South African Party, made concessions to English-speaking South Africans fearful of Afrikaner domination under the Union. Afrikaner nationalists viewed such accommodation as a move to submerge Afrikaner culture under a pro-British dictatorship. Under the leadership of J. B. M. Hertzog, Afrikaners formed the Nationalist Party to halt the erosion of their language and unique society. When the government committed South Africa to support of the British war effort against Germany in 1914, Afrikaners in the Transvaal and the Orange Free State revolted. While the rebellion was eventually crushed, it illustrated the persistence of Afrikaner hatred for Britain and things British, and the determination of the Boers to maintain their own identity.[4]

Aside from the continuing question of Afrikaner nationalism, South Africa also faced the problems of industrialization and race. In the 1920s, the two issues were joined through a series of labor disputes. In 1922, mine owners sought to cut wages for white workers and to move blacks into jobs that had been reserved for whites. The result was an armed uprising in the gold fields as white workers fought police and eventually government troops. The "Rand Revolution" was ended only after martial law was declared and over 200 deaths. While the government suppressed the revolt, it also moved to alleviate white fears of blacks taking their jobs. Continuing the drive towards separation of the races begun prior to 1914, South Africa passed the Apprenticeship Act and the Colour Bar Act of 1926 that effectively excluded blacks from the skilled trades.

While such legislation appeared to many South African liberals as a harsh overreaction, Afrikaner nationalists demanded further efforts to maintain white control. When Hertzog temporarily joined Smuts in a coalition government in the 1930s, conservative Afrikaners deserted their former leader for the "Purified" Nationalist Party under Dr. D. F. Malan. A former Dutch Reformed Church minister, Malan preached the mystical uniqueness and superiority of the Afrikaner people, their continued covenant with God, and the necessity of absolute separatism of white from nonwhite. Malan reiterated the familiar stories of British imperialism and Boer heorism. When the South African government again led the nation into an "English war" in 1939, Malan rallied his followers to the causes of Afrikaner nationalism and racial segregation. By the end of World War II, South Africa was prepared for the plunge into apartheid.

Seizing on the postwar economic problems of inflation, unemployment, and shortages, Malan and the Nationalist Party fused economics with race. Promising economic recovery and racial purity, they won control of the government in 1948. The Nationalist victory was a turning point in South African history. Once in power, Malan and his successors, J. G. Strydom and H. F. Verwoerd, formalized their theories of white supremacy through the apartheid legislation of the 1950s. Social and economic segregation were intensified, black ownership of property in white areas forbidden, the colored population of Cape Province denied the franchise, and critics, both white and black, were silenced under the draconian Suppression of Communism Act. When criticized by Great Britain and its former colonies, South Africa withdrew from the British Commonwealth in 1961.

Until 30 years ago the United States observed the changes in South Africa passively. It was the Nationalist victory in 1948, combined with the emergence of civil rights as an issue within the United States, that rekindled American interest in the area. While Malan triumphed in 1948 on a program of strict segregation, Harry Truman was re-elected in the United States with a civil rights platform that had provoked a Southern walkout at the Democratic convention. As South Africa moved towards apartheid, America has gradually accepted legal equality. Domestic pressure from blacks and white liberals, and international demands from newly independent nations, forced the United States to respond to apartheid. Only recently, however, has America been forced to develop a policy towards South Africa.

The momentous changes in Southern Africa in the past decade, culminating in the Unilateral Declaration of Independence of Rhodesia, the end of colonial rule in the Portuguese colonies, and the mounting international pressure for majority rule in South Africa, have forced America to again search for a South African strategy. Unlike the period 1870-1914, however, the United States has no "British option" to cling to: It now faces the more difficult choice of support of the black majority or continued efforts to preserve or prolong white minority rule.

The Cold War locked the United States into a simplistic and deterministic view of Southern Africa: white rule was necessary to assure stability and anticommunist governments. Rule by the black majority would lead to violence, chaos, and eventually to weak governments that would be easy prey for Moscow. The Congo crisis of the early 1960s seemed to Americans ample evidence of the disastrous results of premature black rule.

Internal and international events in the recent past have now made such a view obsolete. The American civil rights and black power movements increased domestic pressure for a more active interest in Africa and specifically for a commitment to majority rule. The emergence of an independent Africa raised the international importance of American actions towards South Africa. Responding to the pressures of black Americans and black Africa, American policymakers have verbally condemned apartheid and minority rule. It is clear, however, that rhetoric alone no longer satisfies many Americans and most of the world.

To many in the United States the solution to the problem of Southern Africa is inevitable—majority rule. Thus American policy should be anything that will hasten this end. Such critics of American policy argue that the United States should withdraw all political and economic support of South Africa and Rhodesia, uphold the sanctions voted by the United Nations, and, failing a diplomatic solution, even consider assisting a violent end to white rule.

Most Americans and their leaders have been reluctant to accept such an option. This is due to fears of a "bloodbath" in Southern Africa as well as America's traditional commitment to gradual and peaceful change. Much of current American policy is also based on modifications of the same assumptions that controlled its actions in the period 1870-1914. Contemporary versions of the notion of "progress"for Southern Africa are variants of the older ideas of economic penetration, humanitarianism, and racial uplift.

American firms active in Southern Africa face a dilemma: although many condemn apartheid, they have profitably adapted to it. While American businessmen in the period prior to World War I assumed that the supremacy of England was necessary for a stable government and a favorable business climate, contemporary American corporations fear a change in the government might produce instability and hostility to American trade and investment. Seventy-five years ago Americans urged change as necessary for economic progress. They now fear change for the same reason. The "open door" for American business is now threatened not by the Boers or by the British, but by the black African, who may well turn elsewhere for investment or even nationalize American firms. While American companies are increasingly sensitive to criticism of their dealings with minority governments, many argue that it is an economic necessity to avoid any rapid alteration of the South African situation.

The humanitarian element evident in America's pro-British strategy also continues, albeit with an ironic twist. While the United States supported British domination of South Africa out of a paternalistic but sincere belief in the need to "improve" the African, America now fears change will lead to the exploitation not of the black but of the white African. Many Americans assume that a rapid transition to black rule would result in the economic ruin or even the death of the descendants of the English and Boers. While most Americans accept the principle of majority rule, they fear its possible consequences. The pro-Boer lobby within the United States warned that British control would threaten Afrikaner society. Most Americans, however, were willing to accept this as a necessary step in South African development. The contemporary risk, the destruction of the white minority, is not as easily accepted.

While some critics of America's tacit support of white governments in Southern Africa label such a policy "white racism," this is too simplistic and ignores the considerable changes in American racial attitudes in the past decades. Few would deny that American racism has alienated many third-world nations. But the present influence of racial ideas on American policy is covert and subtle rather than overt and obvious. Racial attitudes do remain a perceptible and real element in American policy. The American public's image of the black African parallels the dualism prevalent in the antebellum Southerner's view of the black slave: the African is seen as either "Nat" the savage or "Sambo" the simplistic fool. Ignorance of Africa still prevails in the United States. Most Americans have a stereotyped view of the African drawn from popular fiction, movies, and television. Events such as the rape of white Belgian nuns during the Congo crisis, the murder of white missionaries in Rhodesia, and the plight of the starving babies of Biafra have reinforced the image of the African as savage. Similarly, the "Sambo" image of the African as a lazy, primitive, buffoon also endures. It is hard to consider black leadership seriously when one's image of the African comes primarily from Tarzan and safari movies and Hemingway short stories. Americans perceive the black African as a combination of simplistic "native bearer" and Mau-Mau terrorist. The present American conception of black African leadership is epitomized in Idi Amin of Uganda. Amin is the perfect combination of "Nat" and "Sambo." The uneducated comic opera general is also a dangerous, brutal murderer.

While racism is not now the dominant element it once was in American policy, many white Americans unconsciously still find it hard to accept the notion of blacks as rulers and whites as ruled. Their image of Africa and their experiences within the United States make such a turnabout difficult to imagine. Over a century of identification of white with progress, stability, and Christianity in the "dark continent" has ingrained attitudes that die slowly. Americans strongly endorse the concept of majority rule, but the practical results of this idea in Southern Africa (black control of a sizable white population) demands the abandonment of deeply entrenched attitudes.

In any case, it is likely that the United States will find that its perception of "progress" in Southern Africa is as unrealistic today as it was in 1900. Events in South Africa, Rhodesia, and Namibia make it unlikely that American policy will substantially alter what happens. Just as Americans found, to their disappointment, that their plan for "progress" did not conform with Britain's, so too it is probable that America's hope for a gradual transition to majority rule with stability and a lack of violence will be just as illusory.

# Notes

*Chapter One*
## Strains on Isolation

1. David Pletcher, *The Awkward Years: American Foreign Relations Under Garfield and Arthur* (Columbia, Missouri: University of Missouri Press, 1962), p. 219. On general American interest in Africa in this period see Harold E. Hammond, "American Interest in the Exploration of the Dark Continent," *The Historian,* 18 (Spring 1956), 202-29; Ray Olton, "Problems of American Foreign Relations in the African Area During the Nineteenth Century," unpublished Ph.D. dissertation, Fletcher School of Law and Diplomacy, 1954; Clarence Clendenen, Robert Collins, and Peter Duigan, *Americans in Black Africa, 1865-1900* (Stanford: Hoover Institute on War, Revolution, and Peace, 1966) and Milton Plesur, *America's Outward Thrust: Approaches to Foreign Affairs, 1865-1900* (Dekalb, Illinois: Northern Illinois University Press, 1971), pp. 144-56.

2. Alan R. Booth, "Americans in South Africa, 1784-1870," unpublished Ph.D. dissertation, Boston University, 1964, pp. 142-47; U.S. Bureau of Commerce, *Commercial Relations Between the United States and Foreign Nations, 1870* (Washington: Government Printing Office, 1871), p. 71 (hereafter cited as *Commercial Relations*).

3. For American missionary activities and protests see William Taylor, *Christian Adventurers in South Africa* (New York: Phillips and Hunt, 1881), pp. 76, 91, and Mary Gray, *Stories of the Early American Missionaries in South Africa* (Boston: Pvt. printing, 1935), pp. 51-69. Andrew Foote, *Africa and the American Flag* (New York: Appleton, 1854). For a summary of the dispute over the Confederate raiders see the report of the American consul at Capetown Willard Edgecomb to H. C. Bancroft Davis, Capetown, 4 November 1871 (No. 6), U. S. Department of State, *Despatches from U. S. Consuls in Cape Town, 1800-1906* (Washington: National Archives Microcopy T-191, Vol. 10, Roll 10) (hereafter cited as *C. D.: Capetown*).

4. Frederick Höhne to His Excellency the President of the United States of America, Pretoria, 6 November 1869, *Notes, South African Republic and Orange Free State,* Department of State Archives, National Archives; Fish to Höhne, Washington, October 1870, *ibid.;* Fish to President of the Orange Free State, Washington 19 November 1870, *ibid.*

5. Edgecomb to Davis, Capetown, 18 January 1872 (No. 11), *C. D. Capetown;* Fish to Edgecomb, Washington, 1 August 1871 (no No.), *Records of Consulates: Miscellaneous Letters Received and Sent, Capetown,* Department of State Record Group 84, Department of State MSS., National Archives

(hereafter cited as *Records of Consulates: Capetown*). The treaty was signed by Edgecomb and the President of the Orange Free State, John Brand, on 22 December 1871 and ratified by the U.S. Senate on 24 April 1872.

6. Charles Riley (Consul-General of the Orange Free State) to Fish, New York, 11 March 1872, U.S. Department of State, *Notes from Foreign Consuls in the United States* (Washington: National Archives Microcopy M 664, Vol. 13, Roll 7).

7. Edgecomb to Fish, Capetown, 29 April 1872 (No. 17), *C. D.: Capetown;* "The Diamond Fields of South Africa," *African Repository,* 48 (March 1872), 88-89.

8. "Report on Commerce and Navigation," Edgecomb to Commodore Robert W. Shufeldt, 28 July 1879, Robert W. Shufeldt MSS., Manuscripts Division, Library of Congress, Container 22.

9. John Hay to Edgecomb, Washington, 20 December 1879 (No. 97), *Records of Consulates: Capetown.*

10. M. Russell, "The Republics of South Africa," paper read before the American Geographical Society, 22 December 1876, *Annual Report of the American Geographical Society, 1876* (New York: American Geographical Society, 1877), pp. 235-50. The Boers also sent delegations to major American cities to try to interest businessmen in South Africa. See Riley to Fish, New York, 10 April 1873), *Notes from Foreign Consuls.*

11. Edgecomb to Hay, Capetown, 10 October 1880 (No. 179), *C. D.: Capetown.*

12. See, for example, F. R. Stratham, *Blacks, Boers, and British: A Three-Cornered Problem* (New York: Macmillan, 1881) and "The Future of South Africa," *New York Times,* 19 September 1879, p. 4.

13. Alexander Crummell, "The Obligation of American Black Men for the Redemption of Africa," *African Repository,* 48 (February 1872), 55-61; G. C. Cato, U. S. Consular Agent at Port Natal, to Edgecomb, 5 January 1870, *Records of Consulates: Capetown.*

14. William Strong, *The Story of the American Board: An Account of the First Hundred Years of the American Board of Commissioners for Foreign Missions* (Boston: The Pilgrim Press, 1910), pp. 281-89.

15. "The Possible Future of Africa," *New York Times* 10 August 1879, p. 6.

16. Edgecomb to Charles Hale, Capetown, 1 August 1872 (No. 25); 2 September 1872 (No. 31); Edgecomb to John L. Cadwalder, Capetown, 3 November 1874 (No. 72), *C. D.: Capetown;* Riley to Fish, New York, 1 September 1874, *Notes from Foreign Consuls.*

17. S. M. Pretorius and C. W. Bodenstein to "Minister for Foreign Affairs of America," 15 September 1878, *Notes, South African Republic and Orange Free State;* Kruger to the Department of State, 11 April 1877, *Notes from Foreign Consuls.*

18. J. E. Bok to "Minister of Foreign Affairs of America," 29 January 1882, *Notes, South African Republic and Orange Free State.*

19. *New York Times,* 10 June 1877, p. 4; 4 October 1879, p. 4; 17 January 1881, p. 1.

20. "The English in South Africa," *ibid.,* 23 February 1879, p. 4.

21. Shufeldt toured both Africa and Asia from October 1878 to November 1880. Many of his reports are in "Letters from Commodore R. W. Shufeldt,"

*Ticonderoga:* Africa and Asia, 1878-1880 in the Department of Navy records, National Archives. The bulk of his material on South Africa, however, is in the R. W. Shufeldt MSS., Manuscripts Division, Library of Congress.

22. "World Cruise: Capetown," Shufeldt MSS., Container 22.

23. *Ibid.,* Container 27. The material in the following section comes from this report and a shorter manuscript entitled "South Africa" in the same container.

24. The low salary of the American consul at Capetown was a constant source of complaint. The total budget of the post, including rent and clerical help, was less than $4,000, while European representatives received salaries of over $6,000, plus stipends for rent and numerous aides. Capetown had one of the highest costs of living in the world. See John Siler to the Department of State, Capetown, 29 December 1886 (No. 290), *C. D.: Capetown.*

25. Siler to Davis, Capetown, 10 August 1882 (No. 51), *C. D.: Capetown.* See also Siler's report in *Commercial Relations, 1883,* II, 113.

26. *Ibid.,* 23 August 1882 (No. 57); "The Continent of the Future," *African Repository,* 58 (April 1882), 1-16.

27. "Extension of our Commerce," reprinted in *African Repository,* 58 (April 1882), pp. 57-59.

28. Alfred Aylward, "Dutch South Africa: Its Hydrography, Mineral Wealth, and Mercantile Possibilities," paper read before the American Geographical Society, *Journal of the American Geographical Society,* 15 (1883), 1-44.

29. U. S. Congress, 49th Congress, 3rd Session, Ex. Doc. 98, *Report of Secretary of State Frederick Frelinghuysen on United States Trade with Africa, October 1, 1888,* p. 98.

30. *New York Tribune,* 14 January 1880, p. 4. Britain was very concerned with possible Irish-American support of the Boers. See Edward Thornton, British Minister to the U. S., to Foreign Minister Lord Grenville, Washington, 11 January 1881 (pvt.) in Paul Knapland and E. E. Clewew (eds.), *Private Letters from the British Embassay in Washington to Lord Grenville, 1880-1885* (Washington: U. S. Government Printing Office, 1942), pp. 111-12

31. M. Berliner to Frelinghuysen, 26 January 1882, enclosed in Davis to Siler, Washington, 31 January 1882 (No. 6), *Records of Consulates: Capetown.*

32. See, for example, George Baden-Powell, "New Markets for British Produce," *Nineteenth Century,* 10 (July 1881), 43-55. On British fears of Germany see Great Britain, *Parliamentary Debates,* 3rd Series, 294 (27 February 1885), 1603-04, and Siler to Davis, Capetown, 20 October 1883 (No. 132), *C. D.: Capetown.*

33. Siler to Davis, Capetown, 5 July 1882 (No. 15), *C. D.: Capetown.*

34. *Ibid.,* 10 November 1884 (No. 190). See also *New York Times,* 9 March 1881, p. 4.

35. *Ibid.,* 1 November 1882 (No. 71) and 16 July 1884 (No. 170).

36. William S. Dayton to Frelinghuysen, The Hague, 19 August 1884 (No. 190), U. S. Department of State, *Diplomatic Despatches from U. S. Ministers to the Netherlands* (Washington: National Archives Microcopy M 42, Vol. 24, Roll 28) (hereafter cited as *Diplomatic Despatches: Netherlands*); Van Blokland to Dayton, The Hague, 9 August 1884, and Kruger to Dayton, 13 June 1884, enclosed in *ibid.*

37. Frelinghuysen to Dayton, Washington, 15 September 1884 (No. 49), U.S. Department of State, *Diplomatic Instructions from the Department of State to U. S. Ministers to the Netherlands* (Washington: National Archives Microcopy M 77, Vol. 15, Roll 124) (hereafter cited as *Diplomatic Instructions: Netherlands*); A. A. Adee, "Memorandum Prepared for Mr. Adler re Proposition by South African Republic for a Treaty of Commerce with the United States," 2 November 1884, *Notes, South African Republic and Orange Free State;* Frelinghuysen to Dayton, Washington, 12 February 1885 (No. 73), *Diplomatic Instructions: Netherlands.*

38. Siler to Davis, Capetown, 21 January 1885 (No. 204), *C. D.: Capetown.* For an account of Rhodes's expedition and American participation, see the letters of Jack Carruthers to Howell Wright, 22 November-24 December 1936, Howell Wright Collection, Manuscripts Division, Sterling Library, Yale University, Box 6.

39. See *African Repository,* 63 (January 1887), 31; David Ker, "Africa's Awakening," *Harper's New Monthly,* 72 (March 1886), 546-58 and Clifford Knight to Department of State, Capetown, 13 October 1886 (No. 282), *C. D.: Capetown.*

40. Knight to Porter, Capetown, 3 August 1886 (No. 246), *C. D.: Capetown.*

## Chapter Two
## God, Gold, and Good Government

1. For further discussion of the nature of Boer society and its opposition to modernization see the following excellent studies: C. T. Gordon, *The Growth of Opposition to Kruger, 1890-1895* (Capetown: Oxford University Press, 1970), Chapter I, "The Nature of Transvaal Conservatism"; W. A. De Klerk, *The Puritans in Africa: A Study of Afrikanerdom* (London: Rex Collings, 1975); and John Fisher, *The Afrikaners* (London: Cassell, 1969).

2. G. W. Eybers (ed.), *Select Constitutional Documents Illustrating South African History, 1795-1910* (London: Oxford University Press, 1918), p. 437. see also Gordon, *Opposition to Kruger,* pp. 46-57.

3. *Commercial Relations, 1888-1896.*

4. George Siler to George F. Rives, Capetown, 5 March 1888 (No. 343), *C. D.: Capetown.*

5. Hollis to Rives, Capetown, 27 August 1888 (No. 1); Hollis to William Wharton, Capetown, 25 December 1888 (no No.), *ibid.*

6. Hollis to Rives, Capetown, 17 November 1888 (No. 9); 17 December 1888 (No. 13) 9 January 1889 (No. 14); Hollis to Wharton, Capetown, 1 January 1890 (No. 63): 5 July 1890 (no No.), *ibid.*

7. Wharton to Hollis, Washington, 13 February 1889 (No. 8), *Records of Consulates: Capetown;* Williams to Wharton, Kimberley, 28 March 1890 (no No.), *Records of Consulates: Kimberley;* Williams to the Department of State, Kimberley, 5 May 1890 (no No.), *ibid.*

8. Wharton to Hollis, Washington, 17 July 1891 (No. 78); 19 September 1891 (No. 82), *Records of Consulates: Capetown.* Hollis remained in South Africa and later was appointed to head the American consulate in Lourenço Marques during the Boer War.

9. J. Scott Keltie, "British Interests in Africa," *The Contemporary Review,* 54 (July 1888), 115-25: John Gallagher and Ronald Robinson, "The Imper-

ialism of Free Trade," *Economic History Review,* 6 (1953), 1-15. British exports increased from £ 5,109,000 in 1885 to over £12,000,000 in 1890. Great Britain, *Parliamentary Papers: 1884-5, #82, 35; 1890-91,* #90, 93.

10. Great Britain, *Parliamentary Papers,* Cd. 5918, 1890 "Further Correspondence Concerning Bechuanaland," p. 139.

11. For an account of the expedition see Rhodes to W. T. Stead, 19 August 1891, Howell Wright Collection, Box 26. See also L. H. Gann, *The Birth of a Plural Society: The Development of Northern Rhodesia under the British South Africa Company 1894-1914* (Manchester: Manchester University Press, 1958).

12. *The Commercial and Financial Chronicle,* 51 (25 October 1890), 555-56 and 55 (22 January 1892), 140-44; *New York Times,* 26 November 1893, p. 4, and 6 December 1893, p. 4; Frank Mandy, "Golden Mashonaland," *Scribner's Magazine,* 11 (April 1892), 455-70.

13. See the letter of Edgar Mels to the *New York Times,* 22 May 1890, p. 9, and Henry S. Sanford, "American Interests in Africa," *Forum* 9 (June 1890), 408-29.

14. See the discussion of Rhodes by Herbert Baker, Rhodes's architect, in Baker's letter to Howell Wright, 24 May 1942, Howell Wright Collection, Box 1 and Rhodes to W. T. Stead, 19 August 1891, *ibid.,* Box 26. Gardiner Williams to Hollis, Kimberley, 29 May 1890, *Records of Consulates: Capetown.*

15. See Rhodes's "Confession of Faith," undated, photocopy in Howell Wright Collection, Box 26. See also Ronald Robinson and John Gallagher, *Africa and the Victorians: The Official Mind of Imperialism* (London: Macmillan, 1961), pp. 250-53 and W. T. Stead, *The Americanization of the World* (London: T. Fisher Unwin, 1902), pp. 53-56.

16. J. Njuguna Karanja, "United States' Attitudes and Policy towards the International African Association, 1876-1886," unpublished Ph.D. dissertation, Princeton University, 1962, chapter V, and Leslie E. Meyer, "Henry S. Sanford and the Congo: A Reassessment," *African Historical Studies,* 4 (1971), 19-39.

17. "Germany in Africa," *New York Times,* 28 May 1890, p. 4; *Review of Reviews,* 5 (February 1892), 80-81 and (April 1892), 334-35; E.A. Smith to the Assistant Secretary of State, Lourenço Marques, 20 February 1889 (No. 14), *C. D.: Mozambique.*

18. Jean Van Der Poel, *Railway and Custom's Policies in South Africa, 1885-19100* (London: Longmans, Green and Co., 1933), pp. 111-20.

19. F. W. Rutland, "The Railway from Beria," radio broadcast, Salisbury, Rhodesia, 10 September 1942, copy in Howell Wright Collection, Box 27, 3.

20. McMurdo to Thomas Waller, July 1888. Enclosed in G. L. Rives to Hollis, Capetown, 22 August 1888 (no. 11), *Records of Consulates: Capetown.*

21. Smith to Department of State, Lourenço Marques, 17 June 1889 (No. 38); 24 July 1889 (No. 47), *C. D.: Mozambique;* Henry White to Mrs. E. E. McMurdo, London, 9 May 1889, Henry White MSS., Manuscripts Division, Library of Congress, Box 3.

22. E. G. Woodford to Hollis, Pretoria, 30 June 1889, enclosed in Hollis to Wharton, Capetown, 6 August 1889 (No. 47), *C. D.: Capetown; New York Times,* 29 June 1889, p. 1.

23. James D. Richardson (ed.), *Messages and Papers of the Presidents, 1789-1898* (10 Vols.: Washington: Government Printing Office, 1900), IX, 35;

James Blaine to George B. Loring, *(Confidential)*, Washington, 11 March 1890 (No. 53), *Diplomatic Instructions: Portugal;* Robert Lincoln to Blaine, *(Confidential)*, London, 17 September 1890 (No. 313), *Diplomatic Despatches: Great Britain.*

24. Lincoln to Blaine, London, 13 October 1890 (No. 369), *Diplomatic Despatches: Great Britain;* Blaine to Lincoln, Washington, 9 February 1891, *Diplomatic Instructions: Great Britain.*

25. *Times* (London), 30 March 1900, p. 5.

26. Hollis to Wharton, Capetown, 24 December 1890 (No. 124), *C. D.: Capetown.*

27. Charles Benedict to Edwin F. Uhl, Capetown, 20 October 1894 (No. 65) *ibid.;* W. W. Rockhill to Benedict, Washington, 3 November 1894 and enclosed memo by Adee, *Records of Consulates: Capetown.*

28. The best account of the migration of American engineers to South Africa is Clark C. Spence, *Mining Engineers and the American West: The Lace-Boot Brigade* (New Haven: Yale University Press, 1970), pp. 303-17. See also Eric Rosenthal, *Stars and Stripes in Africa* (London: George Routledge and Sons, 1938), pp. 168-75.

29. Spence, *Mining Engineers,* pp. 304-05; John Hays Hammond, The *Autobiography of John Hays Hammond* (2 Vols.: New York: Farrar and Rinehart, 1935), I, 200-12.

30. Hammond, *Autobiography,* I, 213-14; Spence, *Mining Engineers,* p. 307.

31. Hammond to W. T. St. Auburn, 27 July, 1894, John Hays Hammond MSS., Manuscripts Division, Sterling Library, Yale University, Box 6, Letterbook 1.

32. Hammond to William Hall, 1 August 1894, *ibid.*

33. Hammond to Richard Parker, 29 May 1894; Hammond to W. J. Chalmers (Personal), 2 April 1894; Hammond to H. C. Davis, 11 January 1895; Hammond to Chalmers, 4 February 1895, *ibid.*

34. Gardiner Williams to C. M. Knight, Kimberley, 30 August 1894, *Records of Consulates: Capetown; Commercial Relations, 1895-1896,* I, 99.

35. Williams to Department of State, Kimberley, 6 July 1895, *Records of Consulates: Kimberley;* Hammond to C. J. Clark, 28 April 1895, Hammond MSS., Box 6, Letterbook 2.

36. Hammond to Williams, 28 February 1894; Hammond to E. F. Rhodes, 26 February 1894 *ibid.;* Williams to Department of State, Kimberley, 12 May 1895 and 6 July 1895, *Records of Consulates: Kimberley.*

37. See the letters in the William Taylor File, Box 30, Howell Wright Collection. See also Taylor to Benedict, 11 June 1894; Aultman and Taylor Machinery Company to Benedict, 9 July 1894; Columbus Iron Works to Benedict, 9 October 1894, *Records of Consulates: Capetown.*

38. Hammond, *Autobiography,* I, 222; Hammond to N. H. Harris, 8 October 1895, Hammond MSS., Box 6, Letterbook 2.

39. J. C. Lockhart and C. M. Woodhouse, *Rhodes* (London: Hodder and Stroughton, 1963), pp. 283-84, 446-47; Stead, *Americanization,* pp. 53-56.

40. Hammond to Butters, 17 December 1894 and 3 May 1895; Hammond to Barney Barnato, 5 June 1895, Hammond MSS., Box 6, Letterbook 2.

41. C. J. Clark (Hammond's Private Secretary) to Hammond, 16 April 1894, Hammond MSS., Box 1; Hammond to Clark, 19 April 1894, Box 6, Letterbook 1.

42. Hammond to I. De Dawa Rapose, 20 November 1894, *ibid.*, Box 6, Letterbook 3.

43. Copies of the reports and correspondence concerning them are in Hammond MSS., Box 1. See especially C. J. Clark to Hammond, Buluwayo, 17 April 1895 and Hammond to Robert Williams, 24 January 1894.

44. Hammond to Charles W. Truslow, 2 December 1895, *ibid.*, Box 6, Letterbook 2.

45. Quoted in J. H. Browne, *South Africa: A Glance at Current Conditions and Politics* (Boston: Longmans, Green and Co., 1905), pp. 14-15; *Times* (London), *Letters from South Africa* (London: Macmillan, 1893), pp. 22-23: Clark to Hammond, 27 May 1894, Hammond MSS., Box 1.

46. *New York Times,* 10 October 1894, p. 4.

47. "African Slavery and Civilization," *Commercial and Financial Chronicle* 50 (5 April 1890), pp. 467-68. See also "The Dark Continent," *Century,* 16 (June 1889), pp. 313-14.

48. John Hays Hammond and Jeremiah Jenks, *Great American Issues: Political, Social, and Economic* (New York: Charles Scribner's Sons, 1921), p. 207.

49. E. A. Smith to Eugene Schuyler, Lourenço Marques, 6 May 1889 (No. 29), *C. D.: Mozambique;* Hollis to Wharton, Capetown, 5 February 1890 (No. 74), *C. D.: Capetown.*

50. S. M. Molema, *The Bantu* (Edinburgh: W. Green and Sons, 1920), pp. 241, 368.

51. Lewis Grout, "The Mustard Seed of Missions in South Africa," *Missionary Review of the World,* 2 (June 1889), 488-90; James Scott, "Mission World Among the Zulus," *ibid.* (January 1889), 52-53.

52. Lewis Grout, "The Boers and Missions," *ibid.,* 3 (March 1890), 166-67; Cull Wilcox, *Proud Endeavor: The Story of a Yankee on a Mission to South Africa,* Mark Wilcox (ed.), (New York: Graphic Press, 1962), *passim.*

53. American Bible Society, *77th Annual Report* (New York: American Bible Society, 1893), pp. 150-51.

54. F. F. Ellinwood, "The New Era of Colonization and Its Bearing on Christian Philanthropy," *Missionary Review of the World,* 2 (October 1889), 738-41.

55. Charles P. Groves, *The Planting of Christianity in Africa* (4 Vols.: London: Luttersworth Press, 1948-1958), III, 98-100; *Missionary Herald,* 90 (1896), 392; 93 (1897), 198.

56. Josiah Tyler, "Signs of the Times in South Africa," *Missionary Review of the World,* 6 (January 1893), 48-49.

57. Arthur White, *The Development of Africa* (London: George Phillip and Son, 1891) and "Africa and the European Powers," *Harpers New Monthly,* 82 (November 1891), 924-31.

58. Frederic P. Noble, "The Outlook for African Missions in the Twentieth Century," Address Given at the Congress on Africa, Atlanta, 14 December 1895, *Africa and the American Negro: Addresses and Proceedings of the Congress on Africa, December 13-15, 1895* (Atlanta: Gammon Theological Seminary, 1896), pp. 62-65.

59. O. B. Super, "The Mission of the Anglo-Saxon," *Methodist Review,* 72 (November 1890), 853-67.

60. Thomas Fortune, "The Nationalization of Africa," *Africa and the American Negro,* pp. 199-204.

61. Orishetukeh Faduma, "Success and Drawbacks of Missionary Work in Africa by an Eye-Witness," *ibid.,* pp. 125-36.

62. See the letters from members of the American Board of Commissioners for Foreign Missions in Strong, *Story of the American Board,* p. 428.

63. *Ibid.;* C. J. Clark to Hammond, 12 November 1894, Hammond MSS., Box 1.

64. Hammond, *Autobiography,* I, 288, 305.

65. Benedict to Uhl, Capetown, 23 April 1894 (No. 48), *C. D.: Capetown;* Williams to Benedict, Johannesburg, 14 April 1894, enclosed in *ibid.*

66. W. W. Van Ness to W. J. Leyds, no date, *Records of Consulates: Capetown.*

67. Uhl to Benedict, Washington, 29 May 1894 (No. 26), *Records of Consulates: Capetown;* Benedict to Uhl, Capetown, 2 October 1894 (No. 66), *C. D.: Capetown.*

68. William H. Browne, *On the South African Frontier: The Adventures and Observations of an American in Mashonaland and Matabeleland* (New York: Scribner's, 1899) pp. 31-32.

69. R. L. Beal, "Our Duty to Africa," *Voice of Missions* (October 1896), 13; E. W. Gilliam, "The African Problem," *North American Review,* 336 (November 1884), 417-30; George Shepperson, "Notes on Negro American Influences on the Emergence of African Nationalism," *Journal of African History,* 1 (1960), 299-312.

70. H. K. Carroll, "The Negro in the Twentieth Century," *Africa and the American Negro,* pp. 161-62.

71. M. French-Sheldon, "Practical Issues of an African Experience," *ibid.,* pp. 95-101.

72. Hollis Lynch (ed.), *Black Spokesman: Selected Published Writings of Edward Wilmot Blyden* (New York: Humanities Press, 1971), pp. xxvi-xxx.

73. H. M. Turner, "The American Negro and the Fatherland," *Africa and the American Negro,* pp. 195-98; George Shepperson, "Ethiopianism and African Nationalism," *Phylon,* 14 (1953), 9-18; Edwin S. Redkey, "Bishop Turner's African Dream," *Journal of American History,* 54 (September 1967), 283-301.

74. Louis R. Harlan, "Booker T. Washington and the White Man's Burden," *American Historical Review,* 71 (January 1966), 441-67.

## *Chapter Three*
## Reform and Revolution

1. Quoted in Fisher, *The Afrikaners,* pp. 138-40.

2. Benedict to Adee, Capetown, 29 May 1894 (No. 56), *C.D.: Capetown.*

3. *Ibid.;* Adee to Bayard, Washington, 3 July 1894 (No. 437) *Diplomatic Instructions: Great Britain.* Much of the correspondence concerning the impressment issue is printed in United States Department of State, *Foreign Relations of the United States, 1894* (2 Vols.: Washington: U. S. Government Printing Office, 1895), I, 252-54 (hereafter cited as *Foreign Relations*). See also Bayard to Walter Gresham, London, 19 July 1894 (No. 250), *Diplomatic Despatches: Great Britain.*

4. Hammond, *Autobiography,* I, 342.

5. A wealth of material on Americans and the Johannesburg Reform Committee is in the Howell Wright Collection, Boxes 16-19. See especially Box

17, "Records of the Johannesburg Reform Committee" and letters from Hammond to Alf Brown, Alf Brown folder, Box 17. See also John Hays Hammond, *The Truth About the Jameson Raid* (Boston: Marshall Jones, 1918), *passim*.

6. Hammond, *Jameson Raid*, p. 5. Of the 66 elected members of the Reform Committee, eight were Americans, 34 Englishmen, 17 South Africans (most from the Cape Colony), two Dutch, one Swiss, one Turkish, and three of unknown nationality. Hammond dominated the leadership and drafted most of the protests. See Howell Wright Collection, Box 17.

7. Hammond to C. J. Clark, 12 July 1895, Hammond MSS., Box 6, Letter-book 2; Hammond, *Autobiography*, I, 310-12; Hammond, *Jameson Raid*, pp. 10-11.

8. *Commercial Relations, 1895-1896*, I, 98-99.

9. Quoted in Fisher, *The Afrikaners*, pp. 135-36 See also Eric Walker, *A History of South Africa* (London: Longmans, Green and Co., 1935), p. 449.

10. See, for example, Germany's protests of British attempts to persuade Kruger to relax franchise requirements. *Die Grosse Politik der europäischen Kabinette, 1871-1914* (Berlin: Deutsche Verlagsgesellschaft für Politik und Geschichte, 1922-1927), IX, 2103.

11. Thomas Ross to Howell Wright, 12 April 1937 and 9 June 1937, Howell Wright Collection, Box 27. Ross was an American mining engineer working under Hennen Jennings at Kimberley and Johannesburg. See also Hammond, *Autobiography*, I, 321.

12. Great Britain, *Parliamentary Papers*, Cd. 8380, 1897 "The Select Committee of the Cape of Good Hope House of Assembly on the Jameson Raid," 84; Cable, Hammond to Rhodes, 2 October 1895, copy in Hammond MSS., Box 6; Hammond, *Autobiography*, I, 325-26.

13. J. C. Lockhart and C. M. Woodhouse, *Rhodes* (London: Hodder and Stroughton, 1963), pp. 313-14. This point is also made by Sir Gordon Bower, Personal Secretary to Sir Hercules Robinson, High Commissioner of the Cape Colony, in a letter to Sir Montagu Ommanney, 11 May 1906, Howell Wright Collection, Box 2.

14. Rosenthal, *Stars and Stripes*, p. 190.

15. *Ibid.*

16. Hammond to Poultney Bigelow, 26 August 1896, Hammond MSS., Box 7; Hammond, *Autobiography*, I, 341-44; Clifford Knight to Uhl, Capetown, 8 January 1896 (No. 115), *C. D.: Capetown.*

17. Cable, Olney to Manion, 12 January 1896; cable, Olney to Bayard, 12 January 1896, *Foreign Relations, 1896*, p. 562; Olney to Leyds, 13 January 1896, *Notes, South African Republic and Orange Free State;* cable, Olney to Knight, 18 January 1896, *Records of Consulates: Capetown.*

18. Cable, Manion to Olney, 25 January 1896, *C. D.: Capetown;* Knight to Uhl, Capetown, 5 February 1896, *Foreign Relations, 1896*, p. 573.

19. Bayard to Olney, London, 17 January 1896 (No. 575), *Diplomatic Despatches: Great Britain;* cable, Olney to Manion, 25 January 1896, *Foreign Relations, 1896*, p. 569.

20. Cable, Manion to Olney, 29 January 1896, *Foreign Relations, 1896*, p. 570; cable, Knight to Uhl, 18 February 1896, *ibid.*, p. 573.

21. For details of the campaign to gain Hammond's release see Natalie Hammond, *A Woman's Part in a Revolution* (New York: Longmans, Green and Co., 1897), *passim*, and Hammond MSS., Box 2, folders 40-50.

22. Cable, Hammond to John P. Jones, 30 January 1896, copy in Hammond MSS., Box 2.

23. Hammond, *Autobiography,* I, 360-61.

24. A copy of the petition is in Hammond MSS., Box 3; U. S. *Congressional Record,* 54th Congress, 1st Session, Pt. 5, 4528-29.

25. Cable, Olney to State Secretary, South African Republic, 29 April 1896 and Leyds to Olney, 30 April 1896, *Notes, South African Republic and Orange Free State;* cable, Knight to Olney, 28 April 1896, *Foreign Relations, 1896,* p. 579.

26. Cable, R. W. Chapin to President Grover Cleveland, 2 May 1896, *C. D.: Capetown;* Hammond, *Autobiography,* I, 390-91.

27. Cable, Chapin to Olney, 20 May 1896, *Foreign Relations, 1896,* p. 580; cable, Knight to Olney, 11 June 1896, *C. D.: Capetown.*

28. J. A. S. Grenville, *Lord Salisbury and Foreign Policy: The Close of the Nineteenth Century* (London: Athlone Press, 1964), pp. 103-04.

29. *New York Times,* 3 January 1896, p. 4; 4 January 1896, p. 4; *New York Tribune,* 11 January 1896, p. 3.

30. "The Transvaal and Venezuela," *New York Times,* 1 May 1896, p. 4.

31. Richard Whiteing, "British Opinion of America," *Scribner's Magazine,* 19 (March 1896), 371-77; W. T. Stead, "Cecil Rhodes of Africa," *Review of Reviews,* 13 (March 1896), 317-21.

32. Mark Twain (Samuel Clemens), *Following the Equator: A Journey Around the World* (Hartford: American Publishing, 1897) pp. 659-60. See also Coleman O. Parsons, "Mark Twain: Traveler in South Africa," *Mississippi Quarterly,* 29 (Winter 1975-76), 3-41.

33. *Review of Reviews,* 13 (February 1896), 146.

34. "German Designs in South Africa," *ibid.,* 13 (March 1896), 328-30; H. E. Lawson, "German Intrigues in the Transvaal," *Contemporary Review,* 68 (February 1896), 292-304.

35. Theodore Roosevelt to Henry White, New York, 30 March 1896, Elting E. Morison (ed.), *The Letters of Theodore Roosevelt* (7 Vols.: Cambridge: Harvard University Press, 1951-1954), I, 523.

36. The best discussion of the negotiations and manueverings of this period is Grenville, *Lord Salisbury,* chapter 11, "The Failure of Diplomacy in South Africa, 1898-1899," pp. 235-64. Many of the communications between Britain and South Africa are printed in Cecil Headlam (ed.), *The Milner Papers* (4 Vols.: London: Cassell, 1931).

37. Frank Roberts to Department of State, Capetown, 8 September 1897 (No. 52), *C. D.: Capetown;* "Our Trade with Africa," *Scientific American,* 74 (20 June 1896), 391; Charles Macrum to David Hill, Pretoria, 16 April 1899 (No. 25), *C. D.: Pretoria.*

38. Mallory (ed.), *Treaties,* II, 1313-17.

39. James Bryce, "Impressions of South Africa," *The Century,* 30 (July 1896), 442-53.

40. Hammond to Bigelow, 2 April 1896; Bigelow to Hammond, 12 July 1896, Hammond MSS., Box 3; Poultney Bigelow, "White Man's Africa," *Harper's New Monthly Magazine,* 93-95 (November 1896-August 1897). The articles were later published in book form during the Boer War by Harper and Brothers.

41. "White Man's Africa," *Harper's New Monthly Magazine,* 95 (August 1897), 421-32.

42. Roberts to Thomas Cridler, Capetown, 18 August 1897 (No. 48), *C. D.: Capetown;* Cridler to Roberts, Washington, 27 September 1897 (No. 71), *Records of Consulates: Capetown.*

43. See Hammond's correspondence with American mining engineers in South Africa in Hammond MSS., Boxes 3 and 4; E. A. Wiltsee to Hammond, San Francisco, 28 June 1896, *ibid.,* Box 3.

44. Hammond, "South Africa and its Future," *North American Review,* 383 (February 1897), 233-48. See also Hammond to Editors, *Engineering and Mining Journal,* New York, 18 December 1896, Hammond MSS., Box 7.

45. Hammond, *Autobiography,* II, 446-47.

46. Hammond to Wiltsee, 20 April 1897; Hammond to F. W. Bradley, 21 October 1897; Hammond to Chm., Consolidated Gold Fields of South Africa, 23 October 1897, Hammond MSS., Box 7.

47. "Letter to American Manufactures," enclosure in Stowe to Cridler, Capetown, 10 June 1898 (No. 99), *C. D.: Capetown;* Macrum to the Department of State, Pretoria, 13 June 1899, *C. D.: Pretoria;* Harold C. Dayton to Stowe, New York, 2 March 1899; Milliken Brothers to Stowe, New York, 11 August 1899, *Records of Consulates: Capetown.*

48. Groves, III, 208-09.

49. The best study of the Ethiopian movement in South Africa is Josephus Roosevelt Coan, "The Expansion of Missions of the African Methodist Episcopal Church in South Africa, 1896-1908," unpublished Ph.D. dissertation, Hartford Seminary, 1961. See also L. C. Berry, *A Century of Missions of the African Methodist Episcopal Church* (New York: Gutenberg Printing Co., 1942).

50. Coan, "Expansion of Missions," p. 156.

51. John Dubé, "Zululand and the Zulus," *Missionary Review of the World,* 11 (June 1898), 435-43. See also William C. Harr, "The Negro as an American Protestant Missionary to Africa," unpublished Ph.D. dissertation, University of Chicago Divinity School, 1946, pp. 131-41.

52. Quoted in George Shepperson and Thomas Price, *Independent African: John Chilembwe and the Origins, Setting, and Significance of the Nyasaland Native Rising of 1915* (Edinburgh: The University Press, 1958), pp. 111-12. See also Joseph Booth, "Industrial Missions in Africa," *Missionary Review of the World,* 9 (April 1896), 290-94.

53. The Student Missionary Appeal, *Addresses at the Third Inter-National Convention of the Student Volunteer Movement for Foreign Missions* (Chicago: Student Missionary Campaign, 1898), pp. 418-35; "The Development of Africa," *Methodist Review,* 78 (September 1896), 804-05.

54. Hollis to Rockhill, (Confidential), Lourenço Marques, 30 July 1896 (No. 167), *C. D.: Mozambique;* Hollis to David Hill, Lourenço Marques, 24 August 1899 (No. 79), *C. D.: Lourenço Marques.*

55. William Quinby to Olney, The Hague, 26 May 1896 (No. 236); 20 August 1896 (No. 246), *Diplomatic Despatches: Netherlands.*

56. Howard C. Hillegas, *Oom Paul's People: A Narrative of the British-Boer Troubles in South Africa with a History of the Boers, the Country, and its Institutions* (New York: Appleton, 1899), pp. 145-51.

57. "A Diplomat," "A Vindication of the Rights of the Boers: A Rejoinder to Mr. Sydney Brooks," *North American Review,* 514 (September 1899), 362-74. This was in response to an article by Sydney Brooks denouncing Kruger and defending Britain, "England and the Transvaal," *ibid.* (July 1899), 62-76.

58. There are a great number of works dealing with the growth of Anglo-American friendship in the last decade of the nineteenth century. Most, however, devote scant attention to the role of South Africa in this understanding. See Bradford Perkins, *The Great Rapprochement: England and the United States, 1895-1914* (New York: Atheneum, 1968); Charles Campbell, *Anglo-American Understanding, 1890-1903* (Baltimore: Johns Hopkins University Press, 1957); Alexander Campbell, *Great Britain and the United States, 1895-1903* (London: Longmans, Green and Co., 1960) and Richard H. Heindel, *The American Impact on Great Britain, 1890-1914: A Study of the United States in World History* (Philadelphia: University of Pennsylvania Press, 1940).

59. Quoted in Claude Bowers, *Beveridge and the Progressive Era* (Boston: Houghton-Mifflin, 1932), p. 69.

60. Edward Dicey, "The New American Imperialism," *The Nineteenth Century,* 44 (September 1898), 487-501; White to Hay, London, 2 November, 1898, Henry White MSS., Box 4.

61. Joseph Chamberlain, "Recent Developments of Policy in the United States and their Relations to an Anglo-American Alliance," *Scribner's Magazine,* 24 (December 1898), 674-82.

62. Details of the case are contained in a memorial of Brown to the United States Congress, *Congressional Record,* 56th Congress, 1st Session, Pt. 5, 4347. See also Paul Kruger, *Memoirs of Paul Kruger,* (New York: Century, 1902), pp. 254-57.

63. Macrum to F. W. Reitz, State Secretary, South African Republic, 19 October 1898, enclosed in Macrum to Department of State, Pretoria, 25 October 1898 (No. 8), *C. D.: Pretoria.*

64. Hillegas, *Oom Paul's People,* pp. 262-63.

65. " British Merchants Alarmed by American Inroads," *New York Times,* 22 March 1899, p. 3; "Competing with England," *ibid.,* 7 May 1899, p. 7.

66. Grenville, *Salisbury and Foreign Policy,* pp. 240-41.

67. "The British and the Boers," *New York Times,* 18 May 1899, p. 6.

68. *Memorandum: Bloemfontein Conference,* 5 June 1899, *Records of Consulates: Capetown.* Although unsigned, it would seem, from its pro-British slant, to have been prepared by Macrum and forwarded to Stowe. It has Stowe's initials in pencil.

69. Macrum to Hill, Pretoria, 19 July 1899 (No. 47), *C. D.: Pretoria.*

70. Howison to Macrum, Delagoa Bay, 6 July 1899; 8 July 1899, *Records of Consulates: Pretoria;* Howison to Secretary of the Navy, 17 July 1899, enclosed in Senator W. W. Allen (Democrat-Nevada) to Hay, 15 August 1899, Department of State, *Miscellaneous Letters Received and Sent, 1899,* Department of State MSS., National Archives.

71. See the petition of American businessmen in Johannesburg to the Department of State, no date, enclosed in Macrum to Hill, Pretoria, 21 August 1899 (No. 55), *C. D.: Pretoria; Overland Monthly,* 34 (July 1899), 92; "Transvaal Settlement Problems," *Commercial and Financial Chronicle,* 69 (22 July 1899), 152-53.

72. Stowe to Cridler (Confidential), Capetown, 20 June 1899 (no No.), *C. D.: Capetown.*

73. *Ibid.,* 25 July 1899.

74. *Ibid.,* 20 June 1899.

75. Walter LaFeber, *The New Empire: An Interpretation of American Expansion, 1869-1898* (Ithaca: Cornell University Press, 1963), p. 384.

76. Hollis to Hill, *Lourenço Marques,* 5 October 1899 (No. 95), *C. D.: Lourenço Marques.*

77. Hay to White, 24 September 1899 in William Thayer, *The Life and Letters of John Hay* (2 Vols.: Boston: Houghton-Mifflin, 1915), II, 221.

78. Cable, Stowe to Hay, Capetown, 3 October 1899, *C. D.: Capetown;* cable, Hay to Stowe, Washington, 6 October 1899, *Records of Consulates: Capetown.* Hay also rejected a similar offer from the Transvaal's representative in the United States. See James O'Beirne to Hill, 6 October 1899 and Hill to O'Beirne, 7 October 1899, *Notes from Foreign Consuls in the United States.*

79. Tower to Hay, (Confidential), 8 October 1899, *Foreign Relations, 1899,* p. 350; Hill to Tower, (Confidential), 11 October 1899; Tower to Hay, 13 October 1899; Adee to Tower, 13 October 1899, *ibid;* Cable, Macrum to Hill, 13 October 1899, *C. D.: Pretoria.*

80. *New York Times,* 13 October 1899, p. 6.

81. *Parliamentary Debates,* 77 (19 October 1899), 263-67.

83. *New York Times,* 18 September 1899, p. 6. The letter was from E. L. Finningley, an American businessman who had spent 18 years in the Transvaal.

83. *Ibid.,* 16 October 1899, p. 6. See also the rebuttal by Howard Hillegas, 22 November 1899, p. 22.

## *Chapter Four*
## A British War for American Interests

1. The only previous studies of American policy during the Boer War are John H. Ferguson, *American Diplomacy and the Boer War* (Philadelphia: University of Pennsylvania Press, 1939), and brief sections in Alfred T. Dennis, *Adventures in American Diplomacy 1896-1906* (New York: E. P. Dutton, 1928); Edward W. Chester, *Clash of Titans: Africa and U. S. Foreign Policy* (Maryknoll, New York: Orbis Books, 1974) and Russell Warren Howe, *Along the Afric Shore: An Historical Review of Two Centuries of U. S.-African Relations* (New York: Barnes & Noble, 1975).

2. See the letters to the Department of State from Fraser and Chalmers, M. C. Bullock Company, Gross Printing Company, Manhattan Rubber Company, Ingersoll and Sargent Company, and others in *Miscellaneous Letters Received and Sent, September- October, 1899.*

3. "Who Will Gain by the War?", *Iron Age,* 64 (2 November 1899), 46-47. See also "Opportunities for Trade in Africa," *ibid.,* (12 October 1899), 15-16 and "The War and the Markets," *Commercial and Financial Chronicle,* 69 (28 October 1899), 879-80.

4. *New York Times,* 26 December 1899, p. 6.

5. James Wirgman, "The Boers and the Native Question," *Nineteenth Century,* 47 (April 1900), 593-602. See also the pamphlet by H. R. Fox-Bourne, Secretary of the Aborigines Protection Society, *The Native Question in South*

*Africa* (London: Aborigines Protection Society, 1900) and J. Castell Hopkins, "A British View of the Transvaal Question," *Forum* 28 (December 1899), 385-402.

6. Margherta A. Hamm, "The Secular Value of Foreign Missions," *The Independent,* 52 (26 April 1900), 100-03.

7. Roosevelt to F. C. Selous, Albany, 19 March 1900, *Letters of Theodore Roosevelt,* II, 1233-34; White to Hay, 3 November 1899, Allen Nevins, *Henry White: Thirty Years of American Diplomacy* (New York: Harper and Brothers, 1930), pp. 219-30; Choate to Hay, 29 December 1899 (Private and Confidential), Joseph Choate MSS., Library of Congress, Box 17; Mahan to *New York Times,* 22 January 1900, p. 6.

8. Hay to White, 18 March 1900, in Nevins, *Henry White,* p. 151.

9. Stowe immediately telegraphed Hay asking if he should issue a proclamation of neutrality when the war began. But Hay never issued a formal statement declaring neutrality. For a discussion of the technical aspects of American neutrality see Ferguson, *American Diplomacy,* pp. 44-46.

10. Macrum to Hill, Pretoria, 27 October 1899 (No. 78); 9 November, 1899 (No. 82), *C. D.: Pretoria.*

11. Hay to Macrum, Washington, 24 November 1899 (No. 60), *Records of Consulates: Pretoria;* Hollis to Hill, Pretoria, 2 February 1900 (No. 114), *C. D.: Pretoria.* Later in the war American consuls did deliver mail and money to captured Boer troops.

12. Hollis to Hill, Pretoria, 20 December 1899 (no No.), *C. D.: Pretoria.* Hollis served at Pretoria from 14 December 1899 to 3 February 1900 when he returned to Lourenço Marques. When Adelbert Hay replaced Hollis, he immediately informed the Department of Hollis's close association with the Boers and cautioned his father to disregard Hollis's interpretation of the situation. Cable, Hay to Secretary of State, 9 April 1900, *ibid.*

13. See the interview with W. J. Leyds, the Boer representative in Europe in the *North American Review,* 516 (January 1900), 6-8; Hay to Hill, Pretoria, 10 February 1900 (No. 4), *C. D.: Pretoria.*

14. *Commercial Relations, 1901,* II, 299-300, 487-88; W. L. Penfield, "British Purchases of War Supplies in the United States," *North American Review,* 546 (May 1902), 11-13.

15. Stanford Newel to Hay, The Hague, 12 December 1899 (No. 256), *Diplomatic Despatches: The Netherlands;* F. W. Reitz to Hay, 18 June 1900, *Notes, South African Republic and Orange Free State;* Hay to Pierce, 15 December 1899, *Notes to Foreign Consuls in the U.S.,* IV, 464.

16. Hay to Senator James McMillan, 3 July 1900, in Dennett, *John Hay,* p. 246.

17. See the report by E.H. Crowder to the House Representatives, *Congressional Record,* 57th Congress, 1st Session, Pt. 4, 10 April 1902, 3948. Crowder, Judge Advocate of the U. S. Army, concluded that the sales of mules and the recruitment of muleteers was not a violation of American neutrality; Pierce to Hay, 21 March 1900, *Notes, South African Republic and Orange Free State.*

18. A. Hay to J. Hay, telegram, 18 April 1900, *C. D.: Pretoria.*

19. Hollis to Hay, Lourenço Marques, 2 December 1899 (no No.), *C. D.: Lourenço Marques.*

20. Choate to Hay, telegram, 1 January 1900: Hay to Choate, telegram, 2

January 1900, *Foreign Relations, 1900,* pp. 539-40, 358-59. See also "British Seizures of American Cargoes," *Literary Digest,* 20 (6 January 1900), 3-5.

21. Hay to Choate, Washington, 3 January 1900 (No. 267). *Diplomatic Instructions: Great Britain;* same to same, telegram, 6 January 1900, *ibid;* Hay to Ballard and Ballard Company, 9 March 1900, copy in *Records of Consulates: Capetown.* On the legality of Hay's actions see Ferguson, *American Diplomacy,* pp. 72-83.

22. Cridler to Hollis, Washington, 11 May 1900 (No. 57), *Records of Consulates: Lourenço Marques.*

23. The best summary of European intervention plans is Grenville, *Lord Salisbury,* pp. 269-90. See also William Langer, *The Diplomacy of Imperialism* (2 Vols.: New York: Alfred A. Knopf, 1935), II, 653, and Ferguson, *American Diplomacy,* pp. 121-75.

24. Hay to Stowe (Confidential), Washington, 26 October 1899, *Records of Consulates: Capetown.*

25. Telegram, Holleben to Foreign Office, 2 January 1900, *Die Grosse Politik,* XV, 4661; 2 February 1900, 4466. See also Dennis, *Adventures in American Diplomacy,* pp. 126-27.

26. Telegram, A. Hay to the Secretary of State, 10 March 1900, *C. D.: Pretoria;* telegram, J. Hay to White, 10 March 1900, *Diplomatic Instructions: Great Britain;* telegram, White to Hay, 13 March 1900, *Diplomatic Despatches: Great Britain.*

27. Hay to White, 18 March 1900, Nevins, *Henry White,* pp. 152-53.

28. Newel to Hay, The Hague, 17 March 1900 (No. 284) *Diplomatic Despatches: Netherlands.*

29. *Ibid.,* 29 April 1900 (No. 289).

30. *Ibid.,* 2 May 1900 (No. 290).

31. *New York Times,* 16 May 1900, p. 1; 17 May, p. 6. See also "The Boer Envoys in the United States," *Review of Reviews,* 21 (June 1900), 658-59.

32. "Memorandum of Interview of the Delegates of the South African Republics with the Secretary of State, May 21, 1900," *Notes, South African Republic and Orange Free State.*

33. "How the Press Looks at the Boer Envoys," *Literary Digest,* 20 (26 May 1900), 624-25; White to Hay, London, 26 May 1900, Henry White MSS., Box 17.

34. Roosevelt to Lodge, 14 December 1899; Lodge to Roosevelt, 16 December 1899, *Selections from the Correspondence of Theodore Roosevelt and Henry Cabot Lodge* (2 Vols.: New York: Charles Scribner's Sons, 1925), I, 428-30; Hay to Choate, 3 January 1900 (Private and Confidential), Choate MSS., Box 14; *Times* (London), 14 April 1900, p. 6.

35. *Congressional Record,* 56th Congress, 1st Session, Pt. 1, 98.

36. *Ibid.,* Pt. 2, 1250-54.

37. *Ibid.,* Pt. 5, 5735; Pt. 7, 6127-32.

38. F. A. McKenzie, C. N. T. DuPlessis, and Charles Bunce, *The Real Kruger and the Transvaal* (New York: Street and Smith, 1900).

39. Richard Harding Davis to Arthur Wing Pinero, 13 March 1902, Howell Wright Collection, Box 10; Davis to Roosevelt, (no date), Elihu Root MSS., Library of Congress, "Special Correspondence: Theodore Roosevelt," Box 163; Richard Harding Davis, *With Both Armies in South Africa* (New York: Charles Scribner's Sons, 1900): Poultney Bigelow, *White Man's Africa* (New York: Harper and Brothers, 1900), pp. 73-80, 110-11.

40. Charles Schurz to William Vocke, 8 December 1901, Frederick Bancroft (ed.), *Speeches, Correspondence and Political Papers of Carl Schurz* (6 Vols.: New York: G. P. Putnam's Sons, 1913), VI, 279-80; Andrew Carnegie, "The South African Question," *North American Review,* 517 (December 1899), 798 -804; Henry Adams, *The Education of Henry Adams,* (Boston: Houghton-Mifflin, 1918), pp. 372-73.

41. Roosevelt to Cecil Spring-Rice, 27 January 1900, *Letters of Roosevelt,* II, 1146-47.

42. Hay to Choate, 3 January 1900 (private and personal), Choate MSS., Box 14.

43. White to Mrs. Henry White, 23 January 1900, White MSS., Box 7.

44. Telegram, Macrum to Hay, 6 November 1899, *C. D.: Pretoria;* telegram, Hill to Macrum, 8 November 1899, *Records of Consulates: Pretoria;* telegram, Macrum to Hill, 8 November 1899, *C. D.: Pretoria;* telegram, Hill to Macrum, 2 December 1899, *Records of Consulates: Capetown.*

45. *New York Times,* 7 February 1900, p. 6; 10 February, p. 6; 16 February, p. 6; *Congressional Record,* 56th Congress, 1st Session, Pt. 2, 1940.

46. Ferguson, *American Diplomacy,* pp. 101-04, has a detailed account of the censorship controversy. He concludes that three letters of Macrum, two official and one personal, were opened by the British censor. In addition, several letters by Stanley Hollis were opened and resealed. See Hollis to Hill, Pretoria, 5 January 1900 (No. 115), *C. D.: Pretoria.*

47. Webster Davis, *John Bull's Crime* (New York: Abbey Press, 1901); *New York Times,* 6 July 1900, p. 2; Kirk H. Porter and Donald B. Johnson (eds.), *National Party Platforms* (Urbana: University of Illinois Press, 1961), p. 115.

48. Hollis to Hill, Lourenço Marques, 15 January 1900 (No. 121), *C. D.: Lourenço Marques.*

49. *Ibid.,* 8 June 1900 (No. 140); Hill to Hollis, telegram, 10 August 1900, *Records of Consulates: Lourenço Marques.*

50. Hay to Lodge, 19 February 1902, in Dennett, *John Hay,* p. 243.

51. Lodge to Roosevelt, Washington, 30 March 1901, *Correspondence of Roosevelt and Lodge,* I, 4880.

52. Hay to Choate, Washington, 31 May 1900, Choate MSS., Box 14; White to Hay, London, 16 May 1900, in Nevins, *Henry White,* p. 153.

53. Roosevelt to Spring-Rice, 27 January 1900, *Letters of Roosevelt,* II, 1146-47; Roosevelt to William Sewall, 24 April 1900, *ibid.,* 1269-70.

54. Sydney Brooks, "America and the War," *North American Review,* 520 (March 1900), 337-47.

55. Alfred Thayer Mahan, "The Merits of the Transvaal Dispute," *ibid.,* 312-26; "The Boer Republics and the Monroe Doctrine," *The Independent,* 52 (10 May 1900), 1101-03.

56. Mahan, *The War in South Africa* (New York: P. F. Collier and Son, 1900).

57. Hammond, *Autobiography,* II, 426-27. See also his undated speech before the Century Club of San Francisco, Hammond MSS., Box 10, "Speeches and Addresses: Boer War."

58. Day Allen Willey, "American Interests in Africa," *Arena,* 25 (September 1900), 293-98. See also "American Advocates of the Boers," *Commercial and Financial Chronicle,* 70 (14 April 1900), 714-15; "Wild Men in Public Office," *New York Times,* 23 January 1900, p. 6; Allen Sangree, "Americans in South Africa," *Munsey's Magazine,* 22 (March 1900), 802-08.

59. Stowe to Cridler (Confidential), Capetown, 14 July 1900 (No. 266), *C. D.: Capetown.* See also Stowe's letter in the *New York Times,* 5 December 1900, p. 2.

60. "Some Affairs in South Africa," *Methodist Review,* 82 (November 1900), 978-79.

61. *Parliamentary Debates,* 97 (17 July 1901), 729-34; 98 (25 July 1901), 839-40; 99 (15 August 1901), 1043.

62. "The Boers and Christianity in South Africa," *Missionary Review of the World,* 13 (June 1900), 462-67; "South African Affairs," *ibid.,* 559; "The Missionary Situation in South Africa," *ibid.,* (January 1900), 18-19. See also "Dutch Missions Among the Boers," *Methodist Review,* 83 (March 1901), 309-10.

63. Robert W. Carter, "Queen Victoria: Friend of the Negro," *The Colored American Magazine,* 2 (March 1901), 354-57; *Minutes of the Ecumenical Missionary Conference, New York, April 2-May 1, 1900* (New York: American Tract Society, 1900), p. 470. See also George F. Becker, "Rights and Wrongs in South Africa," *Forum,* 29 (March 1900), 31-37.

64. *New York Times,* 20 June 1900, p. 2.

65. See Churchill's notes and letters in Randolph S. Churchill, *Winston S. Churchill* (Boston: Houghton-Mifflin, 1967), *Companion Volume 2,* 1219-25.

66. Quoted in Ferguson, *American Diplomacy,* p. 183.

67. See Roosevelt to Choate, Washington, 10 November 1901, Choate MSS., Box 12.

68. Newel to Hay, The Hague, 14 December 1900 (No. 352), *Diplomatic Despatches: The Netherlands;* Hay to Newel, 3 December 1900, Dennett, *John Hay,* p. 243.

69. "America as a Home for the Boers," *Literary Digest,* 22 (16 June 1900), 716-17; Stowe to Cridler (Confidential), Capetown, 28 August 1900 (No. 280) *C. D.: Capetown.* See also Rosenthal, *Stars and Stripes in Africa,* p. 203.

70. See Crane's report enclosed in White to Hay, London, 23 November 1901 (No. 712), *Diplomatic Despatches: Great Britain* and W. T. Gordon to Hill, Pretoria, 19 August 1902 (No. 180), *C. D.: Pretoria.*

71. See the letters of inquiry in *Records of Consulates: Capetown* and Gordon to H. H. D. Peirce, Pretoria, 22 June 1902, *C. D.: Pretoria.*

72. *Review of Reviews,* 26 (July 1902), 3-8; Frederick Bunker, "The Crisis in South African Missions," *Missionary Review of the World,* 25 (February 1902), 106-08. See also *86th Annual Report of the American Bible Society* (New York: American Bible Society, 1902), p. 153.

73. See especially James H. Birch to the American consul at Capetown, 9 January 1902; Bullock Electrical Company to the U.S. consul, 10 January 1902; Phillips and Butlorff Co., to William Bingham, 20 August 1902, and National Association of Manufacturers to Bingham, 26 September 1902, *Records of Consulates: Capetown.*

74. Gordon to Peirce, Pretoria, 28 January 1902 (No. 132), *C. D.: Pretoria;* Bingham to Peirce, Capetown, 14 December 1901 (No. 6) *C. D.: Capetown;* Gordon to Peirce, Pretoria, 29 July 1902 (No. 176), *C. D.: Pretoria.*

75. Hammond, "Trade Opportunities in Southern Africa," undated speech, Hammond MSS., Box 11.

76. "Needs of Direct Steamship Service to Africa," *Scientific American: Supplement No. 1360,* 53 (25 January 1902), 21794-95.

77. Stowe to Cridler, Capetown, 29 May 1901 (no No.), *C. D.: Capetown.*

78. "Trade Suggestions from U. S. Consuls: Trade in South Africa," *Scientific American Supplement No. 1347,* 52 (26 October 1901), 21597.

79. Quoted in "Trade Suggestions from U. S. Consuls: Industrial Conditions in South Africa," *Scientific American Supplement No. 1295,* 50 (27 October 1900), 20757.

## *Chapter Five*
## The United States and British South Africa

1. Of the major studies of Anglo-American relations in this period, only Heindel devotes much attention to trade rivalry and British fears of the American economy. See especially pp. 134-50 and 163-68. Edward Crapol, *America for Americans: Economic Nationalism and Anglophobia in the Late Nineteenth Century* (Westport, Conn.: Greenwood Press, 1973) analyzes American response to this conflict.

2. "Statistics on the South African, British, and American Trade," *Scientific American Supplement No. 1407,* 54 (20 December 1902), 22548-49; "Mr. Chamberlain and the Transvaal," *Commercial and Financial Chronicle,* 77 (28 March 1903), 680-81.

3. "The Engineering Requirements of South Africa," *Iron Age,* 70 (4 December 1902), 22. See also "More on South Africa," *ibid.,* (18 December 1902), 66-67.

4. "Conditions in South Africa," *ibid.,* (13, November 1902), 66-68.

5. "Conditions in South Africa," *Commercial and Financial Chronicle,* 78 (9 January 1904), 78-79; "What Peace Brings to South Africa," *Literary Review,* 24 (7 June 1902), 757; "The South African Shipping Trade War," *Iron Age,* 70 (27 November 1902), 76.

6. L. G. Carpenter to Bingham, San Francisco, 24 October 1903, *Records of Consulates: Capetown;* Bingham to Peirce, Capetown, 1 December 1903 (No. 309), *C. D.: Capetown.*

7. Bingham to Peirce, Capetown, 1 December 1903 (No. 309), *C. D.: Capetown.*

8. *Commercial Relations, 1903,* pp. 123-25.

9. *Times* (London), 14 September 1903, p. 5. See also Ross Hoffman, *Great Britain and the German Trade Rivalry* (Philadelphia: University of Pennsylvania Press, 1933), pp. 73-76.

10. Quoted in Heindel, *American Impact,* p. 165.

11. *Report of the National Industrial Association of Great Britain* (London: P. S. King and Sons, 1902), pp. 20-22; *Times* (London), 6 June 1903, p. 5.

12. E. E. Williams, "Made in Germany—Five Years Later," *National Review,* 38 (September 1901), 130-44; "Competition with America and Germany," *Times* (London), 7 May 1903, p. 7.

13. *Parliamentary Debates,* 121 (22 April 1903), pp. 168-69; 134 (19 July 1904), pp. 395-402.

14. Stafford Ransome, *The Engineer in South Africa: A Review of the Industrial Situation in South Africa After the War and a Forecast of the Possibilities of the Country* (Westminster: Constable, 1903), pp. 95-117.

15. F. A. McKenzie, *The American Invaders* (London: Grant Richards, 1902), p. 202.

16. *Ibid.,* pp. 202-03.

17. W. T. Stead, *The Americanization of the World* (London: H. Markley, 1902), pp. 53-68.

18. *Ibid.*, pp. 68-71.

19. J. A. Hobson, "The Approaching Abandonment of Free Trade," *Fortnightly Review,* 71 (March 1902), 434-44.

20. Richard Rempel, "The Impact of American Economic Competition on the Rise of Protectionism in Britain, 1880-1914," paper read before the Organization of American Historians annual convention, Washington, D. C., 6 April 1972. Dr. Rempel has been kind enough to send me a copy of this paper.

21. Bingham to Peirce, Capetown, 15 April 1903 (No. 236), *C. D.: Capetown.*

22. D. J. N. DeNoon,"Capitalist Influence and the Transvaal Government During the Crown Colony Period, 1900-1906," *The Historical Journal,* 11 (1968), 301-31.

23. Joseph Proffit to Peirce, Pretoria, 30 March 1903 (No. 33), *C. D.: Pretoria;* Hay to White, Washington, 3 June 1903 (No. 1210), *Diplomatic Instructions: Great Britain;* Gardiner Williams to Proffit, Kimberley, 10 September 1903, *Records of Consulates: Pretoria.*

24. Proffit to Frederick Loomis, Pretoria, 10 May 1904 (No. 38), *ibid;* High Commissioner of South Africa to the Honourable United States Consul, Capetown, 12 July 1904, *Records of Consulates: Capetown.*

25. Michael Whilby to Proffit, Johannesburg, 26 September 1904, *ibid.;* Proffit to Peirce, Pretoria, 30 September 1904 (No. 116), *C. D.: Pretoria.*

26. Horace Washington to John Nydegger, Capetown, 26 September 1904, *Records of Consulates: Capetown.* See also the recollections of William Wallace Mein in his letter to Howell Wright, 16 March 1937, Howell Wright Collection, Box 22.

27. C. R. Kehler to Proffit, Johannesburg, 20 January 1904, enclosed in Proffit to Peirce, Pretoria, 22 January 1904 (No. 67), *C.D.: Pretoria;* see also Profitt to Adee, Pretoria, 2 May 1904 (No. 54), *ibid.*

28. Proffit to Peirce, Pretoria, 2 February 1904 (no No.), *ibid.;* Clifford Knight to Peirce, Capetown, 31 October 1904 (No. 390), *C. D.: Capetown.*

29. Bingham to Gustavus Loevirger, Capetown, 10 February 1905, *Records of Consulates: Capetown.*

30. Hollis to Francis Loomis, Lourenço Marques, (Confidential), 22 January 1904 (No. 334), *C. D.: Lourenço Marques.*

31. *Parliamentary Papers,* Cd. 43, 1909, "Report of the Royal Commission on Shipping Rates," 6, 62-67. See also Robert Kubicek, *The Administration of Imperialism: Joseph Chamberlain at the Colonial Office* (Durham: Duke University Press, 1969), pp. 118-25.

32. *Ibid.,* Cd. 2977, 1906 "The South African Customs Convention of March, 1906."

33. Reid to Roosevelt, London, *(Confidential),* 24 May 1907, Reid MSS., Box 59.

34. *Rand Daily Mail* (Johannesburg), 12 June 1907, p. 4; H. E. V. Pickstone, "Past and Future of the Fruit Industry," Howell Wright Collection, Box 24.

35. Edward Vorz to Bingham, New Orleans, November 1903, *Records of Consulates: Capetown.*

36. In 1908 the United States accounted for 8.2% of South African imports, while Germany captured 8.7%.

37. *Parliamentary Debates,* 153 (6 March 1906), p. 273.

38. "The South African Trade: A Warning," *Iron Age,* 71 (26 March 1903), 64.

39. Bingham to Peirce, Capetown, 16 February 1904 (No. 327), *C. D.: Capetown;* Williams to Henry Thompson and Son, Kimberley, 6 June 1904, *Records of Consulates: Kimberley;* Proffit to Peirce, 26 June 1903 (No. 48), *C. D.: Pretoria.*

40. *New York Times,* 17 June 1906, p. 12; "South African Trade Conditions," *Iron Age,* 81 (11 June 1908), 1893.

41. Hollis to Loomis, Lourenço Marques, 2 March 1905 (No. 428), *C. D.: Lourenço Marques.* See Adee's comments in Memorandum, Adee to Peirce, 24 April 1905, *Records of Consulates: Lourenço Marques.*

42. Snodgrass to Peirce, Pretoria, 1 September 1905 (No. 21); 2 September 1905 (No. 22), *C. D.: Pretoria.*

43. *Ibid.,* 15 September 1905 (No. 24).

44. Adee to Snodgrass, Washington, 21 November 1905 (no No.), *ibid.;* Reid to Root, London, 17 April 1906 (private), Reid MSS., Box 57.

45. Secretary of Commerce Oscar Straus to Root, Washington, 27 March 1907 enclosure in Huntington Wilson to Julius Lay, Washington, 30 March 1907 (no. 12); Department of State to Lay, 29 May 1908 (no No.), *Records of Consulates: Capetown.*

46. Bingham to Arthur Brown, Capetown, 15 May 1905, *ibid.;* Frederick Burnham to L. D. Strong, 24 September 1908, Howell Wright Collection, Box 3.

47. S. B. Saul, "The American Impact on British Industry, 1895-1914," *Business History,* 3 (December 1960), 19-38.

48. For details of the unification movement see *Parliamentary Papers,* Cd. 3564, 1907 "Papers Relating to the Federation of the South African Colonies"; *Minutes and Proceedings of the South African National Convention held at Durban, Cape Town and Bloemfontein 12th October 1908 to 11th May, 1909* (Capetown: Cape Times Ltd., 1911), G. B. Pyrah, *Imperial Policy and South Africa, 1902-1910* (Oxford: Clarendon Press, 1955).

49. Lay to Department of State, Capetown, 19 September 1907 (No. 33), Department of State Numerical Files, National Archives, Record Group 677, No. 9352.

50. "A Frederated South Africa," *The Nation,* 85 (1 August 1907), 94-95.

51. *Commercial Relations, 1908,* pp. 732-35.

52. *Minutes and Proceedings of the South African National Convention,* 65-67.

53. Olive Schreiner, "The Native Problem in South Africa," *Review of Reviews,* 34 (March 1909), 323-25; J. A. Hobson, *The Crisis of Liberalism* (London: P.S. King, 1909), pp. 245-46. See also Benjamin Sacks, *South Africa: An Imperial Dilemma: Non-Europeans and the British Nation, 1902-1914* (Albuquerque: University of New Mexico Press, 1967), pp. 177-80.

54. "The South African Union," *Independent,* 66 (25 February 1909), 436-37; "The Constitution of South Africa," *The Nation,* 88 (25 February 1909), 185-6. See also "A New Color Line," *Outlook,* 93 (September 1909), 84-85.

55. Strong, *Story of the American Board,* pp. 434-35; "The Union of South Africa," *The Colored American Magazine,* 17 (September 1909), 197-204.

56. Lay to Huntington Wilson, Capetown, 15 June 1909 (No. 129), *Records of the Department of State Relating to Internal Affairs of British Africa, 1909-1912,* Department of State Records, National Archives; Lay to the Department

of State, Capetown, 30 June 1909 (no No.), copy in *Records of Consulates: Capetown.*

57. *Commercial and Financial Chronicle,* 89 (30 October 1909), 1111; "South African Trade Conditions: Emerging from Seven Years' Depression," *Iron Age,* 84 (16 September 1909), 844-45.

58. Many of the letters from American firms are filed in the Department of State Numerical File, Record Group 583, 848a.00; Lay to the Department of State, Capetown, 18 October 1910 (no No.), 583/848b.77; Carr to Lay, Washington, 16 November 1910 (No. 9), *Records of Consulates: Capetown.*

59. Hollis to the Department of State, Lourenço Marques, 10 June 1908 (No. 661), 583/848/14669.

60. Hammond to James B. Connolly, New York, 30 May 1910, Hammond MSS., Box 5; Reid to Philander Knox, London, 1 December 1909, Reid MSS., Box 189: A. L. Smith, "A Nation in the Making," *Yale Review,* 19 (February 1911), 339-56.

61. "Disasters of Free Trade," *Rand Daily Mail,* 11 September 1908; "Tariffs and the Empire," *ibid.,* 21 January 1909, p. 6.

62. *Commercial Relations, 1908-1912.*

63. "British Rule in Africa," an address delivered at the Guildhall, London, 31 May 1910, Theodore Roosevelt, *African and European Addresses:* (New York: G. P. Putnam's Sons, 1910), pp. 159-60; "Speech to the Banquet of the American Society in London," 4 July 1911, Hammond MSS., Box 11.

64. Cornelius H. Patton, "Industrial Storm-Centers in Africa," Address delivered before the seventh international convention of the Student Volunteer Movement for Foreign Missions. *Minutes of the Seventh International Convention* (New York: Student Volunteer Movement, 1914), pp. 223-25. See also "Missionary Influence in South Africa," *Literary Review,* 16 (18 October 1913), 685-86.

65. United States Department of Commerce, *Special Agents Series* (No. 83), "Cotton Goods in South Africa," (Washington: U. S. Government Printing Office, 1914).

*Chapter Six*
## Segregation and the Origin of Apartheid

1. Reid to Hay, London, 17 September 1902, Reid MSS., Box 97; Chamberlain to Hay, London, 5 July 1905, in Dennis, *John Hay,* p. 129.

2. Arthur Hawkes, "The Negro Problem in South Africa," *Review* of Reviews, 28 (September 1903), 325-30.

3. Kenneth J. King, "African Students in Negro Colleges: Notes on the 'Good African,'" *Phylon,* 31 (Spring 1970), 16-30; *Rand Daily Mail,* 26 October 1905, p. 6; Roderick Jones, "The Black Problem in South Africa," *Nineteenth Century and After,* 57 (May 1905), 770-76.

4. Maurice Evans, *Black and White in the Southern States: A Study of the Race Problem in the United States from a South African Point of View* (New York: Longmans, Green and Co., 1916), pp. 131-46;. Alexander Davis, *The Native Problem in South Africa* (London: Chapman and Hall, 1903), pp. 71-72; *Times* (London), 20 June 1903, p. 9.

5. "American Negroes Making Mischief in South Africa," *Missionary*

*Review of the World,* 16 (May 1903), 396-97; "America and the Ethiopian Movement," *Colored American Magazine,* 11 (August 1906), 91-95; Booker T. Washington to E. E. Cooper, Tuskegee, 11 August 1904, Booker T. Washington MSS., Library of Congress, Box 20. For the background and beliefs of the Ethiopian movement see Chapter II, and the materials cited.

6. "A Tuskegee Institute in South Africa: The Zulu Christian Industrial School in Natal," *Missionary Review of the World,* 16 (March 1903), 212-17.

7. Wilcox, *Proud Endeavor,* p. 91.

8. Harlan, "Booker T. Washington and the 'White Man's Burden,'" p. 466; Kenneth King, "Africa and the Southern States of the U. S. A.: Notes on J. J. Oldham and American Negro Education for Africa," *Journal of African History,* 10 (1969), 659-77. See also St. Clair Drake, "Negro Americans and 'the Africa Interest,'" *The American Negro Reference Book,* John P. Davis (ed.), (Englewood Cliffs, New Jersey: Prentice-Hall, 1966), pp. 662-705.

9. William Archer, "Black and White in the Southern States of America," *The State: South Africa,* 2 (December 1908), 751-60; *Rand Daily Mail,* 13 July 1909, p. 6.

10. American Manual Training Company to Julius Lay, 25 February 1909, *Records of Consulates: Capetown.*

11. *American Negro Yearbook: 1912* (Tuskegee, Alabama: Tuskegee Institute, 1913), p. 97. See also Harlan, "Booker T. Washington" 466-67.

12. D.D.T. Jabavu, *The Black Problem: Papers and Addresses on Various Native Problems* (New York: Negro University Press, 1969), pp. 26-27.

13. Speech at Wanders' Hall, Johannesburg, 17 January 1903, in Charles Boyd (ed.), *Mr. Chamberlain's Speeches* (2 Vols.: London: Constable, 1914), II, 112-19.

14. Peirce to Bingham, Washington, 30 December 1903 (No. 158), *Records of Consulates: Capetown;* Peirce to Proffit, Washington, 30 December 1903 (No. 37), *Records of Consulates: Johannesburg;* Bingham to Peirce, Capetown, 7 March 1904 (No. 335), *C. D.: Capetown.*

15. See the petitions in *Records of Consulates: Pretoria.*

16. Proffit to Loomis, Pretoria, 1 October 1903 (No. 31), *C. D.: Pretoria.*

17. W.T. Gordon to Proffit, Johannesburg, 20 December 1903, *Records of Consulates: Pretoria;* Gardiner Williams to the Department of State, Kimberley, 11 March 1904 (no No.), *Records of Consulates: Kimberley.*

18. The petition and a long account of the trial in the *Transvaal Leader* of 2 August 1904 are enclosed in Proffit to Loomis, Johannesburg, 8 August 1904 (No. 103), *C. D.: Pretoria.*

19. *Ibid.*

20. *Ibid.,* 20 September 1904 (No. 114).

21. *Parliamentary Debates,* 129 (12 February 1904), 1151

22. *Ibid.,* 152 (28 February 1906), 1212-47.

23. J. L. Fuller, *South African Native Missions: Some Considerations* (Leeds: Richard Jackson, 1907), p. 57; "The Fighting Tribes of South Africa," *Scientific American,* 95 (21 July 1906), 50-52; J. Du Plessis, "The Native Situation in South Africa: A Missionary Point of View," *Missionary Review of the World,* 30 (December 1907), 919-26.

24. *Voice of the Negro,* 1 (August 1904), 302-03; 3 (June 1906), 400-01; *New York Times,* 19 August 1905, p. 3: James S. Dennis, "The Missionary: Shall he

be Denounced or Decorated?" *Methodist Review,* 88 (March 1906), 262-74.

25. "The 'Ethiopian Movement' in South Africa," *Literary Review,* 27 (19 September 1903), 358-59; "Perils of Ethiopianism," *New York Times,* 23 May 1904, p. 2.

26. See Harold Issacs, "Pan Africanism as 'Romantic Racism,'" in Rauford Logan (ed.), *W. E. B. DuBois: A Profile* (New York: Hill and Wang, 1971), pp. 210-48, and Robert Weisbord, *Ebony Kinship: Africa, Africans, and the Afro-American* (Westport, Conn.: Greenwood Press, 1974).

27. A. Kirkland Soga, "Call the Black Man to Conference," *Colored American Magazine,* 6 (December 1903), 868-73; *ibid.,* Pt. 2, 7 (January 1904), 37-40. For the background of Soga see Sarah A. Allen, "Mr. Allen Kirkland Soga," *ibid.,* 7 (February 1904), 114-16.

28. *Ibid.,* Pt. 3, 7 (March 1904), 197-202.

29. A. Kirkland Soga, "Ethiopians of the Twentieth Century: Questions Affecting the Natives and Colored People Resident in British South Africa," *ibid.,* 6 (August 1903), 562-67.

30. Charles Hall Adams, "Let the Natives of South Africa Have Justice and Education," *ibid.,* 7 (April 1904), 290-92.

31. "The Situation in Africa Through English Eyes," *ibid.,* 8 (April 1905), 268-71.

32. *Voice of the Negro,* 2 (March 1905), 156-58; (June 1905), 368-69.

33. "Africa for the Africans," *Colored American Magazine,* 9 (July 1905), 350-51. See also (September 1905), 470-71.

34. "Anglo-Saxon Civilization in Africa," *ibid.,* 11 (September 1906), 145; Perry Marshall, "Boerland," *Alexander's Magazine,* 4 (15 May 1907), 17-28; Edgar Mels, "Britain and Her Restless Blacks," *Harper's Weekly,* 50 (June 1906), 772-76.

35. South African Native Affairs Commission, *Minutes of Evidence and Reports* (5 Vols.: Capetown: Cape Times, 1905), II, 969-70, IV, 659.

36. Roderick Jones, "The Black Peril in South Africa," *Nineteenth Century and After,* 55 (May 1904), 712-23; "The Black Problem in South Africa," *ibid.,* 57 (May 1905), 770-76.

37. *Ibid.,* 774-75.

38. Frederick Bridgeman, "The Ethiopian Movement in South Africa," *Missionary Review of the World,* 17 (June 1904), 434-45.

39. Bingham to Ernest Lyon, Capetown, 7 March 1905, *Records of Consulates: Capetown.*

40. Captain H. Fowle to Bingham, 20 June 1905, *ibid.*

41. The best study of the revolt is Shula Marks, *Reluctant Rebellion: The 1906-8 Disturbances in Natal* (Oxford: Clarendon Press, 1970). Using recent evidence, Marks concludes that the influence of the Ethiopians and black Americans was greatly overestimated by white officials. Contemporary accounts stressed the role of Americans. See J. Stuart, *A History of the Zulu Rebellion of 1906* (London: Longmans, Green and Co., 1907).

42. John Dubé, "Zulus and the Missionary Outlook in Natal," *Missionary Review of the World,* 30 (March 1907), 205.

43. *American Bible Society: Ninetieth Annual Report* (New York: American Bible Society, 1906), p. 221; *Parliamentary Debates,* p. 167 (17 December 1906), 1097; Evans, *Black and White in South East Africa,* pp. 88-91.

44. Frederic Tatham, "The Native Crisis in Natal," *National Review,* 47 (June 1906), 581-92.

45. *Natal Native Affairs Commission Report on Native Disturbances,* (Bloemfontein: Department of Native Affairs, 1907), p. 5.

46. Horace Washington to the Department of State, Capetown, 12 February 1906 (No. 64), *C. D.: Capetown;* Julius Lay to the Department of State, 11 June 1907 (no No.), *Internal Affairs of British Africa,* 569/7544.

47. Lay to the Department of State, Capetown *(Confidential),* 16 February 1909 (No. 111), *Internal Affairs of British Africa,* 1037/18495.

48. *The Works of Theodore Roosevelt: National Edition* (20 Vols.: New York: Charles Scribner's Sons, 1926), XVI, 260-61.

49. South African Native Races Committee, *The Natives of South Africa: Their Progress and Present Condition* (New York: E. P. Dutton, 1909), p. 200.

50. *Ibid.,* p. 202.

51. Harlan, " Booker T. Washington," 467.

52. Shepperson and Price, *Independent African, passim.*

53. "The Progress of the Negro," *Rand Daily Mail,* 22 February 1909, p. 6. See also Olive Schreiner, "The Native Problem in South Africa," *Review of Reviews,* 39 (March 1909), 324-25.

54. "The Black Vote: A Dead Failure," *ibid.,* 1 December 1908, p. 6; F. A. Stone, "Studies of the American Race Problem," *The Intellectual Review,* 38 (1908), 157-70; H. E. V. Pickstone, *White Civilization and the Problem of Colour* (Capetown: Cape Times, 1909), pp. 11-12.

55. Violet Markham, *The South African Scene* (London: Smith, Elder, 1913), 221.

56. "The Colour Franchise," *Rand Daily Mail,* 4 November 1908, p. 6.

57. South Africans based their interpretation of American reconstruction almost exclusively on historical studies that emphasized the cynical motives of "radical Northerners" and the corruption of "black rule." Most often cited were William A. Dunning, *Reconstruction: Political and Economic, 1865-1877* (New York: Harper and Brothers, 1907) and James Bryce, *The American Commonwealth,* (2 Vols.: New York: MacMillan, 1889). Typical of the South African view of reconstruction, and its lessons for South Africa, are Roderick Jones, "The South African Union and the Colour Question," *Nineteenth Century and After,* 66 (August 1909), 245-56; Sir Henry M. Durand, "The Native Question," *Blackwood's Magazine,* 189 (January 1911), 59-65; William Wybergh, "Native Policy: Assimilation or Segregation?" *The State: South Africa,* 1 (April 1909), 455-64 and Maurice Evans, *Black and White in the Southern States, passim.*

58. *Times* (London), 17 July 1909, p. 11; *Parliamentary Debates,* 184 (16 August 1909), 967, 1000-03; "Mr. Balfour and the American Constitution," *Spectator,* 103 (August 1909), 307. See also J. H. Crocker, "Black Problem: The Solution of Segregation," *Rand Daily Mail,* 25 December 1908, p. 3

59. *Markham, South African Scene,* pp. 228-29.

60. Evans, *Black and White in the Southern States,* pp. 264-65.

61. *Ibid.,* pp. 166-82; Markham, *South African Scene,* pp. 220-23; "Where Black Rules White, *"Rand Daily Mail,* 9 January 1909, p. 6.

62. Lay to the Hon. Braxton B. Comer, Capetown, 7 June 1907; W. T. Carr to

Lay, Washington, 1 August 1907 (No. 24), *Records of Consulates: Capetown.* See also F. G. Stone, "A White South Africa," *North American Review,* 583 (June 1905), 880-84.

63. H. Thoeser to the Department of State, Johannesburg, 29 July 1908 (No. 26), *Internal Affairs of British Africa,* 925/15409.

64. Pickstone, *White Civilization and the Problem of Colour,* pp. 11-13.

65. Durand, "The Native Question," p. 63; Evans, *Black and White in the Southern States,* p. 221.

66. Thoeser to the Department of State, Johannesburg, 29 July 1908 (No. 26), *Internal Affairs of British Africa,* 925/15409.

67. Pickstone, *White Civilization and the Problem of Colour,* p. 19.

68. Wybergh, "Assimilation or Segregation?," 461-62.

69. Evans, *Black and White in the Southern States,* p. 80.

70. *Ibid.,* pp. 269-70.

71. Some black South Africans accepted the concept of separate development and the denial of political rights. See S. M. Molema, *The Bantu* (Edinburgh: W. Green and Sons, 1920), pp. 252-64.

72. W. H. Moor to Proffit, Capetown, 25 March 1903, *Records of Consulates: Capetown;* William Maitland, "The Chinaman in California and South Africa," *Contemporary Review,* 88 (December 1905), 818-28.

73. Memorandum, Division of Far Eastern Affairs to Huntington Wilson, 14 May 1908, Department of State Records, 847/13532; Robert Bacon to Thomas J. O'Brien, 20 May 1908, and Bacon to Whitelaw Reid, 20 May 1908, *ibid.,* 847/13532-5.

74. E. N. Gunsaulus to Lay, Johannesburg, 29 September 1909; Lay to Gunsaulus, Capetown, 7 October 1909, *Records of Consulates: Capetown.*

75. G. M. Tatz, "Apartheid Legislation," in P. J. M. McEwan (ed.), *Twentieth Century Africa* (London: Oxford University Press, 1968), pp. 258-71.

76. Richard Guenther to Carr, Capetown, 15 March 1911 (No. 31), Records of the Department of State, 348b.112od2; Carr to Guenther, Washington, 17 April 1911 (No. 116), *ibid.*

77. Guenther to Carr, Capetown, 22 May 1911 (No. 41), *ibid.,* 348a.112H31. See also William Stretford, "Black, Brown, and White in South Africa," *Contemporary Review,* 103 (January 1913), 404-13.

78. A. W. Baker, "The Color Line in South Africa," *Missionary Review of the World,* 36 (June 1913), 428-34.

79. For education see *Crisis,* 4 (June 1912), 66; 5 (November 1912), 12, 7 (February 1914), 169; on suffrage restrictions see 1 (January, 1911), 14-15 and 5 (September 1913), 219-20; on limits on black employment 5 (December 1912), 53; on mixed marriages 1 (March 1911), 10 and 2 (June 1911), 53; on black missionaries 5 (March 1913), 235.

80. "Slavery," *ibid.,* 6 (August 1913), 186; Francis Hoggan, "A Plea for the Survival of the Proctorates of South Africa," *ibid.,* 5 (October 1912), 300-01.

81. "South Africa," *ibid.,* 6 (September 1913), 23.

82. Dubé to DuBois, 8 May 1914, *ibid.,* 8 (July 1914), 124. See also, Shula Marks, "The Ambiguities of Dependence: John L. Dubé of Natal," *The Journal of South African Studies,* 1 (April 1975), 162-80.

## Conclusion

1. Robert Beisner, *From the Old Diplomacy to the New, 1865-1900* (New York: Thomas Y. Crowell, 1975), pp. 76-77. See also Frederick Merk, *Manifest Destiny and Mission in American History: A Reinterpretation* (New York: Vintage Books, 1963), pp. 261-66.

2. *Ibid.*, pp. 77-81.

3. Marilyn B. Young, *Rhetoric of Empire: American China Policy, 1895-1901* (Cambridge: Harvard University Press, 1968), p. 15.

4. South Africa did eventually provide troops and supplies for the British war effort, and South African forces invaded and seized German Southwest Africa. When Germany was stripped of its colonies at the Paris Peace Conference, South Africa was rewarded with a mandate from the newly-formed League of Nations to rule over Southwest Africa (Namibia). Despite numerous United Nations resolutions and lengthy negotiations, South Africa still occupies this territory.

# Bibliography

## Personal Papers and Manuscript Collections

Manuscript Division, Library of Congress, Washington, D. C.
    Joseph Choate Papers
    John Hay Papers
    Philander Knox Papers
    Elihu Root Papers
    Robert Shufeldt Papers
    Booker T. Washington Papers
    Henry White Papers

Sterling Library, Yale University, New Haven, Connecticut
    John Hays Hammond Papers
    Charles Lorham Papers
    Howell Wright Collection

Records of the Department of Navy, National Archives, Washington, D. C.
    Letters from Commodore R. W. Shufeldt—"Ticonderoga." Africa and Asia, 1878-1880.

Records of the Department of State, National Archives, Washington, D. C.
    Diplomatic Despatches to the Department of State from: Germany, Great Britain, the Netherlands, Portugal
    Diplomatic Instructions from the Department of State to: Germany, Great Britain, the Netherlands, Portugal
    Domestic Letters of the Department of State
    Consular Despatches to the Department of State from: Capetown, Lourenço Marques, Pretoria, Mozambique
    Miscellaneous Records of the Department of State: Boer War
    Notes from the Department of State to Foreign Consuls in the United States

Notes, South African Republic and Orange Free State
Records of Consulates: Miscellaneous Letters Received
and Sent: Capetown, Johannesburg, Kimberley,
Lourenço Marques, Mozambique, Pretoria
Records of the Department of State Relating to the
Internal Affairs of British Africa
Records of the Department of State Relating to the Polit-
ic. Relations between the United States and Brit-
ish Africa

## Unpublished Dissertations and Papers

Bodie, Charles A. "Views of Negro Americans Towards Africa
as Reflected in the Negro Press, 1900-1930." Unpublished Ph.D. dissertation, University of Indiana, 1954.

Booth, Allan R. "Americans in South Africa, 1784-1870,"
Unpublished Ph.D. dissertation, Boston University,
1964.

Chester, Edward. "Robber Barons Overseas: The United
States in the Congo, 1883-1917." Paper read at the African Studies Association Convention, San Francisco,
1975.

Coan, Josephus R. "The Expansion of the Missions of the
African Methodist Episcopal Church in South Africa,
1896-1908." Unpublished Ph.D. dissertation, Hartford
Seminary, 1961.

Fuller, Thomas. "American Travelers in Africa: A Historical
Overview." Paper read at the African Studies Association Convention, San Francisco, 1975.

Goldstein, Myra. "The Genesis of Modern American Relations
with South Africa, 1895-1914." Unpublished Ph.D. dissertation, State University of New York at Buffalo,
1972.

Harr, William C. "The Negro as American Protestant Missionary to Africa." Unpublished Ph.D. dissertation,
University of Chicago Divinity School, 1946.

Karanja, J. Njuguna. "United States' Attitudes and Policy
Towards the International African Association, 1876-
1886." Unpublished Ph.D. dissertation, Princeton University, 1962.

Olton, Ray. "Problems of American Foreign Relations in the
African Area During the Nineteenth Century." Unpub-

lished Ph.D. dissertation, Fletcher School of Law and Diplomacy, 1954.

Phillips, Clifton J."Protestant America and the Pagan World: The First Half Century of the American Board of Commissioners for Foreign Missions." Unpublished Ph.D. dissertation, Harvard University, 1964.

Rempel, Richard. "The Impact of American Economic Competition and the Rise of Protectionism in Britain, 1880-1914." Paper read at the Organization of American Historians' Convention, Washington, D. C., 1972.

## Published Documents and Government Records

Eybers, G. W. (ed.), *Select Constitutional Documents Illustrating South African History, 1795-1910* (London: Oxford University Press, 1918).

Germany, *Die Grosse Politik der Europäischen Kabinette, 1871-1914* (Berlin: Verlagsgesellschaft für Politik und Geschichte, 1922-1926).

Great Britain, *Parliamentary Debates* (Hansards), 3rd, 4th, and 5th Series (London: H. M. Stationery Office, 1872-1914).

———— , Parliamentary Papers. "Commerce of the Cape Colony." (Cd. 3879 of 1866).

———— , "Treaty of Friendship and Commerce between the South African Republic and His Majesty the King of Portugal." (Cd. 3410 of 1882).

———— , "Correspondence Regarding the Railway from Delagoa Bay." (Cd. 5903 of 1890).

———— , "The Select Committee of the Cape of Good Hope House of Assembly on the Jameson Raid." (Cd. 8380 of 1897).

———— , "Further Correspondence Concerning Bechuanaland." (Cd. 5918 of 1898).

———— , "Customs Union Convention Provisionally Agreed to by the Representatives of the South African Colonies at Pietermaritzburg in March, 1906." (Cd. 2977 of 1906).

———— , "Papers Relating to the Federation of the South African Colonies," (Cd. 3564 of 1907).

———— ,"Report of the Royal Commission on Shipping Rates." (Cd. 43 of 1909).

Keith, A. B. (ed.). *Selected Speeches and Documents on British Colonial Policy, 1763-1914* (2 Vols.: London: Humphrey Milford, 1918).

Knaplund, Paul and C. C. Clewes (eds.). "Private Letters from the British Embassay in Washington to the Foreign Secretary Lord Grenville, 1880-1885." *Annual Report of the American Historical Association, 1941* (Washington, D. C.: United States Government Printing Office, 1942).

Malloy, William M. (ed.). *Treaties, Conventions, International Act, Protocols and Agreements between the United States of America and Other Powers, 1776-1909* (2 Vols.: Washington, D. C.: United States Government Printing Office, 1910).

*Minutes and Proceedings of the South African National Convention held at Durban, Cape Town, and Bloemfontein, 12th October-11th May, 1909* (Capetown: Cape Times, 1911).

Natal, *Report of the Native Affairs Commission on Native Disturbances* (Bloemfontein: Department of Native Affairs, 1907).

Porter, Kirk and Donald Johnson (eds.). *National Party Platforms* (Urbana: University of Illinois Press, 1961).

*Report of Secretary of State Frederick Frelinghuysen on United States Trade with Africa, October 1, 1888.* 49th Congress, 3rd Session, Ex. Doc. 98 (Washington, D. C.: United States Government Printing Office, 1889).

Richardson, James D. (ed.). *Messages and Papers of the Presidents, 1789-1898* (10 Vols.: United States Government Printing Office, 1900).

South African Institute of Race Relations, *Survey of Race Relations in South Africa* (Capetown: Cape Times, 1909).

————, *The South African Natives: Their Progress and Present Condition* (New York: E. P. Dutton, 1909).

United States Bureau of Commerce, *Commercial Relations Between the United States and Foreign Countries* (Washington, D. C.: United States Government Printing Office, 1870-1903).

United States Bureau of Statistics, *Commercial Relations of the United States with Foreign Countries* (Washington,

D. C.: United States Government Printing Office, 1905-1912).

United States Congress, *Congressional Record.*

United States Department of Commerce, *Special Agents Series No. 83* "Cotton Goods in South Africa," 'Washington, D. C.: United States Government Printing Office, 1914).

United States Department of State, *Foreign Relations of the United States* (Washington, D.C.: United States Government Printing Office, 1874-1911).

## Memoirs, Letters, and Diaries

Adams, Henry. *The Education of Henry Adams* (Boston: Houghton-Mifflin, 1918).

Bancroft, Frederick (ed.). *Speeches, Correspondence and Political Papers of Carl Schurz* (6 Vols.: New York: G. P. Putnam's Sons, 1913).

Boyd, Charles (ed.). *Mr. Chamberlain's Speeches* (2 Vols.: London: Constable, 1914).

Brown, William H. *On the South African Frontier: The Adventures and Observations of an American in Mashonaland and Matabeleland* (New York: Scribner's, 1899).

Grey, Sir Edward. *Twenty-Five Years* (2 Vols.: New York: Frederic A. Stokes, 1925).

Hammond, John Hays. *The Autobiography of John Hays Hammond* (2 Vols.: New York: Farrar and Rinehart, 1935).

———, *The Truth About the Jameson Raid.* (Boston: Marshall Jones, 1918).

Hammond, Natalie. *A Woman's Part in a Revolution* (New York: Longmans, Green and Co., 1897).

Headlam, Cecil (ed.). *The Milner Papers* (4 Vols.: London: Cassell, 1931).

Kruger, Paul. *Memoirs of Paul Kruger.* (New York: Century, 1902).

Lodge, Henry Cabot and Theodore Roosevelt. *Selections from the Correspondence of Theodore Roosevelt and Henry Cabot Lodge* (New York: Charles Scribner's Sons, 1925).

Lynch, Hollis (ed.). *Black Spokesman: Selected Published Writings of Edward Wilmot Blyden* (New York: Humanities Press, 1971).

Morison, Elting E. (ed.). *The Letters of Theodore Roosevelt* (7 Vols.: Cambridge: Harvard University Press, 1951-1954).

Roosevelt, Theodore. *The Works of Theodore Roosevelt* (20 Vols.: New York: Charles Scribner's Sons, 1926).

————, *African and European Addresses* (New York: G. P. Putnam's Sons, 1911).

Thayer, William. *The Life and Letters of John Hay* (2 Vols.: Boston: Houghton Mifflin, 1915).

*Times* (London). *Letters from South Africa* (London: Macmillan, 1893).

Twain, Mark (Samuel Clemens). *Following the Equator: A Journey Around the World* (Hartford: American Publishing, 1897).

Wilcox, Cull. *Proud Endeavor: The Story of a Yankee on a Mission to South Africa.* Mark Wilcox (ed.), (New York: Graphic Press, 1962).

### Contemporary Accounts

*Africa and the American Negro: Addresses and Proceedings of the Congress on Africa, Atlanta, Georgia, December 13-15, 1895* (Atlanta: Gammon Theological Seminary, 1896).

American Bible Society. *Annual Report of the American Bible Society* (New York: American Bible Society, 1898-1909).

*American Negro Yearbook* (Tuskegee, Alabama: Tuskegee Press, 1913).

Bigelow, Poultney. *White Man's Africa* (New York: Harper and Brothers, 1900).

Bosman, Walter. *The Natal Rebellion of 1906* (London: Longmans, Green and Co., 1907).

Browne, J. H. Balfour. *South Africa: A Glance at Current Conditions and Politics* (Boston: Longmans, Green and Co., 1905).

Chappin, L. J. *The Relation of the British Government to the Natives of South Africa* (Washington, D. C.: Negro Young People's Christian and Educational Congress, 1906).

Davis, Alexander. *The Native Problem in South Africa* (London: Chapman and Hall, 1903).

Davis, Richard Harding. *With Both Armies in South Africa* (New York: Charles Scribner's Sons, 1900).

Davis, Webster. *John Bull's Crime* (New York: Abbey Press, 1901).

Evans, Maurice. *Black and White in South East Africa: A Study in Sociology* (New York: Longmans, Green and Co., 1916).

_____ , *Black and White in the Southern States: A Study of the Race Problem in the United States from a South African Point of View* (New York: Longmans, Green and Co., 1915).

Fitzpatrick, Perry. *The Transvaal from Within* (London: Heinemann, 1900).

Foote, Andrew. *Africa and the American Flag* (New York: Appleton, 1854).

Fox-Bourne, H. R. *The Native Question in South Africa* (London: Aborigines Protection Society, 1900).

Fuller, J. L. *South African Native Missions: Some Considerations* (Leeds: Richard Jackson, 1907).

Gray, Mary. *Stories of the Early American Missionaries in South Africa* (Boston: Pvt. printing, 1935).

Hillegas, Howard C. *Oom Paul's People: A Narrative of the British-Boer Troubles in South Africa with a History of the Boers, the Country and its Institutions* (New York: Appleton, 1899).

Hobson, J. A. *The Crisis of Liberalism* (London: P. S. King, 1909).

Jabavu, D. D. T. *The Black Problem: Papers and Addresses on Various Native Problems* (New York: Negro University Press, 1969).

Leyds, W. J. *The Transvaal Surrounded* (London: Unwin, 1919).

McKenzie, F. A. *The American Invaders* (London: Grant Richards, 1902).

McKenzie, F. A., C. N. T. DuPlessis, and Charles Bunce. *The Real Kruger and the Transvaal* (New York: Street and Smith, 1900).

Mahan, Alfred Thayer. *The War in South Africa* (New York: B. F. Collier and Son, 1900).

Markham, Violet R. *The South African Scene* (London: Smith, Elder, 1913).

Pickstone, H. E. V. *White Civilization and the Problem of Colour* (Capetown: Cape Times, 1909).

Ransome, Stafford. *The Engineer in South Africa: A Review of the Industrial Situation in South Africa After the War and a Forecast of the Possibilities of the Country* (Westminster: Constable, 1903).

Schuyler, Eugene. *American Diplomacy and the Furtherance of Commerce* (New York: Charles Scribner's Sons, 1886).

Stead, W. T. *The Americanization of the World* (London: H. Markley, 1902).

Stratham, F. Reginald. *Blacks, Boers, and British: A Three-Cornered Problem* (New York: Macmillan, 1881).

Strong, William. *The Story of the American Board: An Account of the First One Hundred Years of the American Board of Commissionaires for Foreign Missions* (Boston: Pilgrim's Press, 1910).

Taylor, William. *Christian Adventurers in South Africa* (New York: Phillips and Hunt, 1881).

Williams, E. E. *Made in Germany* (London: Grant Richards, 1896).

Williams, Gardiner. *The Diamond Mines of South Africa* (2 Vols.: New York: Buck, 1906).

White, Arthur. *The Development of Africa* (London: George Phillip and Son, 1891).

## Contemporary Journals and Newspapers

*African Repository*
*Alexander's Magazine*
*American Bible Society Report*
*American Geographical Society Report*
*Arena*
*Blackwood's Magazine*
*Capetown Argus*
*Century*
*Christian Herald*
*Colored American Magazine*
*Commercial and Financial Chronicle*
*Commercial Intelligencer*
*Contemporary Review*
*Crisis*
*Dial*
*Engineering and Mining Journal*
*Fortnightly Review*

*Forum*
*Harper's New Monthly*
*Horizon*
*Independent*
*Intellectual Review*
*International Quarterly*
*Iron Age*
*Journal of the African Society*
*Literary Digest*
*Methodist Review*
*Missionary Herald*
*Missionary Review of the World*
*Munsey's Magazine*
*National Review*
*New York Age*
*New York Herald*
*New York Times*
*Nineteenth Century and After*
*North American Review*
*Overland Monthly*
*Presbyterian Review*
*Rand Daily Mail* (Johannesburg)
*Review of Reviews*
*Scientific American*
*Scribner's Magazine*
*The State: South Africa*
*Times* (London)
*Voice of Missions*

## Articles

Bennett, Norman R. "Americans in Zanzibar, 1865-1915," *Essex Institute Historical Collection,* 98 (1962), 36-61.

Contee, Clarence G. "The Emergence of DuBois as an African Nationalist," *Journal of Negro History,* 54 (January 1969), 48-63.

Davis, R. Hunt. "Charles T. Loran and An American Model for African Education in South Africa," *The African Studies Review,* 19 (September 1976), 87-99.

DeNoon, D. J. W. "Capitalist Influence and the Transvaal Government During the Crown Colony Period, 1900-1906," *The Historical Journal,* 11 (1968), 301- 31.

_____ , "The Transvaal Labour Crisis, 1901-1906," *Journal of African History,* 7 (1967), 481-94.

Gallagher, John and Ronald Robinson, "The Imperialism of Free Trade," *Economic History Review,* 6 (1953), 1-15.

Hambly, W. D. "Racial Conflict in Africa," *Journal of Negro History,* 12 (October 1927), 577-89.

Hammond, Harold E. "American Interest in the Exploration of the Dark Continent," *The Historian,* 18 (Spring 1956), 202-29.

Harlan, Louis. "Booker T. Washington and the 'White Man's Burden,'" *American Historical Review,* 71 (January 1966), 441-67.

Johnson, Abbey A. "Away from Accommodation: Radical Editors and Protest Journalism, 1900-1910," *Journal of Negro History,* 52 (October 1977), 325-38.

Johnson, Edward A. "Is Not the African Negro Undergoing a More Desirable Development than the American Negro?" *Journal of Negro History,* 18 (January 1933), 71-77.

King, Kenneth J. "Africa and the Southern States of the U. S. A.: Notes on J. H. Oldham and American Negro Education for Africans," *Journal of African History,* 10 (1969), 659-77.

_____ , "African Students in Negro American Colleges: Notes on the 'Good African,'" *Phylon,* 31 (Spring 1970), 16-30.

Lane, David. "The Negro in South Africa," *Journal of Negro History,* 6 (July 1922), 296-306.

Marks, Shula, "The Ambiguities of Dependence: John L. Dubé of Natal," *Journal of South African Studies,* 1 (April 1975), 162-80.

Meyer, Leslie. "Henry S. Sanford and the Congo: A Re-Assesment," *African Studies,* 7 (1969), 441-55.

Parsons, Coleman. "Mark Twain: Traveler in South Africa," *Mississippi Quarterly,* 29 (Winter 1975-76), 3-41.

Redkey, Edwin S. "Bishop Turner's African Dream," *Journal of American History,* 54 (September 1967), 283-301.

_____ . "The Meaning of Africa to Afro-Americans, 1890-1914," *Black Academy Review,* 3 (Spring-Summer 1972), 5-38.

Saul, S. B. "The American Impact on British Industry, 1895-1914," *Business History,* 3 (1960), 19-38.

Scheiner, Seth H. "President Theodore Roosevelt and the Negro, 1901-1908," *Journal of Negro History,* 47 (July 1962), 169-82.

Shepperson, George. "Ethiopianism and African Nationalism," *Phylon,* 14 (1953), 9-18.

_____ . "Notes on Negro American Influence on the Emergence of African Nationalism," *Journal of African History,* 1 (1960), 299-312.

Smith, A. L. "A Nation in the Making," *Yale Review,* 19 (February 1911), 339-56.

Van Rhjn, A. J. R. "The Importance of the South African Mining Industry," *African Affairs,* 58 (1959), 229-37.

Yergan, Max. "The Status of the Natives in South Africa," *Journal of Negro History,* 24 (January 1939), 44-56.

## Secondary Books

Aydelotte, William O. *Bismarck and British Colonial Policy* (Philadelphia: University of Pennsylvania Press, 1937).

Beisner, Robert. *From the Old Diplomacy to the New, 1865-1900* (New York: Thomas Y. Crowell, 1975).

Berry, L. C. *A Century of Missions of the African Methodist Episcopal Church* (New York: Gutenberg Printing Co., 1942).

Bowers, Claude. *Beveridge and the Progressive Era* (Boston: Houghton-Mifflin, 1932).

Brown, Thomas. *Irish-American Nationalism, 1870-1890* (Philadelphia: J. B. Lippincott, 1966).

Campbell, Alexander. *Great Britain and the United States, 1895-1903* (London: Longmans, Green and Co., 1960).

Campbell, Charles, *Anglo-American Understanding, 1890-1903* (Baltimore: The Johns Hopkins University Press, 1957).

Chester, Edward. *Clash of Titans: Africa and U.S. Foreign Policy* (Maryknoll, New York: Orbis Books, 1974).

Churchill, Randolph. *Winston Churchill* (Boston: Houghton-Mifflin, 1967).

Clendenen, Clarence and Peter Duigan. *Americans in Black Africa up to 1865* (Stanford: Hoover Institute, 1964).

Clendenen, Clarence, Peter Duigan, and Robert Collins. *Americans in Africa, 1865-1900* (Stanford: Hoover Institute, 1966).

Colvin, Ian. *Life of Jameson* (2 Vols.: London: Edward Arnold, 1922).

Cotton, Walter. *The Race Problem in South Africa* (London: Student Christian Movement, 1926).

Crapol, Edward. *America for Americans: Economic National-ism and Anglophobia in the Late Nineteenth Century* (Westport, Conn.: Greenwood Press, 1973).

David, John P. (ed.), *The American Negro Reference Book* (Englewood Cliffs, New Jersey: Prentice-Hall, 1966).

Dennett, Tyler. *John Hay: From Poetry to Politics* (New York: Dodd, Mead, 1933).

Dennis, Alfred T. *Adventures in American Diplomacy, 1896-1906* (New York: E.P. Dutton, 1928).

De Klerk, W. A. *The Puritans in Africa: A Story of Afrikaner-dom* (London: Rex Collings, 1975).

De Kiewiet, C. W. *A History of South Africa: Social and Eco-nomic* (London: Oxford University Press, 1941).

_____ . *The Imperial Factor in South Africa* (Cambridge: The University Press, 1937).

Doxey, G. V. *Industrial Colour Bar in South Africa* (Capetown: Oxford University Press, 1961).

Du Plessis, J. A. *A History of Christian Missions in South Africa* (Capetown: J. C. Juta, 1939).

Emden, Paul H. *Randlords* (London: Hodder and Stroughton, 1935).

Ferguson, John H. *American Diplomacy and the Boer War* (Philadelphia: University of Pennsylvania Press, 1939).

Fisher, John. *The Afrikaners* (London: Cassell, 1969).

Gann, L. H. *The Birth of a Plural Society: The Development of Northern Rhodesia under the British South Africa Company, 1894-1914* (Manchester: Manchester Univer-sity Press, 1958).

Goodfellow, C. F. *Great Britain and South African Confeder-ation, 1870-1881* (Capetown: Oxford University Press, 1966).

Gordon, G. T. *The Growth of Opposition to Kruger, 1890-1895* (Capetown: Oxford University Press, 1970).

Grenville, J.A.S. *Lord Salisbury and Foreign Policy: The Close of the Nineteenth Century* (London: The Athlone Press, 1964).

Groves, Charles P. *The Planting of Christianity in Africa* (4 Vols.: London: Lutterworth Press, 1948-1958).

Hammond, John Hays and Jeremiah Jenks, *Great American Issues: Political, Social, Economic* (New York: Charles Scribner's Sons, 1921).

Heindel, Richard H. *The American Impact on Great Britain, 1890-1914: A Study of the United States in World History* (Philadelphia: University of Pennsylvania Press, 1940).

Hoffman, Ross. *Great Britain and the German Trade Rivalry* (Philadelphia: University of Pennsylvania Press, 1933).

Howe, Russell Warren, *Along the Afric Shore: An Historical Review of Two Centuries of U. S.-African Relations* (New York: Barnes & Noble, 1975).

Kendle, John E. *The Colonial and Imperial Conferences, 1887-1911: A Study in Imperial Organization* (London: Longmans, Green and Co., 1967).

Kubicek, Robert. *The Administration of Imperialism: Joseph Chamberlain at the Colonial Office* (Durham: Duke University Press, 1969).

LaFeber, Walter. *The New Empire: An Interpretation of American Expansion, 1869-1898* (Ithaca: Cornell University Press, 1963).

Langer, William. *European Alliances and Alignments, 1870-1890* (New York: Alfred A. Knopf, 1931).

————. *The Diplomacy of Imperialism* (New York: Alfred A. A. Knopf, 1935).

Latourette, Kenneth S. *A History of the Expansion of Christianity* (New York: Harpers, 1943).

Le May, G. H. L. *British Supremacy in South Africa, 1899-1907* (London: Clarendon Press, 1965).

Lockhart, J. C. and C. M. Woodhouse. *Rhodes* (London: Hodder and Stroughton, 1963).

Logan, Rauford (ed.). *W. E. B. DuBois: A Profile* (New York: Hill and Wang, 1971).

Lynch, Hollis R. *Edward Wilmot Blyden: Pan-Negro Patriot, 1832-1912* (London: Oxford University Press, 1967).

Marais, J. S. *The Fall of Kruger's Republic* (Oxford: Clarendon Press, 1961).

Majorie, Jula. *The Pace of the Ox: The Life of Paul Kruger* (London: Constable, 1937).

Marks, Shula. *Reluctant Rebellion: The 1906-8 Disturbances in Natal* (Oxford: Clarendon Press, 1970).

McKinley, Edward H. *The Lure of Africa: American Interests in Tropical Africa, 1919-1939* (New York: Bobbs-Merrill, 1975).

Meier, August. *Negro Thought in America, 1880-1915: Racial Ideologies in the Age of Booker T. Washington* (Ann Arbor: University of Michigan Press, 1963).

Merk, Frederick. *Manifest Destiny and Mission in American History: A Reinterpretation* (New York: Vintage Books, 1963).

McEwan, P. J. M. (ed.). *Twentieth Century Africa* (London: Oxford University Press, 1968).

Mitchell, Lewis. *The Life of the Rt. Hon. Cecil Rhodes, 1853-1902* (2 Vols.: London: Arnold, 1910).

Molema, S. M. *The Bantu* (Edinburgh: W. Green and Sons, 1920).

Nevins, Allen. *Henry White: Thirty Years of American Diplomacy* (New York: Harper and Brothers, 1930).

Newlyn, W. T. and O. C. Rowan. *Money and Banking in British Africa* (Oxford: Clarendon Press, 1954).

Oldham, J. N. *Christianity and the Race Problem* (London: Student Christian Movement, 1924).

Paullin, Charles. *The Opening of Korea by Commodore Shufeldt* (Boston: Ginn, 1910).

Perkins, Bradford. *The Great Rapprochement: England and the United States, 1895-1914* (New York: Atheneum, 1968).

Pletcher, David M. *The Awkward Years: American Foreign Relations Under Garfield and Arthur* (Columbia, Missouri: University of Missouri Press, 1962).

Plesur, Milton. *America's Outward Thrust: Approaches to Foreign Affairs 1865-1890* (DeKalb, Illinois: Northern Illinois University Press, 1971).

Porter, Bernard. *Critics of Empire: British Racial Attitudes towards Colonialism in Africa, 1895-1914* (New York: St. Martin's Press, 1968).

Pyrah, G. B. *Imperial Policy and South Africa, 1902-1910* (Oxford: Clarendon Press, 1955).

Robinson, Ronald and John Gallagher. *Africa and the Victorians: The Official Mind of Imperialism* (London: Macmillan, 1961).

Rosenthal, Eric. *Stars and Stripes in Africa* (London: George Routledge and Sons, 1938).

Roux, Edward. *Time Longer than Rope: A History of the Black Man's Struggle for Freedom in South Africa* (Madison: University of Wisconsin Press, 1964).

Sacks, Benjamin. *South Africa: An Imperial Dilemma: Non-Europeans and the British Nation, 1902-1914* (Albuquerque: University of New Mexico Press, 1967).

Shepperson, George and Thomas Price. *Independent African: John Chilembwe and the Origins, Setting, and Significance of the Nyasaland Native Rising of 1915* (Edinburgh: The University Press, 1958).

Spence, Clark C. *Mining Engineers and the American West: The Lace-Boot Brigade* (New Haven: Yale University Press, 1970).

Spender, J. A. *The Life of the Rt. Hon. Sir Henry Campbell-Bannermann* (London: Hodder and Stroughton, 1923).

Stuart, J. *A History of the Zulu Rebellion of 1906* (London: Macmillan, 1913).

Van Der Poel, Jean. *Railway and Custom's Policies in South Africa, 1885-1910* (London: Longmans, Green and Co., 1933).

Walker, Eric. *A History of South Africa* (London: Longmans, Green and Co., 1935).

Weisbord, Robert. *Ebony Kinship: Africa, Africans, and the Afro-American* (Westport, Conn.: Greenwood Press, 1974).

Weston, Rubin Francis. *Racism and United States Imperialism: The Influence of Racial Assumptions on American Foreign Policy, 1893-1946* (Columbia, South Carolina: University of South Carolina Press, 1972).

Williams, William A. *The Roots of the Modern American Empire: A Study of the Growth and Shaping of Social Consciousness in a Marketplace Society* (New York: Random House, 1969).

Wilson, Monica and Leonard Thompson. *The Oxford History of South Africa* (New York: Oxford University Press, 1971).

Younger, Edward. *John Kasson* (Iowa City: University of Iowa Press, 1955).

Young, Marilyn B. *Rhetoric of Empire: American China Policy, 1895-1900* (Cambridge: Harvard University Press, 1968).

# Appendix

**American Exports to South Africa
1890 to 1912 in dollars***

| Year | Total |
|------|-------|
| 1890 | 1,866,000 |
| 1891 | 2,099,000 |
| 1892 | 2,034,000 |
| 1893 | 2,929,000 |
| 1894 | 3,078,000 |
| 1895 | 6,221,000 |
| 1896 | 14,031,840 |
| 1897 | 13,956,000 |
| 1898 | 14,054,000 |
| 1899 | 16,694,700** |
| 1900 | 20,086,128** |
| 1901 | 9,350,000*** |
| 1902 | 15,332,000 |
| 1903 | 30,053,790 |
| 1904 | 14,145,800 |
| 1905 | 11,040,235 |
| 1906 | 11,072,242 |
| 1907 | 9,877,730 |
| 1908 | 9,774,822 |
| 1909 | 10,620,421 |
| 1910 | 12,959,908 |
| 1911 | 13,762,583 |
| 1912 | 15,736,321 |

In 1896 the United States surpassed Holland and Germany and was second only to Great Britain in exports to the area. It held this position in all years except 1908 and 1909 when it slipped to third behind Britain and Germany. In 1910 the United States again passed Germany.

*Figures are based on reports by American consuls in their despatches and in *Commercial Relations.*
**Estimated by consuls due to disruption of the Boer War.
***Capetown only.

# INDEX

Abolition of slavery: effect on South Africa, 6
Act of Union, 105, 110
Adams, Charles Hall, 119
Adams, Henry, 80
Adee, A.A., 18, 45, 101
Africa; early U.S. interest in, 3
"Africa for the Africans," 59. *See also* Ethiopianism
African Methodist Episcopal Church, 42, 59, 112; racial activities condemned, 118, 120, 123; ministers barred from Transvaal, 121; blamed for Natal uprising, 121. *See also* Ethiopianism; Turner, H.M.
Afrikaners. *See* Boers
*Alabama, U.S.S.,* 5
Allen, William, 79
Allis-Chalmers Co., 102
American Bible Society, 37
American blacks: pro-British stance of, 86-87; disillusionment with British, 114-17; South African restrictions on, 116-17; as example to South African blacks, 112; linked to Ethiopianism, 120-24. *See also* African Methodist Episcopal Church; Ethiopianism; Washington, Booker T.; Du Bois, W.E.B.
American Board of Commissioners for Foreign Missions, 4, 37-38; condemns Boer brutality toward blacks, 9-10; and South African race laws, 107
American Geographical Society, 8
American Institute of Mining Engineers, 51
American Missionary Congress on Africa, 38
American Zulu Mission. *See* Natal Zulu Mission
Amery, Leopold, 93
Amin, Idi, 143

Anglophobia: effect on U.S. policy, 16
Anglo-Saxonism, 38, 62-63, 68-69, 86, 90, 111, 136
Anti-imperialism, 17
Apartheid; origins of, 129, 140; and U.S. business, 142; effect on U.S. policy, 141-44
Apprenticeship Act, 140
*Arena,* 85-86
Armour & Co., 102
Australia: and South African grain, 99
Aylward, Alfred, 16

Balfour, Arthur, 126
Bantu language, 118
Barnato, Barnett, 25, 31
Basutoland: Americans denied permits in, 97
Bayard, Thomas A., 45, 50
Bechuanaland, 18, 26
Beelaerts Van Blokland, G.J.T., 18
Beisner, Robert, 135-37
Beit, Alfred, 25
Belgian Congo, 27
Benedict, Charles, 40, 45
Beveridge, Albert, 62
Bigelow, Poultney, 57, 80
Bingham, William, 93, 101, 103, 115
Birchenough, Henry, 93
"black week," 72
Blacks. *See* American blacks; South African Blacks
Blaine, James G., 29
Bloemfontein, Orange Free State: U.S., consulate at, 25; fall of, 72, 83; conference at, 64
Blyden, Edward, 41-42
Boers: origin of name, 6; emigrate to U.S., 88; blamed for lack of racial progress, 118; fear erosion of culture, 139

187

189